Why Stocks Go Up (and Down)
A Guide to Sound Investing

WILLIAM H. PIKE

Why Stocks Go Up (and Down)
A Guide to Sound Investing

DOW JONES-IRWIN
Homewood, Illinois   60430

This publication is designed to provide accurate and
authoritative information in regard to the subject matter
covered. It is sold with the understanding that the
publisher is not engaged in rendering legal, accounting, or
other professional service. If legal advice or other expert
assistance is required, the services of a competent
professional person should be sought.

From a Declaration of Principles jointly adopted by a Committee
of the American Bar Association and a Committee of Publishers.

ISBN 0-87094-314-6
Library of Congress Catalog Card No. 82–71875

Printed in the United States of America

5 6 7 8 9 0 M 9 8 7 6

Preface

The purpose of this book is to give you a sound understanding of what determines value in the stock market, *and that — determining value —is the key to successful investing.* This book is the outgrowth of a course I have taught for the Boston Security Analysts Society for the past 10 years. The students are newcomers to the investment industry who have had no experience with accounting, finance, or the stock market.

Part One introduces the basic concepts of business ownership and record keeping. The heavy emphasis on accounting may not seem relevant at first, but stock values are always related to accounting reports. To not write about income statements and balance sheets would cheat you, the reader.

Parts Two and Three will increase your breadth and depth of knowledge, but can be skipped without losing the continuity of Parts One and Four. Part Two is about bonds and preferred stock (which is quite different from common stock). While it is not necessary to understand bonds and preferred stock in order to understand common stock, Part Two will add to your perspective. Part Three explains more fully how income statements and balance sheets relate to stock prices.

It is my hope that Part One will correct misconceptions you did not even know you had, and that Part Four will answer the questions you have most frequently asked.

Chapter 18 is an 18-year history of Polaroid's stock. It is written like a mystery story and you should always assume that the future is unknown. The discussions of the optimistic and pessimistic cases for the stock allow the reader to come to his own "buy" or "sell" conclusion before turning the page to see what actually happened. This chapter repeatedly introduces seemingly new factors not previously discussed. That is a fact of life in the stock market. New factors are always coming up, and the investor who recognizes them first will be the most successful.

This book, and especially Chapter 18, is like a movie, in that any one frame simply does not tell the story. By reading the whole book and studying the charts and tables, you should develop an excellent feel for why stocks go up (and down).

ACKNOWLEDGMENTS

The time and efforts of many individuals other than myself contributed to making this book what it is. In particular, Patricia Ostrander, for her assistance on the bond chapters, and William Devin, for his assistance on the trading chapters, are gratefully acknowledged. Their advice and reviews of those chapters were of enormous help. The selection of Polaroid as the real-world example in this book was in part the result of the analysis of that company through the years by many conscientious Wall Street analysts. In particular I would like to acknowledge Gary Bridge and Brenda Landry, whose knowledge and recollections of company history were most helpful. To keep my legal and SEC facts accurate, I have relied on Arthur Loring, who was invariably available at his desk late in the evening when I needed him. Finally, there were students too numerous to mention whose questions in class and discoveries of ambiguities in the manuscript have added to its clarity.

After the above type was set, I discovered an additional deserving acknowledgement. My aunt, Ethel Pike, indexed and proofread the entire manuscript. Her keen eye caught mistakes that all other readers missed. Her contribution to the book's readability and accuracy is gratefully acknowledged.

William Pike

Contents

PART ONE

Basics: Starting a Business, Financial Statements, and Common Stock

1

Getting started

Our story begins in late 1977 when Mr. Jones had the inspiration that he could build a better mousetrap. He immediately decided to go into business and see if he could make some money. He was handy in the workshop, and he knew where to go to buy some wood and metal to make the mousetraps, as well as where to buy a screwdriver, a saw, and other tools. He even had a friend who owned a department store and who would probably be willing to sell his traps. Jones knew that he would have to keep financial records of what he bought and sold and the profit he made, but he recognized that his knowledge of business and accounting was limited. So he asked his good friend, Mr. Greenshades, who had been an accountant for years, if he would advise him. Greenshades was quite willing, knowing that once the business was under way, he would be able to charge a fee for his services. Greenshades's first advice to Jones was to open a separate bank account for his mousetrap business, and keep it independent of his personal account. Legally, of course, there is no distinction at all between Jones's personal account and his business account. For example, if both bank accounts draw interest, Jones would have to pay the income tax on both.

On January 1, 1978, Jones deposited $100 into the mousetrap company account and declared himself in business. He named his company the Jones Mousetrap Company, or JMC for short. At this point, JMC is called a *sole proprietorship*. This means the company is owned by one person and is not yet incorporated (discussed in Chapter 2).

Greenshades advised Jones to keep accounting records in the same manner as most other companies, which means having two financial statements: a *balance sheet* and an *income statement*. The balance sheet has three major categories, which show, *for a given point in time:* (1) *Assets*, which are anything of value that the company owns or has claim to; (2) *Liabilities*, which are debts the company owes at the same point in time; (3) *Ownership Equity*, which reflects the combination of the amount of money put into the company by the owners *and* the total amount of profit it has earned down through the years, less any dividends the company has paid down through the years.

The common form of the balance sheet is: all Assets are recorded on the left side of the balance sheet and Liabilities and Ownership Equity are recorded on the right side, as shown.

Assets	*Liabilities*
	Ownership Equity

Since Jones put $100 into the company on January 1, the balance sheet at that time looked like this:

Assets	*Liabilities*
Cash $100	
	Ownership Equity
	Jones Put In. $100

What this really says is that the company has $100 worth of assets, and Jones (since he is the sole owner of the company) has a claim, or equity, of $100 in the company. The terms *equity* or *ownership equity* are frequently a source of confusion because, as we will see, they are used in many different contexts. At this point it will be helpful to just memorize the definition above and remember where it goes on the balance sheet. It will become clearer later. Since JMC has not made or sold any mousetraps there is no statement of income, yet.

After opening the bank account, Jones set out to make his initial purchases. He spent $30 on wood and metal, from which the traps will be made, and another $20 on screwdrivers, saws, and other equipment that will be used to make the traps. The $30 worth of wood and metal is called *inventory*. The $20 worth of tools is called *equipment*. The difference is this: inventory consists of the raw materials from which the traps will be made; it will be used up and ultimately become part of the mousetraps that are to be sold. Equipment does not become part of the mousetraps; it is only used to make the mousetraps. Equipment will not be used up during the manufacturing process, although it may wear out, get lost, or be disposed of because it became obsolete and was replaced by better equipment.

DEFINITIONS

Inventory is that raw material or those materials that will be used to make the products that will ultimately be sold. It is usually used up within one year.

Equipment is the tools which are used to help produce the goods that are to be sold. Usually they are expected to last longer than one year.

At this point, then, the JMC balance sheet looked like this:

Assets		Liabilities	
Cash	$ 50		
Inventory	30		
		Ownership Equity	
Equipment	20	Jones Put In	$100
Total	$100	Total	$100

All that has happened thus far is that one asset (cash) has been changed into two others (inventory and equipment). It is customary to distinguish on the balance sheet between *Current assets*, consisting of cash and items that are expected to be converted into cash within one year, and *Long-term assets*, those items which are expected to be around for over one year. The most common long-term assets include tools, buildings, company cars and trucks, and the like. We will see other types of long-term assets later. If Jones wanted to build a factory in which to make his traps, the cost of the factory and the cost of the property on which it was built would obviously be long-term assets, because they would be around for well over one year. Buildings, tools, motor vehicles, and so on are often categorized on the balance sheet as *Property, plant, and equipment*. Thus, a more formally drawn balance sheet would look like this:

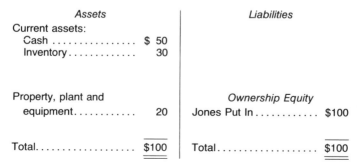

Assets		Liabilities	
Current assets:			
Cash	$ 50		
Inventory	30		
Property, plant and		*Ownership Equity*	
equipment	20	Jones Put In	$100
Total	$100	Total	$100

At this point, Jones began making mousetraps. After a week's work, he had used up $20 worth of wood and metal and had built 10 traps. He brought the traps to the store that had agreed to sell them. The store, however, said it would not pay Jones for the traps until they were sold.

If Jones wanted to be more accurate on his balance sheet, he could now separate inventory into two groups:

Inventory:
Finished goods...................... $20
Raw materials....................... 10

By the end of January, all 10 mousetraps were sold, for $6 each. The store, however, kept $1 per trap for its trouble, as was the agreement between Jones and the store. Thus the store owed Jones $50 which he collected. At this point, Jones decided to redo his balance sheet and draw up his first income statement. What has happened?

1. Sales of $50 were made and the $50 was received in cash.
2. Finished goods worth $20 were sold.

Thus the income statement for the month of January might look like this:

JMC
Statement of Income
From 1/1/78 to 1/31/78

Sales............................. $50
Less: Cost of goods sold .... − 20
Equals: Profit...................... = $30

Jones knew he would have to pay income tax on his profit. Even though it did not have to be paid until later, tax is a legal liability so it would be most accurate to put it into the income statement immediately. Since Jones owned the entire company, which was still a sole proprietorship (not yet incorporated), the Internal Revenue Service would treat the profit as part of Jones's total income including his salary from his regular job. Therefore, the actual tax rate paid on the mousetrap profit could vary, depending on Jones's other job salary that year. We will assume a tax rate of 50 percent, which is close to the 46 percent basic tax rate for most large corporations. Since 50 percent is an easy number to work with, we will assume a 50 percent tax rate throughout this book. The income statement therefore, would be more complete like this:

JMC
Statement of Income
From 1/1/78 to 1/31/78

Sales..........................	$50
Less: Cost of goods sold	− 20
Equals: Profit before tax...........	= 30
Less: Income tax @ 50 percent ...	− 15
Equals: Net profit after tax	= $15

Since the tax has not yet been paid, but will have to be paid, Jones put the following entry on the balance sheet under Liabilities:

Taxes payable $15

The liability group on the balance sheet, like the asset group, is usually broken into two parts, *Current liabilities* (those due within one year), and *Long-term liabilities* (those due after one year). Since taxes are paid quarterly by most businesses—and by individuals who don't have their tax deducted from each pay check— *Taxes payable* is a current liability.

The net profit of $15 that was earned is classified as *Retained earnings* in the *Ownership equity* section of the balance sheet. Thus, the balance sheet now looked like this:

JMC
Balance Sheet
1/31/78

Assets		Liabilities and Stockholders' Equity	
Current assets:		Current liabilities:	
Cash	$100	Taxes payable	$ 15
Inventory:		Long-term liabilities	
Raw materials	10		
		Ownership equity:	
Property, plant, and		Jones put in	100
equipment...........	20	Retained earnings.....	15
Total..................	$130	Total..................	$130

Reviewing the right-hand side of the balance sheet, notice that Ownership equity is not a liability. Ownership equity is not owed to anybody, except in the sense that the company is "owed to" or belongs to Jones. What actually does belong to Jones? The company has $130 worth of assets, but the United States government has a claim on $15 worth. In other words, if Jones liquidated the company (i.e., sold all the assets for what they were worth), he could not legally pocket the entire $130. He first would have to pay the $15 in taxes. Thus, Jones would be left with $115. Thus, one might say Jones's equity (or ownership) in the company is $115, not just the $100 that he put in. Nevertheless, it is conventional to list separately the amount of money put into the company and the amount of money earned by the company (retained earnings).

DEFINITIONS

Balance sheet   The balance sheet reflects the financial condition of the company *at a point in time*. It shows what assets are held, what liabilities are owed, what money (or capital) was initially put into the company, and how much was earned by the company. It is sometimes called the "Statement of Financial Condition."

Income statement   The income statement shows the revenue (sales) that the company has made and the expenses that have been incurred to make those sales, and the profit or loss derived therefrom. The income statement shows what has happened *over a period of time*. It should always say on it "Income Statement from (date) to (date)." This statement is also called the Profit and Loss Statement, or just the "P and L."

Book value   Book value is defined as total assets less total current and long-term liabilities. In other words, JMC's book value is currently $115—exactly equal to the Ownership Equity account. This is not always so, for reasons that will be seen in later chapters, but book value often closely approximates ownership equity.

Jones was pleased with his successful mousetrap sales and his profit and wanted to make some more. Thus, he went out and bought some more raw materials. During the first week of February, he spent $60 on metal and wood. He also used $30 worth of inventory to build mousetraps, which he brought to the store. At that time, the *Current assets* portion of the balance sheet would have looked as follows:

```
Current assets (as of 2/7/78):
    Cash.............................. $40
    Inventory:
        Finished goods...................   30
        Raw materials....................   40
```

Because Jones planned to take a vacation in the latter part of the month, he hired a trusted friend, Mr. Arbetter, as an employee. Jones agreed to pay Arbetter $4 per hour. Jones expected Arbetter would work 15 hours before the end of the month, so he knew the company would need $60 to pay Arbetter's wages. Since the store only pays for the traps after the end of the month, and Arbetter wanted to be paid weekly, it was obvious that JMC would need to borrow some cash to pay Arbetter until the store came through with JMC's money. Therefore, since Jones did not want to put any more of his own money into the company, he went to a bank. To be on the safe side, and to have enough money for new raw materials, Jones asked to borrow $100 for 30 days, from February 15 to March 15. The bank, however, felt the business was too risky (i.e., if the traps were unable to be sold, it was unlikely the bank could get all its money back). The bank did say, however, that if Jones was willing to put in another $50 of equity it would be willing to loan JMC $50 for the month. The bank stipulated, however, that if the traps did not sell, and if the company had no money to pay back the loan at the end of the month, the company could be declared legally bankrupt and therefore would be legally required to sell its equipment and raw materials for whatever they would bring in order to pay back the bank. Actually, in a case like this where JMC was a sole proprietorship (owned entirely by Mr. Jones), he personally would be responsible to the bank. The bank, however, did not know Jones very well and felt safer knowing there were assets that could be sold to raise the money, should the company default on the loan (i.e., not pay it back on time). To compensate for the risk of the loan, the bank asked interest of $4 for the month.[1] Jones agreed to the stipulations and the loan was made on February 15. The new balance sheet of February 15 appeared as follows:

JMC
Balance sheet, 2/15/78

Assets		Liabilities and Stockholders' Equity	
Current assets:		Current liabilities:	
Cash	$140	Taxes payable	$ 15
Inventory:		Bank debt payable	50
Finished goods	30		
Raw materials	40	Long-term liabilities	
Property, plant, and equipment:		Ownership equity:	
		Jones's equity	150
Equipment	20	Retained earnings	15
Total..................	$230	Total..................	$230

At the end of February, all the mousetraps (in this case 15) had been sold. The store and Jones, however, had agreed to raise the price, and this time Jones received $6 per trap, or a total of $90. On February 28, the store informed JMC that although all the traps had been sold, the

---

[1] The $4 interest on the $50 loan for one month is unrealistically high, but the numbers work well in the example.

store was a little short on cash and would not be able to pay JMC until the 10th of March.

At this point, February 28, Jones wished to set up a new balance sheet and income statement. He had a number of things to enter:

1. Although cash had not yet been received, JMC had a legal claim again.st the store, so JMC recorded $90 in *Sales*, and set up a new account on the balance sheet, *Accounts receivable* (i.e., money that was owed to the company).

2. *Finished goods* of $30 had been sold, so must be removed from the balance sheet. Even though the money for the traps had not yet been received, the traps had been sold, so JMC recorded $30 in *Cost of goods sold* for the month of February.

3. Arbetter had worked diligently and had converted another $20 of raw materials into finished goods. He received his $60 for wages as expected. To reflect these wages, JMC lowered *Cash* by $60.

4. Arbetter had spent one third of his time building mousetraps, and two thirds had been spent keeping the books, sweeping the floor, and doing other chores. Therefore, $20 (reflecting his time working on mousetraps) should go into *Inventory*, specifically *Finished goods*. (None of Arbetter's traps had actually been sold yet. The traps that were sold during February had been built by Jones.) The other $40 of Arbetter's pay was taken directly to the income statement. Since that $40 cannot be attributed to any particular mousetraps, yet was a necessary expense of doing business, it must be recorded as an expense in the period (February) during which it was incurred. Rather than being listed under *Cost of goods sold (CGS)* it is listed separately as *General and administrative expense (G &A)*.

Notice these distinctions carefully:

a. *Cost of goods sold* is the dollar cost of the goods that *have actually been sold*.

b. The dollar cost of goods that have been manufactured but *not yet sold* is put on the balance sheet as *Finished goods*. Even though the cost of their manufacture has been paid for, they are not put on the income statement as Cost of goods sold until the goods are actually sold.

c. The $40 cost attributable to keeping the books, sweeping the floor, and so on is not attributable to any specific mousetrap. Therefore, it is not put in *Cost of goods sold* but into *General and administrative expense* (or something similar) and put on the income statement for the period in which it occurred. General and administrative expense (G&A) is almost never put on the balance sheet. The exceptions are too minor to consider here.

Other things to enter:

5. Of the 30 days the bank loan was to be outstanding, 15 had elapsed.[2]
    Thus, since one half of the time had gone, it might be assumed that
    half of the interest had been "earned" by the bank. Since the interest
    had not actually been paid yet, JMC set up a new current liability
    account, *Interest payable*, of $2. Also, since the bank's money was
    used to conduct business, the interest on the money must be consid-
    ered an expense. Accordingly, a new account, *Interest expense*, was
    set up on the income statement in the amount of $2. Again, even
    though the money had not actually been paid yet, it had been
    "earned" by the bank, so must be accounted for.
6. Note also that *Taxes payable* have increased to reflect the February
    profit.

Thus, for the month of February, the income statement looked like
this:

JMC
Statement of Income
From 2/1/78 to 2/28/78

Sales		$90
Expenses:		
CGS.....................	$30	
Gen. and adm.		
expense................	40	
Interest expense	2	
	$72	72
Profit before tax		18
Taxes at 50 percent		9
Net profit after tax		$ 9

At this point, Jones decided to take some of the profit out of the
company for himself, and he chose to do this by declaring a $5 dividend.
Alternatively, he could have taken out the $5 and called it his salary. If
he had taken the $5 as salary, it would have appeared under *expenses* in
either CGS or G&A, or on the balance sheet under Finished goods,
depending on how he attributed the $5 of salary. In fact, he might have
been better off if he took the $5 as salary, because if it then appeared as
an expense he would have had higher expenses; therefore, less profit
before tax; and therefore, paid less tax. However, for illustrative purposes, let us assume he declared a dividend. Note the difference. Salary
is a cost incurred while attempting to make a profit. A dividend is
something you *may* choose to pay with the profit you earned. Although
$5 gets deducted from cash in either case, the rest of the accounting is

---

[2] Actually, February is a shorter month, so not quite 15 days had elapsed. For simplicity, we shall assume 30-day months.

quite different. Since Jones chose to pay himself the $5 as a dividend, he deducted $5 from the *Cash* account and $5 from the *Net profit after tax* account, and therefore left only $4 of the profit to add to *Retained earnings*. Retained earnings, for now, means any profit earned by the company that was not paid out as a dividend. The definition will be made more precise later on. Thus Jones could put the following at the bottom of the income statement:

Net profit after tax	$ 9
Less: Dividend	− 5
Retained earnings	$ = 4

Some companies do not put this on the bottom of the income statement, but leave it as a separate statement, the Statement of Retained Earnings.

As of February 28, the balance sheet looked like this:

JMC
Balance Sheet, 2/28/78

Assets			Liabilities + Stockholders' Equity		
Current assets:			Current liabilities:		
Cash		$ 75	Interest payable	$	2
Acc't. receivable		90	Bank debt payable		50
Inventory:			Taxes payable		24
Finished goods		40	Total current liabilities. . . .		76
Raw materials		20			
Total current assets		225	Long-term liabilities		
			Ownership equity:		
Property, plant and equipment:			Jones put in		150
Equipment		20	Retained earnings		19
			Total liabilities and		
Total assets		$245	owners' equity		$245

The $40 under *Finished goods* may present some confusion. It is the dollar cost of the finished goods, which in this case consists of two components: the $20 worth of raw materials and the $20 worth of labor paid to Arbetter. On the earlier balance sheets the *Finished goods* had only a raw materials component, because Jones was not paying himself any wages. Generally, the cost of finished goods consists of all costs that are normally attributable to making the goods. These almost always include both labor and raw material costs, as well as some other smaller items. On the other hand, such costs as interest and wages paid for general and administrative functions usually are not attributed directly to making goods and are therefore *not* included in *Finished goods*. These types of costs, sometimes called "overhead" costs, are not put on the balance sheet but rather are put directly on the income statement as general and administrative expense, or interest expense, or whatever is appropriate.

Note the convention of subtotalling both current assets and current liabilities. It is also conventional to place the current liabilities due first at the top, and those due latest at the bottom. Similarly, in current assets, cash comes first, the current asset most easily converted into cash comes second, and so on. The current assets that would be most difficult to convert into cash come last.

Note also that the balance sheet "balances," that is, the left side and the right side both total the same amount. There is absolutely no significance to the actual dollar amount, in this case $245. The only thing that matters is that they balance. If they do not, an error was made someplace.

2

Ownership and stock

In the month of March, Mr. Jones decided it was time to move the business out of his one-room flat and to buy some land and build a small factory. He estimated that buying the land and building and equipping the factory would cost about $500. This seemed like a lot of money for a company this small, but Jones knew the plant would last for years and the land would probably appreciate in value, so he decided to go ahead. But with only $75 in cash, and that needed to buy raw materials and pay wages, not to mention paying off the bank loan, it was clear the company needed more money. Because it was very unlikely that a bank would loan $500 to a new risky venture with so few assets, Jones decided to raise more equity money, that is, permanent money which does not have to be paid back like bank-borrowing. Having no desire to risk any more of his own money, he decided to see if his friends would be willing to invest in his company. Why should they risk their money? Because they knew that if the venture was profitable it would be able to pay them dividends. Should profits grow, so presumably would dividends. Each investor, then, would hope to eventually receive in dividends more than he or she had initially put in as equity money. Obviously, if one didn't expect dividends, one would not put any money in.

In fact, many of Jones's friends had faith in him, and four of them agreed to put in $75 each. At this point Jones was afraid that, since his friends had put up a total of $300, or two thirds of the total equity money paid in, they might think they owned two thirds of the company. (Recall Jones had only put in $150.) Jones turned to Mr. Greenshades for help, and Greenshades made the following points. First, Greenshades pointed out that percentage ownership in a company does not have to be proportional to the amount of money put in. It is entirely up to the people putting money into a company to negotiate with the people already owning the company what their percentage will be. Obviously, Jones wanted to maintain as large a percent of the company as possible. Similarly, his friends wanted as large a share of the company as they could have for their money. There is no law to say who gets what percent of the company. Percentage ownership in a company does not have to be proportional to the amount of money put in. In this case, all agreed that, since Jones had invented the mousetrap and would be putting a lot of time into the company, he deserved a larger share of the ownership than his proportion of the money put in. It was agreed that Jones would keep 60 percent of the company and the four other investors would get 10 percent each.

Next, Greenshades explained the use of stock as a way to reflect ownership of a company. Very simply, stock represents ownership. A share of stock is a piece of paper that says the owner of this piece of paper owns whatever portion of the company this share represents. Until now, Jones owned the entire company. Therefore, he owned all the company's stock; he could have had one share worth the entire company, or two shares each worth half the company, or 10 shares each worth one tenth of the company. It made no difference—Jones could have printed up as many shares of stock as he pleased. He owned all of them, totalling 100 percent of the company. Now he had agreed to give up 40 percent of the company to his friends. They decided to draw up 100 shares of stock. Jones would keep 60 shares and each of the four investors would get 10 shares. They could just as easily have printed 200 shares and Jones would have kept 120, and the four investors 20 each. It makes no difference how many shares there are as long as each partial owner of the company has a proper proportion.

Finally, Greenshades explained that, with the addition of the four investors, JMC would no longer be a sole proprietorship and would either become a partnership or could incorporate and become a legal corporation. The primary advantage of being a corporation is called the *limited liability* feature, which means that neither Jones nor the partners could be held liable for the debts of the company. For example, when the company was a sole proprietorship, if business had been bad and the company was unable to repay the bank loan when it was due, Jones would have had to come up with the money out of his own pocket; or if the company had become a partnership, the partners would have had to come up with the money from their own pockets. Similarly, if Arbetter had broken his hand while working for the company, he might have sued JMC for medical expenses. If he won and if the company did not have enough cash to pay the settlement, even after having sold off all its assets, Jones (or the partners) would have had to come up with their personal cash. The limited liability feature of a corporation means that neither the bank nor Arbetter would have been able to collect from Jones (or the partners). They could have collected as much as the assets of the company could have been sold for, but beyond that, the owner or owners would have no liability from their personal money for the debts of the corporation. Jones and the four investors readily agreed that incorporation was a good idea.

Another factor that distinguishes a corporation from a sole proprietorship or partnership is the way its profits are taxed. In a sole proprietorship, the profits are taxed as a part of the income of the proprietor. In a partnership, the profits are taxed as part of the partners' income in proportion to their ownership of the partnership. In a corporation, however, profits are taxed at rates based on how much profit the corporation made. Corporate tax rates are independent of the earnings of the owner or owners of the corporation.

Incorporation in most states usually involves no more than filing a simple statement at the statehouse and paying a nominal fee. Thus, JMC became a corporation. The company name was changed to JMC, Incorporated. Greenshades now explained the following to Jones and the four investors.

Every person who owns one or more shares of a company is called a "shareholder" of that company. He has the right to attend stockholders' meetings and has as many votes as he has shares on all issues that come up before the stockholders at the meeting. In the case of a large company like IBM or Eastman Kodak, the stock is very widely held and no person is likely to hold more than 1 or 2 percent. Most stockholders own far less. Kodak's ownership, for example, is divided into 164 million shares of stock. Therefore, a person owning 100 shares owns less than one ten-thousandth of 1 percent of Kodak!

A corporation must have at least one stockholder meeting each year. The primary purpose of the meeting is to elect the board of directors. Usually, any stockholder can nominate anyone he wants for the board of directors. Anyone can be nominated, whether or not he works for the company and whether or not he is a stockholder of the company. The board of most companies, however, includes the president and some of the officers. Directors who are not employees of the company are called "outside directors." Typically, a board of directors is made up of between 7 and 13 members. The board's most important functions usually include choosing the president of the company, reviewing the president's performance, and declaring dividends. If a large number of stockholders are dissatisfied with the way their company is being run, they can elect new directors at the next meeting who can replace the president with someone more acceptable. To do this, of course, requires a large number of unhappy stockholders. As a practical matter, in most large companies the board is similar from year to year with only one or two changes every year or two. Nevertheless, all directors have to be reelected periodically. In some companies, all directors come up for reelection each year; but in other companies, only some of the directorships come up for election (or reelection) each year. There is usually no limit to the number of terms a director can serve.

Stockholders are notified well in advance of the meeting when and where it will be held. Those who cannot attend, however, are allowed to vote by proxy, which is essentially an absentee ballot. The term *proxy fight*, which is often heard in the financial community, refers to a case where a group of unhappy stockholders want to elect new directors who they feel will more adequately represent them (i.e., make the changes in the company that they feel are necessary). Since most stockholders do not actually attend the meeting, the dissident group tries to get the nonattending stockholders to vote their proxies in favor of the dissidents' candidate. The incumbent directors, of course, will endeavor to get the stockholders to vote them in again.

In the case of JMC, Jones owns 60 percent of the stock and he can therefore elect himself as at least 60 percent of the board of directors and appoint himself president. In a closely held company (very few stockholders) the stockholders' meeting might be quite informal, particularly if one shareholder has a majority (over 50 percent) of the shares.

Besides voting, the importance to the four investors of owning as much of the stock as possible is that whenever a dividend is declared the same amount of dividend will be paid *on each share*. Thus a person owning 60 shares would receive six times as much as a person owning 10 shares. A stockholder with 10 shares would receive twice as much as a stockholder owning 5 shares. The final reason for wanting to own as many shares as possible is that should the company be dissolved or liquidated (i.e., if all the assets were sold and all the debts paid off), the remaining money would be distributed to the stockholders in proportion to the number of shares owned.

Greenshades now proposed setting up the *Ownership Equity* portion of the balance sheet in the format used by most companies, which is as follows:

Ownership Equity

Paid-in capital:
Common stock (at par value $1 per share) $100
(authorized 100 shares, outstanding 100 shares)
Additional paid-in capital   350
Retained earnings.   19
Total ownership equity $469

Paid-in capital, Greenshades explained, represents money put into the company in exchange for stock. Since the total capital paid in by the five investors (including Jones) was $450, the items under *Paid-in capital* must, by definition, total $450. *Retained earnings* represents profits earned by the company's operations (i.e., making and selling mouse-traps), less the amount of dividends paid.

Par value, Greenshades went on, was an anachronism with essentially no meaning today, but he thought JMC should put it in for the sake of formality. *Par value* is an arbitrary dollar value assigned to each share of stock. In this case, the assigned par value was $1 per share. Thus the dollar figure in Common stock (at par value $1 per share) is $100 ($1 × 100 shares outstanding = $100).

Additional paid-in capital, by definition, is the difference between the total money (capital) paid into the company for stock, less that portion of it which is arbitrarily assigned to par value. Therefore:

Paid-in capital = Common at par + Additional paid-in capital

The "additional" just means the portion of the paid-in capital above what is assigned to common at par. Usually, the only way to calculate additional paid-in capital is to take the total paid-in capital and subtract common at par. Additional paid-in capital is sometimes called *paid-in surplus, capital surplus*, or *capital paid-in above par*. The terms are synonymous, although the latter is the most accurate description. The word *surplus* is undesirable here, because it may imply there is surplus cash lying around the company. This, of course, is not true. The cash in this case, for example, will shortly be used to buy some land and construct a factory unit. All of these items—*Paid-in capital, Common at par*, and *Additional paid-in capital*—are just accounting entries reflecting the fact that sometime in the past some money was paid into the company in exchange for stock. If in fact the cash is still there, it would be in the *cash* account on the left-hand side of the balance sheet. From looking at the accounting entries, there is no way to know when the cash was paid in or what has since been done with the cash.

Suppose the par value had been declared at $2, then the *Ownership Equity* portion of the balance sheet would have looked like this:

Ownership Equity

Paid-in capital:
Common stock (at par value $2 per share)	$200
(authorized 100 shares, outstanding 100 shares)	
Additional paid-in capital	250
Retained earnings................................	19
Total ownership equity	$469

Authorized 100 shares simply means that the stockholders agreed that the company's ownership *may* be split into as many as 100 shares. In the case of JMC, the ownership has been split into 100 shares, and therefore 100 shares are both authorized and outstanding. If the stockholders thought they might want to sell more shares later on, they would first have to vote to authorize the president or officers of the company to sell more. For example, JMC really wanted to raise $500 and so far has only raised $300 from the four new stockholders. Thus, if they wanted to raise more money by selling even more shares, the stockholders would have to authorize more, perhaps a total of 200 or 300, even though only 100 are currently *outstanding*. Once the company (its officers) has been authorized to sell more shares than are currently outstanding, it may sell such shares at any time in the future or it may never sell such shares. *Authorize* simply means permission. It does not require that such authorized shares actually be sold. Suppose, for example, a total of 200 had been authorized, and besides the 100 outstanding, an additional 50 shares were sold for $6 each. Assume also that the par value = $1. Then the *Ownership Equity* section would appear as follows:

Ownership Equity

Paid-in capital:
    Common stock (at par value $1 per share) $150
    (authorized 200 shares, outstanding 150 shares)
    Additional paid-in capital 600
    Retained earnings   19

Total ownership equity $769

    As it happens, JMC stockholders had only authorized 100 shares. But if they wanted to sell more they could always authorize them at next year's annual stockholders meeting, or in an emergency, management or the board of directors could even call a special shareholders meeting expressly for authorizing more shares. Of course, the stockholders might vote not to authorize more shares, in which case the company would not be legally allowed to sell any more shares.

DEFINITIONS

Paid-in capital The total amount of dollars paid into the company by stockholders for stock. This figure is made up of the sum of *Common stock at par value* and *Additional paid-in capital*. The total dollars in *Paid-in capital* almost never changes unless the company issues more stock.

Par value An arbitrary figure set by the company that distinguishes one of the two components of paid-in capital. Some companies used *stated value* in place of *par value*. There is a minor distinction that is irrelevant for most purposes. Par value is the same for all common shares. Additional paid-in capital probably is not.

Additional paid-in capital This can be calculated by taking *Paid-in capital* and subtracting *Common stock at par value*.

Retained earnings The total profits earned by the company for all years since its inception, less any losses in any years since inception, less all of the dividends paid since inception. Retained earnings is often called *earned surplus*, or *retained profits*. Again, the word *surplus* is considered undesirable since it might imply that surplus cash is lying around in the company. It is likely that this cash has long since been spent.

Notice that the categories *Common stock at par* and *Additional paid-in capital* do not tell you how much was paid for each share or when the shares were sold. In fact, most companies have sold new shares on more than one occasion, and received a different price on each occasion. Again, the *Paid-in capital* portion of the *Ownership equity* account only tells you how much money was received in total for all those times when the company sold shares. Do not confuse (1) the company's selling *new* shares, and (2) individuals who already own shares selling their shares to another individual. This will be discussed later. For now, we are only interested in how to account for money that comes into the company when the company writes up new shares and sells them to someone for cash.

3

Borrowing money as the company grows

JMC has now raised $300 of the $500 it is seeking. Having improved its equity position (i.e., put more equity, or cash, permanently into the company), it is now possible that another $200 can be raised by borrowing. Note the difference between equity money and money borrowed. Equity money is money put permanently into the company in exchange for stock (ownership rights). The equity money itself will never be paid back, although the individual who paid it in did so with the idea that either (1) he will get back more in dividends later, or (2) he will be able to sell his stock to another individual for more than he paid for it.

Money that is borrowed, or debt money, must be paid back in the exact amount and with interest according to a specified time schedule. Therefore, people who lend money to the company have the disadvantage of not having ownership rights, but instead have the advantage of a fixed time schedule and legal rights for getting their money back with interest.

Since $200 is more than the company expects to earn this year, it would not make much sense to borrow $200 on a short-term basis (i.e., to plan to pay it back within one year). Furthermore, since the factory to be constructed with the money should be usable for many years, there seemed no reason why it should not be paid for over many years. Hence,

JMC went to an insurance company and asked for a five-year term loan.[1] The insurance company said it would consider making a loan to JMC, and assigned one of its investment officers to examine the books (financial records) of JMC and study the mousetrap and its potential market. The insurance company decided that although risky, it would go ahead and loan JMC the $200, but asked the following stipulations:

1. JMC was to pay back the loan at the rate of $30/year for four years, and then pay the remaining $80 at the end of the fifth year. Each payment was due on December 31 of that year.
2. JMC must pay 8 percent interest annually on the outstanding balance, to be paid at the rate of 4 percent semiannually, on June 30 and December 31.[2]
3. In the event JMC could not meet any one of its interest or payback requirements, the insurance company could immediately declare the company "in default" and require the entire loan to be repaid immediately. In other words the company could be forced to liquidate its assets (i.e., sell its property and factory in order to raise money to meet the interest and payback obligations. In the event that the entire assets of the company were not enough to meet the insurance company's and other creditors' claims, the insurance company asked to be first to be paid with whatever cash could be raised.

JMC had no objections to the first two requirements. The firm felt certain it could meet the annual $30 payback requirement, called a *sinking fund,* with little difficulty. It was also confident that it could meet the large $80 payment at the end of the fifth year. This large payment at the end is called a *balloon*. Both the $30 payments and the $80 payment are called return of principal (as distinguished from interest). In the language of finance, JMC borrowed $200 principal amount under a term loan agreement.

On the third requirement, JMC said it could not let the insurance company have the first, or senior, claim on assets in the event of forced liquidation because the bank had already been promised that. As it happens, the bank loan was due to be paid back within one week, but Jones knew the monthly cash problem might come up again; that is, JMC

---

[1] A "term" loan typically implies a loan of three to seven years. Borrowing for longer than that is more often done by selling bonds (discussed in a later chapter).

[2] To understand how the interest payment schedule works, assume the loan was made on January 1. In that case, the first interest payment would be $8 on June 30 of the first year. This is 4 percent of $200, the amount outstanding during that period. Similarly, the second interest payment on December 31 would also be $8 since the entire $200 was outstanding during the period. But on December 31, $30 of the loan would be paid back. This leaves an "outstanding balance" of $170. Thus the third and fourth interest payments, June 30 and December 31 of the second year, would each be $6.80, which is 4 percent of $170. Similarly, the third-year payments would each be $5.60, and so on.

would have to go on buying raw materials and paying wages during the month even though JMC would not be paid for the sold traps until 10 or more days after the end of the following month. In other words, Jones knew the company would need future bank loans to meet the late-month cash needs while the company had large accounts receivable (i.e., money owed to it). In the language of Wall Street, JMC would need bank loans *to finance receivables*. What this means is that JMC will need bank loans to pay the bills it would be able to pay itself as soon as Accounts Receivable are received.

The insurance company understood the problem because many of its loan customers had the same difficulty, and said it would waive that requirement. The loan was consummated.

DEFINITIONS

Short-term debt Loans which must be repaid within one year, whether payable to banks, suppliers, insurance companies, individuals, or whomever. On the balance sheet, however, this term frequently means just short-term bank debt.

Long-term debt Loans that will be paid back after one year.

Term loan A term loan is usually for a period of three to seven years and is therefore long term. It often has a sinking-fund requirement in addition to a balloon.

Sinking fund Required partial repayment on a long-term loan. It can be payable annually, semiannually, or in any manner the borrower and lender agreed upon at the time the loan was made. The sinking fund (or annual "sinker") is a return of principal that must be paid, in addition to the interest.

Balloon A large payment to complete the repayment of a long-term loan. It is possible that a long-term loan can have no sinking fund, and the balloon, when the loan is due, is therefore equal to the entire value of the loan. It also happens frequently that the sinking fund pays out in equal installments and there is no balloon at all.

On March 1, the loan and sale of stock to the four new investors had been completed. The new balance sheet appears on page 24.

In the month of March, JMC continued to make and sell mousetraps. From the list of events that took place in March (see below) it is possible to derive the income statement for March and the balance sheet on March 31. Although the derivation is presented, it is not necessary for the reader to follow each calculation. If the reader comes away with an understanding of the various terms on the financial statements and understands how they arise, and where they belong on the balance sheet or income statement, he or she is sufficiently prepared to go on. It is important, however, to read through the example as some new terms are explained.

Balance Sheet JMC 3/1/78

Assets		Liabilities + Ownership Equity	
Current assets:		Current liabilities:	
Cash	$575	Interest payable	$ 2
Acc't receivable	90	Short-term debt (bank)	50
Inventory:		Tax payable	24
Finished goods	40	Total current liabilities	76
Raw materials	20		
Total current assets	725	Long-term liabilities:	
		8% Term loan	200
		Ownership equity:	
		Paid-in capital	
		Common stock (par value	
Property, plant, and equipment:		$1) (authorized 100 shares,	
Equipment	20	outstanding 100 shares)	100
		Additional paid-in cap.	350
		Retained earnings	19
		Total ownership equity	469
Total assets	$745	Total liabilities and equity	$745

During the month of March, the following events occurred:

1. Raw materials costing $80 were purchased. JMC could have paid the $80 with its now abundant cash, but it was still uncertain how much of that would be needed for the new land and factory, so JMC asked if it could delay the $80 payments for a while. Since JMC was now a good customer, the company selling the raw materials to JMC agreed to extend credit for one month. Thus, instead of deducting the $80 from cash, JMC set up a new account under *Current liabilities,* called *Accounts payable,* for $80.

2. Raw materials costing $60 were converted into finished goods, of which two thirds were sold.

3. At the end of the month, $10 worth of raw materials were partially converted into mousetraps not yet completed. Since this could no longer be called raw materials, and was not yet finished goods, it gave rise to a new inventory account—*Work in progress.*

4. The store paid the $90 it owed to JMC for February sales.

5. The store sold the 10 mousetraps it had left over at the end of February, which included all of those that were in JMC's *Finished goods* inventory as of March 1. The store also sold 20 more traps that it had received from JMC during March. All of them were sold, for a total of $200, after subtracting the store's fee. The store said it would pay JMC the $200 as usual, 10 days after the end of the month.

6. Mr. Arbetter received $120 in wages, of which $80 was attributed to

time spent building traps and $40 was considered general and administrative expense. Actually, some of Arbetter's time was spent talking to two new stores, which were considering carrying the line of mousetraps. Thus, the $40 might more properly be termed *Selling, general and administrative expense (SGA)*. Of the $80 of Arbetter's wages attributed to trap building, $60 was apportioned to traps sold, $15 to traps finished but not yet sold, and $5 to the time spent on the traps that were partially completed at the end of the month.

7. Property on which to build the factory was purchased for $100. The factory was not yet started.

To derive the March 31 financial statements, the following calculations were made:

Cash as of 3/1/78 .... $575
    Add: Received from store 90

Subtotal 665
    Less: Paid to Mr. Arbetter 120
    Less: Property purchase.. 100
    Less: Bank loan paid back 50
    Less: Interest on bank loan 4

    Total as of 3/31/78... $391

Accounts receivable as of 3/1/78 .... $ 90
    Less: February sales receipts paid to JMC during March............... 90

Subtotal 0
    Add: March receipts of store not to be paid to JMC until April 200

    Total as of 3/31/78... $200

Inventory: Finished goods as of 3/1/78 .... $ 40
    Less: All finished goods as of 3/1/78 were sold during the month 40

Subtotal 0
    Add: Raw material converted but not yet sold....................... 20
    Add: Arbetter's wages attributable to traps finished
        but not yet sold 15

    Total as of 3/31/78... $ 35

Inventory: Work in progress as of 3/1/78 .... $ 0
    Add: Raw material converted but not yet completed 10
    Add: Labor on raw material of not yet completed traps................. 5

    Total as of 3/31/78... $ 15

Inventory: Raw material as of 3/1/78 .... $ 20
    Add: New purchases 80

Subtotal 100
    Less: Amount converted to finished goods............................ 60
    Less: Amount converted to work in progress......................... 10

    Total as of 3/31/78... $ 30

Property, plant, and equipment as of 3/1/78 .... $ 20
  Add: Purchase of property 100
    Total as of 3/31/78 .... $120

Interest payable * as of 3/1/78 .... $ 2
  Less: This was paid when due on 3/15/78 (along with the other $2
    of interest) 2
    Total as of 3/31/78 .... $ 0

Short-term debt as of 3/1/78 .... $ 50
  Less: Paid off when due 3/15/78 50
    Total as of 3/31/78 .... $ 0

Taxes payable as of 3/1/78 .... $ 24
  Add: Expected tax on income for March 9
    Total as of 3/31/78 .... $ 33

Accounts payable as of 3/1/78 .... $ 0
  Add: Credit extended to JMC for raw material 80
    Total as of 3/31/78 .... $ 80

Retained earnings as of 3/1/78 .... $ 19
  Add: Profit for March 9
  Subtotal .... $ 28
  Less: Dividends paid 0
    Total as of 3/31/78 .... $ 28

The *Cost of goods sold* for the month of March was calculated as follows:

Transferred from finished goods .... $ 40
Transferred from raw materials[†] 40
Transferred from Arbetter's wages[†] 60
                                             $140

JMC
Statement of Income from 3/1/78 to 3/31/78

Sales		$200
Expenses		
CGS	$140	
SGA	40	
Interest expense[‡]	2	
	$182	182
Pretax profit		18
Income tax expense		9
Net profit after tax		$ 9

* For simplicity, we have ignored the interest payable on the $200 term loan.

† Actually, both these figures would have been first added to finished goods and then, when the product was sold, subtracted from finished goods and transferred to *Cost of goods sold.* We have ignored that step for simplicity.

‡ Note that although the entire $4 interest was paid in March, only $2 was taken as an expense. This is because the other $2 previously had been "expensed" in February. Again, we have ignored the interest on the $200 term loan for simplicity.

JMC
Balance Sheet, 3/31/78

Assets		Liabilities and Stockholders' Equity	
Current assets:		Current liabilities:	
Cash.........................	$391	Accounts payable	$ 80
Acc't receivable	200	Taxes payable	33
Inventory:		Total current liabilities.........	113
Finished goods................	35		
Work in progress..............	15	Long-term liabilities:	
Raw material	30	8% Term loan..............	200
Total current assets	671		
		Ownership equity:	
		Paid-in capital	
		Common stock	
		(par value $1) (authorized	
		100 shares, outstanding	
Plant, property, and equipment:		100 shares)..............	100
Property.......................	100	Additional paid-in cap.	350
Equipment.....................	20	Retained earnings..........	28
		Total ownership equity	478
Total assets......................	$791	Total liabilities and equity	$791

An interesting and worthwhile exercise for the reader, to check his understanding of the material thus far presented, would be to try to derive one income statement for the period from January 1 through March 31. An easy check to see if it has been done correctly is to see if the retained earnings and the taxes from the three-month income statement are equal to the retained earnings and taxes payable accounts on the balance sheet of March 31, 1978. (Don't forget the dividend.)

Jumping ahead to year end

Through the end of the year the company continued to prosper. The new factory, designated Plant Number 1, had been completed by June and then expanded in September. Some automatic machinery for making mousetraps had been installed. The expansion and automatic machinery had been paid for by money coming from three sources: (1) profits from operations, (2) another term loan, and (3) more new stock that had been sold to some other friends.

There were now 12 stockholders. According to the Securities and Exchange Acts, as long as there are "not more than a small number of sophisticated investors," the company is deemed to be private. The "small number" has never been precisely defined, but it is generally taken to mean 35 or fewer individuals. When a company is private, its owners have no legal obligation to print financial statements or to report to the Securities and Exchange Commission (SEC), and thus the profitability of the company need be revealed to no one except, of course, the Internal

Revenue Service. If the company were to sell stock to over 35 individuals, then under federal law it might be deemed a public corporation. In this case, the company would be required to file with the Securities and Exchange Commission in Washington, D.C., its annual income statements and balance sheet, as well as certain other information.

In practice, there are a number of ways a company can sell to more than 35 individuals and still be deemed a private company. For example, if a company sold stock on two separate occasions, but each issue was to less than 35 people, then each of those stock sales could be considered "private" offerings and the company would still qualify as private although there would be perhaps 70 stockholders. The detailed requirements that determine whether a company will be deemed private or public are more of legal interest than investment interest. A new company such as JMC should have little difficulty remaining private even if it has a second or third private stock offering.

At December 31, the financial statements of the company appeared as shown below. Note the numbers have been expanded and modified considerably for clarity and realism.

JMC
Balance sheet
12/31/78

Assets		*Liabilities and Stockholders' Equity*	
Current assets:		Current liabilities:	
Cash...................	$ 5,000	Accounts payable...........	$ 10,000
U.S. govt. securities......	25,000	Short-term debt.............	6,000
Acc't receivable	10,000	Taxes payable	2,000
Inventory:		Sinking-fund payments	
Finished goods........	20,000	on long-term debt	
Work in progress	5,000	due within one year.......	2,000
Raw materials.........	15,000	Total current liabilities	20,000
Total current assets........	80,000		
		Capitalization:	
		Long-term debt	
		8% Term loan..............	10,000
		9% First mortgage bonds	20,000
Fixed assets:		Stockholders' Equity:	
		Common stock (par value	
Property...............	3,000	$1.00) (authorized 1,000	
Buildings	13,000	shares, outstanding 500	
Equiipment.............	44,000	shares)...................	500
Total fixed assets..........	60,000	Capital surplus	4,500
		Retained earnings	85,000
		Total stockholders' equity......	90,000
Total assets..............	$140,000	Total liabilities and equity......	$140,000

JMC
Income Statement for the Year Ending 12/31/78

Sales.....................		$100,000
Expenses		
Cost of goods sold.........	$70,000	
Selling, gen. and adm.		
expense...............	18,000	
Interest charges...........	2,000	
	90,000	90,000
Pretax profit................		10,000
Income tax.................		5,000
Net profit after tax...........		$ 5,000

Besides the changes in the numbers, the following changes should be noted:

1. The company had quite a bit of cash lying around. Rather than leave it in a checking account at the bank where it earns no interest, Jones thought it wiser to buy some government bonds, which pay interest and can always be sold for cash immediately, either through JMC's bank or through a broker. This is a common practice among corporations with large balances of cash. Besides U.S. government securities, there are other means of investing cash that are very safe and readily convertible into cash. Therefore, instead of *U.S. government securities*, one often sees *Marketable securities*. This does *not* refer to common stocks, whose prices are much less dependable and can be difficult to sell on short notice.

2. The *Property, buildings, and equipment* accounts were increased substantially.

3. The company once again went to the bank for short-term debt. This time it was for $16,000, of which $10,000 has already been paid back.

4. Note that the *Taxes payable* account is less than the full taxes for the year, because being a corporation, JMC had to begin estimating and paying taxes quarterly. Thus, only the estimated tax for the last three months remains on the balance sheet, as all the earlier quarters' taxes have been paid. When the final tax bill for the year is figured in early 1979, the taxes payable figure can be adjusted accordingly.

5. Recall that liabilities due within one year are classified as short-term. When JMC first took down the 8 percent term loan, it was for $12,000.[3] But one of the stipulations was that a sinking-fund payment

---

[3] The term loan was actually for $200, of which $30 was due within one year, but again the numbers have been modified for realism.

of $2,000 would be paid each year on December 30 beginning in 1979. Therefore, of the original $12,000 loan, $2,000 was due within a year and the remaining $10,000 was still classified as long-term debt.

6. The 9 percent First Mortgage Bonds were sold to a group of insurance companies in October 1978. They are called First Mortgage because, if JMC should fail to make its payments to the insurance companies, they have the right to take possession of the building and sell it in order to get their money back.

7. The *Retained earnings* figure is obviously out of proportion. For a company that has been in business only one year, the retained earnings figure should be equal to the profits of the company that year, less the dividends paid by the company that year. The large figure presented would be more typical of a company that had been in business and making profits for many years. We shall use the large number for convenience.

8. *Capitalization.* This is a hard-to-define word, which comes up in many contexts within the business world. On the balance sheet, it usually refers to the combination of long-term debt plus stockholders' equity. In this sense, it refers to the money (or capital) used by the company to manufacture the products it sells. In other words, the machinery and equipment that were bought with this money can be thought of as "capital." This, in fact, is the economist's definition of capital—goods (machinery) used to make other goods. Such machinery, or capital goods, can be paid for by (*a*) money put into the business by individuals who bought stock from the company (which may have happened on more than one occasion), and/or (*b*) profits earned by the company, and/or (*c*) money raised by selling debt (bonds, term loans). Inventory, however, is not thought of as capital, but rather as the raw materials that are acted on by the capital (machinery) to make the company's products. Whereas long-term debt and equity are usually thought of as financing capital equipment, short-term debt and other current liabilities are usually thought of as financing inventories or receivables until these can be converted into cash in what might be called the inventory cycle, or receivables cycle. Although we usually think of the balance sheet this way, it is not necessarily true. For example, there are many companies that use short-term debt to finance capital equipment or use long-term debt or equity to finance inventories.

4

Ratio analysis

When a financial analyst first looks at a balance sheet or income statement, all she sees is the same morass of numbers that the layman sees. To make sense of these figures, to evaluate the company's financial strength or weakness, and to get insights into possible stock market performance, she must look at the relationships between the figures. The ratios discussed below are among those frequently used by analysts. The figures used are taken from JMC's financial statements of December 31, 1978, which are found at the end of Chapter 3.

PROFITABILITY RATIOS

1. Net earnings per common share outstanding

This ratio is one of the most important factors helping to determine what one should pay for a share of stock. The discussion here will set the stage for further discussion in later chapters. This ratio is usually called earnings per share or abbreviated as EPS. It is simply the net earnings of the company for the year, $5,000, divided by the number of shares of common stock outstanding, 500. Therefore, JMC's earnings per share for 1978 were $10 per share.

$$\frac{\text{Net earnings}}{\text{Number of shares}} = \frac{\$5,000}{500 \text{ shares}} = \$10/\text{Share}$$

This ratio helps one to decide what he should pay for a share of stock by telling him how much money that share can "earn" for him. The earnings per share are not, of course, paid directly to the stockholder; they are kept in the company. The company may, however, declare a dividend from time to time, which *is* paid directly to the stockholder. Thus, the higher the earnings per share, the higher the dividend per share is likely to be. The astute reader should realize, then, that what someone should be willing to pay for a share of stock is not really related to what the share of stock is "earning" today, but *what it is expected to be earning (and therefore potentially paying in dividends) over a period of time.* Thus, if a share of stock were earning $10 per share this year, expected to earn $20 next year, and $30 the following year, and the company was expected to pay out 50 percent of earnings as a dividend in each year, then the holder of one share of stock would expect to receive $5 + $10 + $15 = $30 over a period of three years. Thus, he would certainly be willing to buy the stock for more than the $10/share that the stock is earning today. How much more he would be willing to pay is related to two factors; first, his evaluation of the risk that his estimates of the company's next three years' earnings and dividends are wrong, and second, his evaluation of what the company can be earning, and therefore potentially paying as dividends beyond three years out. The exceptionally astute reader will now realize that what one should be willing to pay for a share of stock is not necessarily related to what he expects the company to earn and pay out as a dividend in the near future, but rather what one expects other investors will be expecting for potential earnings and dividends for the period beginning some time in the future. If this seems confusing, it is , but this is what stock prices are all about. Let's look at some examples.

The table below shows three hypothetical companies' expected dividends for six years, and the bank interest that can be had if one chooses to put one's money in the bank at 5 percent interest rather than buy any of the three stocks. Presuming $100 is put into the bank, the investor (bankbook holder) would expect to get $5 per year interest and get back one's original investment of $100 at the end of six years (or any other time, for that matter).

| | Put in | Interest or dividend payment during year | | | | | | Get back |
		(1)	(2)	(3)	(4)	(5)	(6)	
Bank	$100	$ 5	$ 5	$ 5	$ 5	$ 5	$ 5	$100
Company A		5	6	7	8	9	10	
Company B		5	7	9	12	16	21	
Company C		0	0	0	20	30	40	

For Company A, dividends are expected to grow as shown for six years and then either go higher or stay at $10. If one had the same degree of confidence in receiving these dividends that she has in receiving bank interest, she would presumably be willing to pay more than $100 for a share of stock of Company A. Again, how much more is related to the confidence that these estimated dividend payments will actually come to pass. The problem is that one almost always has less confidence in receiving dividends from a company than getting interest from a bank. Also, as one looks further out in time, confidence in earnings and dividend estimates gets lower and lower, whereas confidence in bank interest remains fairly high.

For the sake of the discussion, assume Company A will continue to pay a dividend of $10 for every year in the future after the sixth year and that investor confidence in Company A's dividend-paying ability is as high as confidence in a bank's interest-paying ability. In that case, Company A would be worth $200 per share at the end of six years. Why? Because a $10 return (dividend) per year on a $200 investment is obviously identical to a $5 return per year on a $100 investment. Therefore, what would you be willing to pay now for a stock with Company A's dividend expectations and a "known" value of $200 at the end of six years? Obviously over $100. If the future amount and timing of dividends is known with 100 percent confidence, the value the stock is worth today can be figured out mathematically. [1] The math is beyond this book, but under these assumptions a share of stock in Company A works out to be worth $187. In the real world, however, there is never 100 percent certainty so the stock would presumably sell for less than $187, given these best-guess dividend estimates.

Company B is expected to pay even higher dividends over six years and therefore a share of its stock should sell for more than a share of Company A's stock, provided there is similar confidence in the dividend estimates, and a similar expectation for receiving a steady dividend (in this case $21 per year) in each year beyond the sixth year. Company C pays no dividend today and is not expected to for three years, but then its dividend-paying power will be much higher than Company A or B. Would you pay more today for a share of Company C or Company B? Once again, the answer depends to an important degree on your confidence that the dividends will actually be received, and, of course, the further out in the future the lower the confidence.

In this example we talked about dividends, but we said earlier that the price of the stock is related to its expected earnings. Wall Streeters generally talk about earnings because it is presumed that what a company

---

[1] Presuming interest rates do not change and ignoring taxation consequences

earns is a good measure of what it can pay as dividends. The more a company earns, the more it can presumably pay in dividends. In reality, dividends are not paid from earnings but are paid from cash. In a given year, a company may earn nothing—or even lose money—but choose to pay the dividend anyway, provided, of course, it has the cash available to do so. Thus, if a company is losing money in a given year and still pays the dividend, we might say (from an accounting point of view) that it was paid out of retained earnings rather than current earnings. However, if a company is losing money over a period of years and sees no immediate expectation of a good profit, it is unlikely that it would continue to pay a dividend and deplete all its cash reserve. It is, however, common practice today for a company to maintain a dividend for a year if just that year's earnings are expected to be low (or a loss). But over a period of years, it is generally presumed that if there is not a continuing flow of earnings there cannot be a continuing flow of dividends.

Remember that when a dividend is declared and paid, it is deducted from cash on the left side of the balance sheet and deducted from retained earnings on the right. The cash account reflects the actual dollars belonging to the company, and the retained earnings account is just an accounting entry. Review the definition of retained earnings at the end of Chapter 2.

There are no rules about how much one should pay for any given amount of earnings per share, or dividends per share. Thus in the example above it is not clear whether Company C or Company B is worth more today. Only by long experience of studying the relationship between the price of a stock per share and its expected earnings per share, called the *price-to-earnings ratio*, does one begin to develop a feeling for what a stock is really "worth." At this point, however, we are ahead of our story. We will return to it later.

2. Book value per common share

This is simply the book value, previously defined, divided by the number of shares outstanding.

$$\text{Book Value} = \frac{\text{Total assets} - \text{Total liabilities}}{\text{Number of shares}}$$

$$= \frac{140,000 - 50,000}{500} = \frac{90,000}{500} = \$180/\text{Share}$$

This ratio tells you about how much each share of common stock can be expected to receive if the company were liquidated. When a company is liquidated, it means all the assets are sold and the money received is initially used to pay off the debts (liabilities). Then, if there is any money left over, it is split up among the common stockholders in proportion to how many shares of stock each owns. As a practical matter in the case of a liquidation, after all the debts are paid off it is unlikely that the stockholders would realize book value. The exact figure of $180/share above assumes that all the assets could be sold for exactly their book value (i.e., the value at which they are carried on the balance sheet). Normally, however, when a company is liquidated, its inventories are often sold for less than their book value. If the plant and equipment are obsolete they might not be able to be sold for anything, or just for scrap value, which is probably much less than the value at which it is carried on the books. Even so, an efficient operating plant might sell for more than book value since another company buying the plant would be able to save all costs of building it. Land is often worth more than what it originally cost.

When a company is liquidated, the amount of money raised selling off the assets is sometimes not enough to pay off all the liabilities. In this case it is usually known in advance what liabilities get paid off first. Recall that the bank and the insurance company who made loans to JMC both wanted to be paid first in the event of liquidation, but JMC told the insurance company that it had promised the bank first priority. Similarly, the priority of all other liabilities is usually determined in advance, either by negotiation, as with the bank and insurance company, or by law. The law in most states specifies that in the event of liquidation the first priorities are any back wages owed to employees and any taxes owed.

Liquidation can occur either voluntarily, because the board of directors decides to do it, or more likely because the company is bankrupt. Bankruptcy usually occurs when a company is unable to pay a debt or debts that are legally due. This debt can be a bank loan, an interest payment, an account payable to a supplier, or any other debt. Then, either the party owed the money goes to court and asks that the company be legally declared bankrupt, or sometimes the company voluntarily goes to court to declare bankruptcy.

Once the court declares the company legally bankrupt, the company and all the parties owed money (or goods or services) go to court and try to make an arrangement that is satisfactory to all. If they cannot come to an agreement, then the company is liquidated, or dissolved. When a company is liquidated under bankruptcy, the court oversees the selling of the assets and then decides which of the creditors will get how much money if there is not enough to pay off all of them. Despite the previously determined order of priority in liquidation, the court in bankruptcy has a lot of flexibility in deciding which creditors get how much, and they do not always follow the established priorities. The bankruptcy laws are very complex and not relevant here. We are more concerned with successful companies.

Even ignoring the value in bankruptcy, it is important to understand book value per common share because some investors like to use this ratio as a benchmark against which to measure the price of stock. For example, book value per share is often thought of as a price below which a stock will not fall for long, for the following reason: if the book value of a company were $10 per share and its stock was selling for $4, someone could attempt to buy all the stock and voluntarily liquidate the company, thereby realizing a $6 per share profit. In the real world, however, this does not happen often to a public company with widely held stock (many stockholders) but it is a real enough possibility that many stocks do seem to stop going down when the stock is selling well below book value, say 25 to 50 percent below. When a stock does go that far below book value, it often does not stay there long—the low price attracts buyers. But it frequently occurs that a stock sells at slightly below its book value, perhaps up to 25 percent below.

3. Yield

The yield on a common stock is defined as the dividend received by the investor divided by the price of the stock. The dividend received usually refers to the dollar amount of dividends expected to be received over the next 12 months. Since the yield also depends on the price, it is important to know what price you are talking about. If a stock pays a $5 dividend per year and the price of the stock is $100 today, the yield to the investor today is 5 percent.

$$\frac{\text{Dividend}}{\text{Stock price}} = \frac{\$5}{\$100} = 5\%$$

If the current price of the stock is $83, the yield is 6 percent.

$$\frac{\text{Dividend}}{\text{Stock price}} = \frac{\$5}{\$83} = 6\%$$

However, an investor who purchased the stock at $50 a few years ago might say his yield, based on his purchase price of $50, is 10 percent.

$$\frac{\text{Dividend}}{\text{Stock price}} = \frac{\$5}{\$50} = 10\%$$

When investors talk about the yield on a stock without otherwise specifying, they generally mean the dividend expected over the next 12 months divided by the price of the stock today. Since the price of the stock generally changes daily, the expected yield over the next 12 months also changes daily.

Yield usually refers to the return to an investor. The word occasionally has other uses, but you would know this by the context of the discussion. Bond yield, like stock yield, refers to the return to an investor but is more complicated and will be discussed in Chapter 8.

4. Return on total capital employed in the business (after taxes)

Return, in this case, means net profit after taxes. *Capital employed in the business* means the total value of everything under *Capitalization* on the balance sheet, which for now means long-term debt plus equity. Recall that capitalization may be thought of as the sources of money that bought the capital assets (i.e., the machinery and equipment that the company uses to make its finished goods). Therefore, *return on capital* is a measure of how efficiently the company is able to use its assets to generate profit.

$$\frac{\text{Net profit after tax}}{\text{Total capitalization}} = \frac{\$5,000}{\$120,000} = 4.2\%$$

The return on capital is regarded by many analysts as one of the most important ratios in analyzing a company. By showing how efficiently a company is able to use its assets to generate profit, the analyst has an excellent basis for comparison of two or more companies. Such a comparison is particularly useful for comparing companies in the same industry. For example, if three shoe manufacturers had returns on capital of 12, 8 and 6 percent, respectively, regardless of the size of the companies it could be concluded that the company with the 12 percent return had the potential to be the fastest growing, since, proportional to its capital assets, it will be generating the largest amount of cash to use to buy even more capital assets to enable it to keep growing.

5. Return on common shareholders' equity

This ratio is very similar in meaning to return on total capital. In this case, it is presumed that part of the measure of the efficiency of a company is its ability to borrow money (long-term) to help make the company grow. A company usually cannot borrow money unless it has a good equity base to begin with (i.e., has a high proportion of equity relative to the amount of debt it wishes to borrow). Thus, the profits earned by the use of assets, whether these assets were bought with equity money or debt money, are really all a return to the fact that the equity money was there in the first place.

$$\frac{\text{Net profit after tax}}{\text{Stockholders' equity}} = \frac{\$5,000}{\$90,000} = 5.6\%$$

6. Pretax profit margin

This ratio, also called the *pretax return on sales,* is the profit before taxes divided by the total sales for the same period.

$$\frac{\text{Pretax profit}}{\text{Sales}} = \frac{\$10,000}{\$100,000} = 10\%$$

Like the previous two ratios, profit margin is also a measure of the efficiency of a company. If two companies of roughly the same size, which sell the same products, have differing profit margins, the one with the larger margin is probably the most efficiently managed. Again, the company with the highest margin is likely to be the fastest growing since it is able to generate the most cash to plow back into the business.

Within a given industry, the company with the highest pretax profit margin is also likely to be the safest investment because, if sales or profitability were to decline, the company that started with the higher profit margin might only have its profit reduced, but the company that had a low profit margin to begin with could show a loss and eventually go out of business.

7. Return on sales after tax

This is also called the *profit margin after taxes* or just *net profit margin.* It has about the same meaning as the pretax profit margin. The only case where it would make a difference when comparing two companies is if the two companies had differing tax rates. When the companies being compared have approximately the same tax rate, the analyst can use either the pretax or aftertax profit margin with the same comparative results.

8. Tax rate *or* Effective tax rate

This is simply the total tax paid divided by the pretax profit.

$$\frac{\text{Tax paid}}{\text{Pretax profit}} = \frac{\$5,000}{\$10,000} = 50\%$$

The term arises because corporate tax laws are so complex that even though the ordinary tax rate on income may be 46 percent, by the time all the additions (e.g., surtaxes) and subtractions (e.g., deductions, credits) have been added in, it is unlikely that any company will actually be paying precisely 46 percent.

FINANCIAL CONDITION RATIOS

Ratios 4 through 8 related primarily to the profitability of the company (i.e., its ability to generate new cash). Another set of important ratios relates more to the financial condition or solvency of the company. Even a company of high potential profitability is of little investment worth if it is about to run into debts greater than it can afford to pay. The financial ratios that follow help to assess the ability of the company to meet its cash needs in the future.

9. Current ratio

This defined as current assets divided by current liabilities.

$$\frac{\text{Current assets}}{\text{Current liabilities}} = \frac{\$80,000}{\$20,000} = 4{:}1$$

The current ratio is a measure of the company's ability to pay off its short-term debt. Recall that current assets are those expected to be converted into cash within a year. Current liabilities are those which must be paid within one year. Since, in the normal course of business, current assets are continually being added (inventory, accounts receivable) and current liabilities are continually being paid off, the current ratio can be regarded more generally as a measure of the company's ability to meet day-to-day needs. An old rule of thumb is that a current ratio of two to one (2:1) is a minimum safety margin, but that is not particularly meaningful today. The ratio varies a lot, depending on the nature of a given company's business. An electric utility, for example, has little day-to-day fluctuation in its costs. Since utility costs are so predictable in advance, there is little need to keep extra cash around beyond what is known to be needed. When a current ratio is very low, say 0.2:1, it could indicate that the company will need to go out and borrow money in the near future. Again, this would vary from company to company.

10. Quick ratio *or* Acid test

This is defined as current assets, less inventories, divided by current liabilities.

$$\frac{\text{Current assets} - \text{Inventory}}{\text{Current liabilities}} = \frac{\$80,000 - \$40,000}{\$20,000} = 2{:}1$$

The quick ratio, like the current ratio, is a measure of the company's ability to pay off debt in the short run. This assumes that, if the company were forced to pay off its debt in a hurry, it would not have time to sell inventory. The rule of thumb is that a quick ratio of 1:1 or better would be considered good. Again, this will vary from company to company, depending on individual circumstances. A company could have a quick ratio of well under 1:1 and be in good financial shape.

11. Cash ratio

The cash ratio is cash plus marketable securities divided by current liabilities.

$$\frac{\text{Cash} + \text{Marketable securities}}{\text{Current liabilities}} = \frac{\$5,000 + \$25,000}{\$20,000} = 1.5{:}1$$

This is merely a more stringent version of the acid test.

The significance of the last three ratios lies not so much in the actual ratios, since they vary widely from company to company, especially companies in different industries, but in the changes that occur over a period of time in the same company. If a financial analyst saw the following figures, she would immediately conclude that the financial status of the company was weakening, and it may need to raise some outside money, either by borrowing or by selling stock.

	XYZ Company			
	1979	1980	1981	1982
Current ratio	$\frac{2.4}{1}$	$\frac{2.5}{1}$	$\frac{1.2}{1}$	$\frac{0.7}{1}$
Quick ratio	$\frac{1.1}{1}$	$\frac{0.9}{1}$	$\frac{0.6}{1}$	$\frac{0.5}{1}$
Cash ratio	$\frac{0.8}{1}$	$\frac{0.8}{1}$	$\frac{0.4}{1}$	$\frac{0.3}{1}$

This would be a flag telling her something is wrong in the company. She would try to confirm this by looking at the profitability ratios and seeing if they, too, were declining. She would also ask the company directly what has caused this deterioration of financial position. Often the company will explain things that the analyst cannot read from the financial statements.

The next two financial ratios relate directly to the ability of the company to raise more money if needed.

12. Interest coverage (sometimes called Times-interest-earned *or* Earnings coverage)

This is a measure of the company's ability to meet its interest charges. If a company owing money were unable to meet these interest charges, the bank or person to whom the loan (and interest) was owed, usually has the legal right to force the company to liquidate as much of its assets as is necessary to pay off the *entire* loan. Thus, a company unable to meet its interest charges is risking being thrown into bankruptcy.

The interest coverage ratio answers two questions: (1) how much money is available to pay interest, and (2) how many times larger is that amount available than it needs to be. In other words, how safely is the interest covered? Interest is paid with cash, so we could simply look at Cash on the balance sheet and see if it is enough to cover interest payable. But that really is not satisfactory, because if a company used all its cash to pay interest the company would be unable to continue operating. What we are really interested in is the ability of the company to generate sufficient cash over a period of time to meet its interest payments over the same period. Thus, the way this ratio is usually calculated is to look at the income statement to see how much money came in and how much money had to go out before interest was paid in order to keep the company going. The calculation is usually done using a full year's results, either the past year, or the expected results for the current year, or some future year.

Ratio calculation

Sales.	$100,000	(Came in)
Less: Cost of goods sold	− 70,000	(This money had to be spent or there would be no products to sell)
Less: Selling, general and administrative expense	− 18,000	(This money also had to be spent or the company could not function)
Equals:	$ 12,000	

Therefore, there is $12,000 *available* to pay interest. Thus interest is "covered" six times (6x).

$$\frac{\text{Money available to pay interest}}{\text{Total interest}} = \frac{\$12,000}{\$2,000} = 6x$$

Note that the taxes do not enter into the calculation. This is because interest charges are deducted before pretax profit and taxes are calculated. Thus, if interest charges were $12,000 in the above example, there would be no pretax profit and therefore no taxes to be paid.

While the ratio calculation above is perfectly correct and shows you exactly what you are calculating, it is usually presented differently in the financial press. Note that this statement says exactly the same thing in a different way:

$$\frac{\text{Earnings before interest and taxes}}{\text{Total interest}} = \frac{\$12,000}{\$2,000} = 6x$$

In the language of Wall Street, interest coverage is 6 times (6x). This means pretax, pre-interest earnings ($12,000) would have to fall to one sixth of its existing level before the company would be in jeopardy. With interest covered 6 times, this company probably would be able to borrow a limited amount of additional money without too much difficulty. But if interest were covered 44 times (for example, earnings of $88,000 before interest and taxes, and interest charges of $2,000), the analyst would know that the company could borrow money very easily and be able to do so at a lower interest rate than the company with earnings coverage of only 6 times. If interest were only covered 2 times, and if perhaps the current and quick ratios were weak or deteriorating, the analyst would suspect that this company might be in trouble and could have difficulty borrowing additional money.

In addition to interest coverage, many investors also use a similar ratio called the *fixed charge coverage ratio*. This ratio is calculated much like the interest coverage ratio; but, in addition to interest, it also takes into account certain other fixed charges, such as fixed lease payments and perhaps some other minor items. JMC Corporation is not leasing any assets so we will not do that calculation here.

13. Debt to total capitalization

This usually refers to long-term debt only, divided by total capitalization.

$$\frac{\text{Long-term debt}}{\text{Total capitalization}} = \frac{\$30,000}{\$120,000} = 25\%$$

The less debt already in the total capitalization, the more easily (i.e., at lower interest) the company will be able to borrow money. What constitutes a "safe" ratio depends, again, on the nature of the company and its industry. An electric utility, for example, where earnings are very predictable, can easily borrow money above a 50 percent debt/total capital ratio, even if interest coverage is low. However, a company in which earnings fluctuate widely may have trouble borrowing more than 30 percent of its total capitalization, primarily because the ability to cover interest or to meet sinking-fund payments might be seriously impaired in a year when earnings are low.

5

Going public

A common difficulty of students trying to understand the stockmarket is the confusion between the company's stock and stock of the company owned by individuals (or mutual funds, trusts, and the like).[1] The confusion is best cleared up by pointing out that both categories are identical. All of a company's stock is owned by someone.

Shares of stock merely represent percentages of ownership in a company. The company has no stock of its own. It cannot own itself. A company may buy back its stock from individuals with the company's money, but that stock, called *treasury stock*, no longer represents partial ownership of the company. These treasury shares may not be voted by the company at the stockholders' meeting and they do not get dividends. Such shares are without value unless reissued by the company.

"JMC, Inc., has 500 shares outstanding." That doesn't mean JMC, Inc., has them. It means JMC ownership is divided into 500 equal parts, each share representing one five-hundredth. Individuals own them. It would be clearer to say, "JMC, Inc., has 500 shares outstanding, which are owned by individuals." If some of the individuals who owned the stock sold their shares to other individuals, it simply means that part of the ownership of the company has changed hands. Regardless of the

---

[1] From here on, we will use the term *individual*, when referring to buying or selling stock, to mean either persons, mutual funds, trusts, and so on.

price at which the stock changed hands, there is no change in any of the company's accounts. There are still only 500 shares outstanding. The *Common stock at par value* and *Additional paid-in capital* accounts do not change. Those figures only represent the total amount of money that was paid into the company when each share of stock was issued *by the company* to its *first* owner. By way of analogy, if I buy a new Oldsmobile, the money goes to General Motors. If I then sell my Oldsmobile to my neighbor, he pays me. General Motors never sees the money that he paid me. That car can now change ownership every day and it has no effect on the financial statements of General Motors.

JMC is currently a private company. This means all of its stock is owned by a small number of investors, and none is legally able to be sold to the public. The Securities and Exchange Acts require that before any stock can be sold to the public, it must first be registered with the SEC. Thus, prior to the company going through the registration process (discussed below), JMC's 12 stockholders are extremely limited in their ability to sell their stock.

There are two reasons a company may want to go public (i.e., make stock of the company legally available to the public):

1. The *company* wishes to raise more capital, and does not want to borrow or have another private stock offering. In this case, the company writes up new shares (provided they have been authorized by the stockholders) and sells them to new (or old) investors. All the money from this sale goes *to the company*.
2. Existing stockholders wish to sell their stock and raise money for themselves. In this case, all the money from the sale of the stock goes directly *to the stockholders*.

In the latter case, we say it is the existing stockholders who are "bringing the company public," and the company officers may not have any choice in the matter. In practice, when a new company is formed, the investors who are putting up the money in exchange for the initial "private" stock decide among themselves, right at the beginning, when and under what circumstances the stockholders will have the right to sell their stock to the public. For example, the initial stockholders may agree that "any time after the company has been profitable for at least two years, and if a majority of us are in favor, then we will have the legal right to force the company officers to do what is necessary to have a public offering." The agreement might also add something like, "each of us may sell up to 30 percent of his or her shares at the time of this offering and up to another 30 percent of the shares at the time of the next offering, which cannot be forced for at least two years. In addition, however, if the company itself is offering new shares to the public *at any time,* then each of us may also join the offering and sell up to 20 percent of our already outstanding shares." Every company's agreement with its initial stockholders is different.

For whichever of the above reasons the company is going public, the shares to be sold to the public must first be registered with the SEC. This means the company must send to the SEC a statement of (1) how much stock will be sold, whether it is new shares being sold by the company or already outstanding shares being sold by current stockholders to other individuals, or some of each, and (2) certain financial and other information about the company to help potential investors (buyers) to make a proper evaluation of the risks involved in buying this stock. This information is put together in a small booklet called a *prospectus*. The SEC examines the prospectus and, if it is not satisfied that enough information has been presented, it requests more. The SEC does not attest that the information presented is truthful, or even that it is adequate for investors to make an informed decision. But when the SEC gives its permission for the stock to be sold to the public, investors generally assume there is enough information presented that, if truthful, an investor should be able to make an informed decision about the worth of the stock. If the information is found to be fraudulent, however, the people who bought the stock based on the information contained in the prospectus may be able to return the stock to the company and have their money refunded. Furthermore, the perpetrators of the fraud are subject to criminal prosecution.

While the prospectus is pending with the SEC, the company is allowed to print and distribute a *preliminary prospectus*, sometimes called a *red herring*. This name derives from the fact that the company is required to print in red ink on the front page that this is only a preliminary prospectus and is subject to change. When the SEC is satisfied that the prospectus is sufficiently informative, it declares the registration to be "effective," which means that any time within the next 90 days the company or selling stockholders, or both, may sell all or just some of the shares *which have just been registered*. They may not sell any other shares. If any of the stock that has just been registered has not been sold during the 90-day period, it must be reregistered before it can be sold. The reason for this is that after the 90 days, it is possible that circumstances have changed sufficiently that the old prospectus is out of date and potential investors no longer have enough current information to make an informed decision. Once the registered shares have been sold, *they are registered forever* and may be sold from one individual to another every day without another prospectus.[2]

---

[2] There are some special circumstances when already registered shares must be registered again. Discussion later in this chapter.

There is an exception to this formal registration procedure, under Rule 144 of the Securities and Exchange Acts.

Under Rule 144, a stockholder who has held unregistered stock of a public company at least two years may sell it to the public without registering it—provided that the amount is small and that certain conditions are met. Once it is sold, that stock would then be free to trade forever, as if it had been registered.

When a company sells new stock, either privately (to fewer than 35 individuals), or publicly (registered stock to any number of individuals), it is called a *primary offering*. When existing stockholders sell their already outstanding stock, either to other private individuals or to the public, it is called a *secondary offering*. Therefore, in a primary offering, the money from the sale of the stock goes to the company. In a secondary offering, the money from the sale of the stock goes to the selling stockholders. If this distinction is clear, it should be apparent that there is no limit to the number of primary offerings a company can have. Similarly, there can be many secondary offerings of the "company" stock until all the shares have been registered once or have been sold under Rule 144 and therefore do not have to be registered. "Company" is in quotes because it is not really the company having the secondary offering; rather, it is stockholders. Nevertheless, the company must still file a prospectus to register the shares of the selling stockholders. The first time any stock of a company is sold to the public, whether a primary or secondary offering, it is called the company's *initial public offering*.

Actually, every time an individual sells one or more shares of registered stock to another individual, he or she has made a secondary offering. Therefore, every purchase or sale on a stock exchange is technically a secondary offering. In Wall Street jargon, however, the word *secondary* usually refers to stock that has just been registered. Shares that are sold from one individual to another are just called "trades." *Trade*, of course, is a poor word because stocks are bought and sold, not traded.

Registered secondary offerings, or just "secondaries," can arise from a number of sources. First, the shares can come from the founder or founders of the company, such as Mr. Jones. Second, shares can come from investors who got their stock in a private offering, such as the four investors who put money into Jones Mousetrap Company back in March or the other investors who put money in later in the year.

A third way a secondary can arise is as follows. Sometimes, when a public or private company decides it wants to raise money quickly (rather than filing with the SEC, which is both expensive and time-consuming), it will choose to sell new stock privately. Note that new stock can be sold privately even though the company is already public. While such private shares do not have to be registered, because they are not being sold to the public, they do have to be authorized by existing shareholders. This kind of private offering, as before, must be sold to a "small group of sophisticated investors." This is sometimes called a *private placement.*

Private placements are typically made with trust departments of banks, insurance companies, mutual funds, and the like. When buying a "private placement" of stock, the bank or mutual fund must sign a "letter of investment representation," which says it is purchasing the stock for "investment" and will not sell it for at least a specified period of time. Such stock is sometimes called *investment letter stock*, or just *letter stock*. The laws governing the sale of letter stock are ill-defined, but the period for which the holder of the letter stock cannot sell has usually been interpreted to mean at least two years. Whatever the holding period, when the holder finally decides to sell, he or she must first register the stock with the SEC (unless it is sold under Rule 144). This then, would also be a secondary. To review a point made previously: a secondary offering from any of these sources would be the company's intitial public offering, only if the company has not yet gone public.

Less frequently, a secondary may refer to previously registered stock. For example, if a large fund or individual holds a major block of stock, usually more than 10 percent of the company's total outstanding stock, and wishes to sell it all at once to the public, the holder must first have the company file a prospectus with the SEC. This usually occurs when the holder of the stock is an *insider*, which means either he or she is an officer of the company, or otherwise has access to information about the company that the general public does not. While a prospectus obviously cannot reveal every bit of information that an insider knows, it is theoretically required to reveal at least "all material information" about the company that the prospective buyer would need to make an informed decision about whether or not to buy the stock. This "material disclosure" requirement applies to all prospectuses, whether for stock that is being reregistered, or stock being registered for the first time.

Let us now return to why a company goes public. The first reason, for the company to raise money, is obvious. The second reason, for the stockholders to raise money, requires further explanation. Assume Mr. Smith owns 100 shares of JMC and JMC's earnings-per-share are $10. Assuming the company is paying out 50 percent of earnings as a dividend (i.e., $5 per share per year), Smith will receive a total of $500 per year in dividends. If Smith were to sell the stock, however, he could get more for it than the $5 per share it brings him this year. This is because the purchaser of the stock can look forward to a future stream of hopefully increasing earnings and dividends. The rationale for this was discussed in the Earnings Per Common Share Outstanding discussion in Chapter 4. If it is not familiar to the reader, now would be a good time to review it. Let us assume that experienced investors have told Smith that they would be willing to pay $100 per share for JMC stock. If the stock is earning $10 per share and investors are willing to pay $100 per share, we would say the price-earnings ratio of the stock is ten (10x).

$$\text{Price-earnings ratio} \ = \ \frac{\text{Price/Share}}{\text{Earnings/Share}} \ = \ \frac{\$100}{\$10} \ = \ 10x$$

In other words, investors are willing to pay 10 times (10x) current earnings per share (or 20x the current dividend) for a share of JMC stock. In Wall Street language one would say, "Investors are willing to pay 10 times earnings for JMC," or, "JMC's price-earnings ratio is 10x," or, "The investment community will capitalize JMC's earnings at 10 times." Note the use of the word *capitalize*. Again, this is a word with many meanings. In this case, it refers to what price-earnings ratio people are willing to pay for a stock.

If Smith sells his 100 shares at $100 per share, he will have a total amount of $10,000 in cash, compared with the $500 per year he might have expected to receive if he held his stock. This is the main reason why initial stockholders in a company want the company to go public—because the public's willingness to pay a high price-earnings ratio enables the original stockholders to receive in cash today what they would not otherwise get for years, if ever, in dividends.

An initial investor does not, of course, have to sell all of his shares to get rich. For that matter, he does not have to sell any. Suppose Mr. Smith chose to hold all of his stock. Instead, assume the company itself, or other individuals, sold stock to the public to raise money. If the public paid $100 per share to the company, and assuming the stock continued to trade at about that price, Smith would know that he was "worth" $10,000 because he could always sell his stock for that (after registering it, of course). Knowing this, he could probably borrow whatever money he needed, putting up his stock for collateral.

It is this willingness of the stockmarket to pay a high multiple of current earnings (some companies have gone public with price-earnings ratios of over 40x) that provides incentive for people with good ideas to start their own companies. Similarly, this is the incentive that causes people with excess capital to invest in new ventures, as did the four individuals who invested in Jones Mousetrap Company in Chapter 2.

This incentive is also one reason why companies sometimes lose their best people. An engineer with a new idea might get a bonus from his company for the idea, but it is far less than what he will make if he forms his own company and keeps a lot of the stock for himself, as did Jones in JMC. Recall that Jones had only put up one third of the money, but kept 60 percent ownership in the company.

One way that companies are able to prevent their key employees from leaving is to give them stock options. Stock options offer an individual a way to make a lot of money in a stock even if he or she did not put any money into the company at the beginning. Assume, for example, that Ms. Appel is a valued employee of XYZ Corporation, and management of XYZ has given her a stock option on 100 shares of XYZ stock. The stock option may say something like the following:

> Ms. *APPEL* has the right, anytime in the next *three* years, to purchase from the company *100* shares of stock at $100 per share.

What this says is that Ms. Appel is being offered the right to buy a given number of shares (100 in this case) of XYZ stock *anytime* within a specified period (up to three years in this case) for a price that is decided today ($100 per share). Say, for example, Ms. Appel was given this stock option on January 4, 1980, at which time XYZ's stock was selling at $100 per share. It is now May of 1982 and XYZ's stock has appreciated to $400/share, which Ms. Appel thinks is as high as it is likely to go before January 4, 1983. Thus she decides to exercise her option. So she calls whomever is administering the plan and says she wishes to exercise her option and buy 100 shares at $100 per share. She can now turn around and sell it the same day at $400, and make a $300 profit per share. Since her option was for 100 shares, she has made a gain of $30,000 on top of her regular salary.

If, however, the stock goes down while she is holding the option, she has lost nothing since she has not paid anything yet and does not have to. In most large companies, management can offer enough shares in options to keep most good employees happy without having to give away a significant portion of the company. Options also work to keep employees because, in most companies' stock option plans, if the employee leaves the company, he or she must forfeit options. Before management can offer any stock options to any employees, however, the company's whole stock option plan must be approved by the stockholders at their annual meeting.

6

JMC Corporation goes public

In March of 1979, JMC decided business was going so well that it was time to build a second mousetrap factory, to be designated Plant Number 2. Once again, the question arose as to where the money would come from to build the plant? In other words, how would the plant be financed?

With long-term debt comprising 25 percent of total capitalization and earnings coverage of 6 times (6x; see ratio calculations in Chapter 4), it is doubtful that JMC could borrow the $10,000 it needed for the new plant.

A bank or insurance company, which might have considered making the loan, might have accepted the 25 percent debt-to-total capitalization ratio and even the 6x earnings coverage, but these figures were computed *before* the loan would have been made. The potential lender obviously would want to know what the ratios would be *after* the loan had been made. Assuming JMC would have to pay 10 percent interest per year on a $10,000 loan, the annual interest would be $1,000. Thus, the interest coverage would be reduced to 4x.

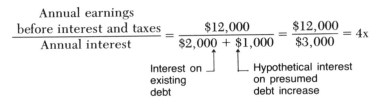

$$\frac{\text{Annual earnings before interest and taxes}}{\text{Annual interest}} = \frac{\$12,000}{\$2,000 + \$1,000} = \frac{\$12,000}{\$3,000} = 4x$$

Interest on existing debt ⤒ ⤒ Hypothetical interest on presumed debt increase

The debt-to-capitalization ratio would be raised to 31 percent.

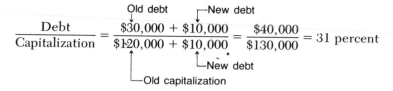

With this lower earnings coverage and higher debt ratio, Mr. Jones realized that it was unlikely that his small company would be able to get a $10,000 loan. (For large established companies like General Motors, these ratios might be quite acceptable.)

Thus, JMC decided it would have to raise more equity money, which is another way of saying, "sell new stock." Since none of the initial 12 investors wanted to put any more money into the company (i.e., buy any more stock from the company), it was decided that the company would have to sell stock to the public. It also occurred to some of the 12 initial stockholders that, as long as the company was writing up a prospectus to file with the SEC, they might take advantage of this registration to sell some of *their* stock, too. So, it was decided to register some new shares (primary) as well as some of the already outstanding shares (secondary).

Since neither Jones nor the others knew how to go about selling stock to the public, they consulted Mr. Greenshades, who suggested they contact an investment banker. An investment banking firm has nothing to do with banking in the usual sense of checking accounts and personal loans. Rather, an investment banker is a firm that helps businesses raise money by selling new stock or bonds to either the public or as private placements to large financial institutions such as banks and insurance companies.

Jones contacted three investment bankers, all of whom visited the company within the next few weeks. Mr. Stodge, from the firm of Stodge Brothers, Investment Bankers, Inc., explained to Jones that his firm had brought many companies like JMC public and were quite experienced. Stodge suggested Jones keep a number of considerations in mind. First, Stodge explained that the price of a stock is at all times related to how well the company has been doing and is expected to do. But within that constraint, there is quite a bit of room for the price to move around. For example, Stodge thought that in the current stockmarket environment, if the mousetrap company were growing (in terms of earnings per share) at an average rate of about 12 percent per year, the stock might be expected to sell at a price-earnings (P-E) ratio of perhaps somewhere between 10x and 15x. (Thus, in a given year, if the company were earning $2 per share, the stock might be expected to sell between $20 and $30 per share.) Whether the stock would tend to sell at the low end of this range (or even lower), or at the high end of this range (or even higher) would be hard to predict, but would be related to; (1) how well the investment community regarded JMC stock, (2) the price-earnings ratios of similar companies, and (3) other factors we will see more about in Chapter 15.

Second, Stodge pointed out that JMC would obviously want to sell its shares for as much as possible, for two reasons: (1) so the selling stockholders could get the most possible money for their shares, and (2) so the company could raise its money selling as few shares as possible, to give away the least possible percentage ownership of the company (i.e., have the current shareholders suffer the least dilution).

Dilution is an important concept in understanding the stock market. Dilution occurs when shares of stock in a company become worth less as a result of the company's issuing more shares. Look at the following example.

Currently, JMC has 500 shares outstanding and is earning $5,000; thus it has earnings per share of $10.

$$\frac{\text{Earnings}}{\text{Shares outstanding}} = \frac{\$5,000}{500} = \$10/\text{Share}$$

Assume the company pays 50 percent of earnings as a dividend. Thus, the dividend per share is $5. Assume also that JMC stock will sell at a price-earnings (P-E) ratio of 10x, therefore one share of stock will sell at $100.

$$\underline{EPS} \quad \underline{P\text{-}E} \quad \underline{Stock\ price}$$

$$\$10 \times 10x = \quad \$100$$

At first glance, with the stock selling at $100, it appears that JMC would have to sell 100 shares to raise $10,000.

$$100\ \text{Shares} \times \$100/\text{Share} = \$10,000$$

But, adding 100 new shares will lower EPS as follows:

$$\text{EPS} = \frac{\text{Earnings}}{\text{Shares outstanding}} = \frac{\$5,000}{500 + 100} = \$8.33/\text{Share}$$

$$\begin{array}{cc} \uparrow & \uparrow \\ \text{Old} & \text{New} \\ \text{shares} & \text{shares} \end{array}$$

Therefore, if the stock sells at a price-earnings ratio of 10x, it would now only sell at $83.33. Thus, we could say the issuing of 100 new shares has diluted JMC earnings from $10.00/share to $8.33, or about 17 percent dilution.

Note also that, with the stock at $83, JMC cannot raise $10,000 by selling 100 shares as long as the P-E remains at 10x.

EPS	P-E	Stock price	New shares	Money raised
$8.33	× 10x	= $83	× 100 Shares	= $8,333

Thus JMC still has to sell more stock to raise the $10,000. But that will lower EPS even further. It turns out that to raise $10,000, 125 new shares must be sold, which produces a 20 percent earnings dilution.

$$\text{EPS} = \frac{\$5,000}{500 + 125} = \frac{\$5,000}{625} = \$8 \times 10x = \$80 \times 125 = \$10,000$$

with columns EPS, P-E, Stock price, New shares, Money raised.

The 20 percent dilution reflects the fact that earnings would be $8/share after the new stock was issued, but were $10/share before the new stock was issued. Thus each share's earnings were diluted by 20 percent as a result of the issuing of new shares.

If the new stock were to sell at a price-earnings ratio of 10x earnings, it would sell at $80 per share after the new stock was issued, compared to $100 per share before the new stock was issued, a 20 percent decline. Similarly, if the dividend payout ratio remained at 50 percent, the dividend would now have to be reduced to $4/share, also a 20 percent decline.

The dilution calculations above were based on a price-earnings ratio of 10x. What if the stock were selling at a P-E of 20x earnings? In that case, it works out that only about 56 new shares are needed to raise $10,000, and earnings dilution is not as severe.

$$\text{EPS} = \frac{\$5,000}{500 + 56} = \frac{\$5,000}{556} = \$8.99 \times 20x = \$180 \times 56 = \$10,080$$

with columns EPS, P-E, Stock price, New shares, Money raised.

Thus, with a higher price-earnings ratio the same amount of money can be raised selling fewer shares. This results in less dilution, only about 10 percent, which lowers earnings to $8.99. Therefore, if the dividend payout ratio remains at 50 percent, the dividend would be $4.50 per share, instead of the $4.00 per share in the case with the P-E of 10x. Reasonably, current stockholders would like to have the highest P-E possible when new shares are being sold (issued).

The dilution calculations above are not complete. They would be complete if we assumed the $10,000 raised from the sale of stock were not used for anything. In fact, it was to be used to build a new mousetrap plant that would generate more earnings. Moreover, since it takes time to build a new plant, let's assume JMC invested the $10,000 in Treasury bills earning 5 percent interest. Assuming the money was going to be there for one year while the plant was being built, it would earn $500 interest. Thus, assuming a P-E of 10x, a more correct dilution calculation would be:

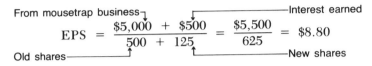

$$\text{From mousetrap business} \quad \text{Interest earned}$$
$$\text{EPS} = \frac{\$5,000 + \$500}{500 + 125} = \frac{\$5,500}{625} = \$8.80$$
$$\text{Old shares} \qquad\qquad \text{New shares}$$

Under these assumptions, EPS were only diluted from $10.00 to $8.80, or 12 percent, not the 20 percent shown previously. Similarly, the 10 percent dilution calculation, assuming a P-E of 20x, was not exactly correct, either.

In the real world, when a company announces an equity financing (intention to raise money by selling new stock) investment analysts immediately go through the calculations above, making assumptions where necessary, to see what the dilution will be and how much it will affect the stock price. If the offering was a total surprise to the financial community, the stock would be very likely to go down by at least as much as the dilution. If the investment analysts thought the financing was being done because the company was having serious problems, the P-E ratio would probably also decline and the stock would fall even further. If the new financing was because the company had a great new opportunity, the P-E might expand and the stock go down less than the dilution. Often, an announcement of an equity financing is not a surprise. Analysts who closely watch a company's financial statements can often see in advance a need to raise new cash. Similarly, management will often state publicly that they would like to do an equity financing sometime in the next year or so. When a financing is expected, the stock market usually adjusts gradually in advance and the market's reaction when the announcement is made is minor.

An interesting and unusual example of dilution in an equity financing occurred in the Polaroid equity offering in 1969. Since Polaroid did not need the money immediately, it invested the money at about 6 percent interest. At the time, Polaroid was selling at a very high P-E, over 50x. Thus, when analysts did the dilution calculation, it turned out that the interest on the money that Polaroid would receive would add so much to earnings that, even with the increased number of shares outstanding, Polaroid actually showed an increase in EPS rather than a decrease. This is called *negative dilution;* it is very unusual. The calculations, shown below, are based on 1968 earnings because the stock offering was in March of 1969 when it was much too early to make a close estimate of 1969 earnings. Also, it was assumed that Polaroid would be earning the interest for the full year, even though the offering did not occur until March. Dilution calculations are often done on an annualized basis.

Polaroid's 1968 earnings per share as reported:

$$\frac{\text{Earnings}}{\text{Shares}} = \frac{\$58.9 \text{ Million}}{31.7 \text{ Million}} = \$1.86/\text{Share}$$

Polaroid's 1968 earnings per share, adjusting both earnings and shares for the equity offering:

Additional earnings from interest received after investing the $100MM raised from the equity offering

$$\frac{\text{Earnings}}{\text{Shares}} = \frac{\$58.9 + \$2.7}{31.7 + 1.1} = \frac{\$61.6}{32.8} = \$1.88$$

New shares from the offering

Dilution points to a key concept in the relationship of the stock market to capitalism. We showed earlier that the stock market will pay a higher P-E for a company with faster earnings growth and, therefore, potential dividend growth. Thus, the greater the company's potential, the higher the P-E and, therefore, the less dilution that will be suffered in a new stock offering. In the language of Wall Street, a company with a high P-E can do an equity financing (sell new stock) much cheaper (i.e., at less dilution) than a company with a low P-E. This seems socially desirable because the high P-E, reflecting a high expected growth rate, implies the market's expectation that this company's products will be in great demand. If a company's products are in great demand, then it indeed seems desirable that the company be able to raise money cheaply in order to expand its ability to make its products and satisfy that demand.

Thus, we see the two sides of the capitalism "coin." On one side are the investors who wish to invest their capital (money) where they see the fastest growth. On the other side are the companies that wish to raise capital. The result is that the companies with successful products (i.e., what consumers want), have the easiest (cheapest) ability to raise money to increase production of those products. So the profit motive is not the *purpose* of capitalism, as some people erroneously believe; rather, the profit motive is a *mechanism* which causes capital to be directed to those areas of the economy that are growing rapidly reflecting consumers' demands.

Selling the stock

When a company is offering new stock, it can attempt to sell it for whatever price it wants. Obviously, if it is too high, nobody will buy it.

If the price of the stock appears unreasonably low, the existing stock-holders may try to prevent its sale because their stock is being diluted too much. In the real world, the company, usually with the help of its investment banker, decides on a price that appears likely to attract investors. The actual price can be adjusted up or down as the date of effective registration approaches and market conditions indicate that it was priced too high or could have been priced higher.

Stodge had now explained why it was desirable from both the company's and current stockholders' points of view to sell the shares for as much as possible. However, Stodge recommended not pricing the stock too high because it might not all be sold, in which case the price would have to come down to sell the remaining shares. In that case, most of the initial buyers would have a loss right away, which is considered un-desirable for establishing a good market for a new issue of stock. Conversely, if the stock came (was sold) at an attractive price (i.e., was sold to the public at slightly less than it was "worth"), there would probably be a great demand for the stock and, not only would it be sure to be sold, it would probably rise in price immediately after it was free to trade on the open market. That way, everyone who initially bought the stock would have a profit, and people would remember it favorably as a very successful offering—or as a "hot" issue. This can make it easier for the company to sell additional stock offerings in the future.

Next, Stodge explained that it was desirable to have an active, stable public market for the stock. This would also make it easier for either JMC or existing shareholders to sell more of their stock on another occasion.

Due to the above considerations, Stodge said it was important that the stock be "widely held," or "widely distributed," that is, there should be a large number of stockholders because if a large number of people each owned a few shares of the stock, rather than a small number of people each owning a large number of shares, it was more likely to produce an active market for the stock. Also, Stodge suggested placing some stock "in strong hands" (i.e., should be sold to insurance companies, trust companies, or investors who have a reputation for holding stock for a while and not selling the minute they see a small profit, or panicking and selling just because the stock might fall a point or two, even though the company is in perfectly good shape). Thus, Stodge suggested that about half of the stock ought to be sold to large institutions (insurance companies, banks, trust companies, mutual funds) and the other half ought to be widely distributed to individual investors. Stodge explained that his firm had many wealthy individual clients, as well as close contacts with major institutions, and was sure he would have no trouble selling the stock.

Jones then asked how much he could get for the stock. Stodge explained that he would first have to study JMC's books (financial records) and the potential growth rate of the company, but from his experience the public would probably be willing to pay a price-earnings ratio of between 10 and 12 times earnings. Stodge said he would want a commission of $.50 per share and that he would underwrite, or guarantee, to sell the entire issue. That is, if any stock could not be sold on the offering, Stodge's firm would buy it, with the idea of reselling it later on. Jones liked that idea but thought it only reasonable to meet the other two investment bankers, anyway.

Mr. Slick then arrived, representing the firm of New Ventures, Inc. New Ventures had a reputation for dealing with highly speculative stock issues. For example, many of the companies New Ventures had brought public had gone bankrupt within a year or two and the stockholders had lost all their money. Other issues, however, had made millions for New Ventures' clients. Jones was afraid, therefore, that the type of client Slick dealt with would be a very nervous stockholder, and the panic selling that Stodge had referred to might be more likely to occur if Slick's clients were the initial stockholders. Jones, of course, had every bit of confidence that JMC would not go bankrupt and, therefore, even if the stock did at some time go down, he presumed it would come back up as soon as the investment community realized there was nothing wrong with JMC. Nevertheless, it is this type of wild fluctuation in the price of a stock that may scare away some potential buyers of the stock who prefer more stable, steady prices.

Slick was quite aware of his company's reputation, and he explained to Jones that, besides the highly speculative companies New Ventures had brought public, it had also done offerings for many conservative companies like JMC. Slick also pointed out that New Ventures had a large number of clients and for a company like JMC it would place (sell) the stock with the more stable customers. Slick said he thought JMC could be brought public at about 14 times earnings and that New Ventures would ask a $.60 per share commission.

Jones stopped to think. "If Slick takes us public (sells the stock to the public) at 14 times earnings, rather than at 10 times earnings, as Stodge suggested, then we will get more money for each share and have less dilution, so it would certainly be worth paying the slightly higher commission." Slick also said that since JMC was a small company and did not make a particularly glamorous product, it might be hard to sell the stock. Thus, New Ventures would only take the deal on a "best-efforts" basis. This means New Ventures would sell as much of the stock as it could, but if it was unable to sell all the stock, it wanted to return the unsold shares to JMC (or the original owners) rather than buy it itself. Slick's reason was that New Ventures was a much smaller firm than Stodge Brothers and had much less capital that it was willing to risk if it had to retain some JMC stock in the event the offering was not completely sold out (i. e., sold to the public).

Jones, being conservative, decided he would rather take slightly less money for his stock but have the offering guaranteed. When a stock offering is guaranteed we say it is "underwritten" by the investment banker. Thus, Slick was told the best-efforts basis was unsatisfactory and, after being thanked for his trouble, was shown the door.

The third investment banking firm was quite similar to Stodge Brothers, but would only underwrite or guarantee the offering at 9x earnings, less commission. Also, Stodge Brothers not only had a better reputation and quality image, but offered a number of financial consulting services which the other firms did not. Finally, Stodge Brothers could do more to help JMC stock later on because of its stock brokerage and investment research contacts with a large number of institutional customers. So Jones called Stodge and asked him to handle the offering. Stodge immediately came out to JMC's office and examined the books.

Splitting the stock

One of his first suggestions was a 10 for 1 stock split in order to get wider distribution. If the stock were split 10 for 1, that means each stockholder would mail in his old stock certificates and get back new certificates for ten times as many shares. Thus, instead of having 500 shares outstanding, the company would have 5,000. There would be no change in any of the company's accounts. The only difference would be that instead of having 500 shares outstanding, each representing one five-hundredth of ownership in the company, there would now be 5,000 shares outstanding and each would represent one five-thousandth of ownership in the company. Actually, there would be a minor change on the balance sheet as follows: first, the stockholders (in this case the original 12) would have to vote to authorize at least 5,000 shares; second, if the stock is being split 10 for 1, the par value would have to be divided by 10. Thus, the Stockholders' Equity portion of the balance sheet would now look like this:

Stockholders' Equity

Paid-in capital
   Common stock at par value ($.10) (authorized
     5,000 shares, outstanding 5,000 shares) . . . . $ 500
   Capital surplus 4,500
Retained earnings 85,000

Total stockholders' equity $90,000

Compare this to the stockholders' equity section of JMC's balance sheet at the end of Chapter 3. The reason for the change in par value is this: the number of shares outstanding multiplied by the par value must always equal the dollar figure in the *Common stock at par value* account. Since no new money comes in because of a stock split, the $500 figure remains the same. Thus, with 5,000 shares now outstanding and $500 in the *Common stock* account, the par value must be reduced to $.10 to make the figures balance.

The reason for the stock split, Stodge explained, was to get wider distribution. JMC currently had 500 shares outstanding. If JMC sold an additional 125 shares, it would raise the desired $10,000, *but only 125 shares would be in the hands of the public.* This would be a very thin market, exactly opposite the wide distribution Stodge had recommended. However, if the stock split 10 for 1 before the public offering, the $10,000 could be raised just as easily, but there would be 1,250 shares in public hands rather than 125 shares, hence more stockholders, hence wider distribution.[1]

Therefore, after the 10 for 1 split, but before the new issue, the earnings per share would be reduced to $1.

$$\frac{\text{Earnings}}{\text{Shares}} = \frac{\$5,000}{500 \text{ Shares} \times 10} = \frac{\$5,000}{5,000 \text{ Shares}} = \$1 \text{ Per share}$$

After the stock split and after the new issue of 1,250 shares, the EPS would be $.80 per share.

$$\frac{\text{Earnings}}{\text{Shares}} = \frac{\$5,000}{5,000 + 1,250 \text{ Shares}} = \frac{\$5,000}{6,250 \text{ Shares}} = \$.80 \text{ Per share}$$

Note that although the stockholders' percentage of ownership in the company was diluted by the new issue, it was not diluted by the split. To demonstrate this, let's look at Smith's original holding of 100 shares. After the new issue, but before the split, he could expect to sell at $80 per share for a total of $8,000. After the split, he would have 1,000 shares that he could now expect to sell at $8 per share, still totalling $8,000.

Jones saw the logic of the split and the other 11 owners (stockholders) of JMC agreed. So it was voted to increase the authorized shares to 6,250. This authorized enough shares for both the stock split and the new offering.

Since some of the 12 investors wanted to sell some of their shares to the public, it was decided to have a "combined" offering. This means that some of the shares being offered are from the company—a primary

---

[1] Actually, 1,250 shares is still too thin for a real world example; 100,000 shares might be considered a minimum, but dealing with such large numbers would make the example hard to follow.

offering—and some of the shares are being offered by selling stockholders—a secondary offering. All the shares will be sold at the same price, and Stodge Brothers will keep the same commission per share.

The selling stockholders, who now owned 5,000 shares after the split, decided to sell 1,000 of *their* shares to the public. Thus, the combined offering was 2,250 shares, 1,250 being primary—the proceeds of which would go to the company—and 1,000 being secondary—the proceeds going to the selling stockholders. *After the offering there would be 6,250 shares outstanding, not 7,250. The 1,000 shares being sold by selling stockholders were already outstanding, they are merely changing ownership. Only the new shares being sold by the company add to the outstanding.*

With Stodge's help, JMC put together a prospectus and registered with the SEC to sell 2,250 shares. Even though the company was selling only 1,250, the entire 2,250 being offered had to be registered. After about three months of letters back and forth between the SEC and JMC, the SEC was satisfied that the prospectus contained enough information for potential buyers to make an informed decision. On September 1, 1979, the SEC declared JMC's registration to be effective.

Stodge Brothers could have placed (sold) the entire 2,250 shares itself, but as is customary, it only placed some of the stock, in this case 800 shares, and distributed the rest to other investment bankers and stockbrokers to distribute to their clients. Stodge Brothers and all the other dealers (investment bankers and stockbrokers) participating in the offering are called the selling group. Stodge Brothers, of course, splits the commission with the other dealers. There are two reasons Stodge is willing to give some of the offering to other dealers. First, since other investment bankers are willing to give Stodge some of their business, everybody has a more even flow of business. Second, most investment bankers have only a limited number of clients. By having many dealers selling the stock, it gets better publicized among all potential investors. Thus, there is more demand for the stock and less risk that the issue will not be able to be sold. Also, if the issue cannot be sold, rather than have to buy all the remaining stock itself, and risk its going down, Stodge Brothers will split the risk with the other members of the underwriting syndicate. The underwriting syndicate is usually comprised of only some of the dealers in the *selling group* (i.e., those dealers who have agreed to participate in the purchase of any shares of stock that were not able to be sold to the public). Not all of the dealers in the selling group are part of the underwriting syndicate. Those who are not in the underwriting syndicate simply sell as many shares as they can and return the rest to the syndicate. The syndicate then either sells them directly to the public, or redistributes the shares to other members of the selling group who have more demand for the stock. Those members of the selling group who are part of the underwriting syndicate get a higher commission than those who are not because they are taking some risk if all the shares cannot be sold. Those dealers in the selling group who are not in the underwriting syndicate are taking no risk and therefore get a very small commission.

With the wide exposure the selling group provides, it hopes there will be excess demand for the stock (i.e., there will be people who wanted some of the stock but were unable to get any on the offering). Some of these people, it is hoped, will still want the stock and will then try to buy it on the open market after the offering is completed. This is called the *after market*. The after market literally refers to any trade made between members of the public after the investment banker or underwriter has completed the offering. In common usage, however, "after market" refers to the hour or two, or even day or two, immediately following the offering when there is a lot of trading among people who were unable to get any stock in the offering, and people who did get stock during the offering but are selling it immediately either to make a quick profit (if the stock is going up) or cut their loss (if the price is going down).

By the time the JMC registration had become effective, the selling group had already called its clients to see who was interested in buying the JMC stock. Since there was a lot of interest in JMC stock, the issue was "fully subscribed" before the registration became effective, which meant each dealer (underwriter or not) had enough customers who wanted to buy the stock and it could all be sold.

Shortly after registration became effective at 10:00 A.M., September 1, 1979, the stockbrokers and underwriters immediately called the clients to whom they were selling the shares and told them the stock was "free to trade." This meant that as of that moment those individuals who had subscribed to the stock were now the legal owners and could sell it if they wished. Where could they sell it?

7

Over-the-counter trading

When a stock initially goes public, it is not traded on any exchange. Rather, it is traded *over-the-counter* (OTC). This does not mean there is an actual counter where people get together to buy and sell stocks. It means that brokers can buy or sell an OTC traded stock for their clients by telephoning directly to one or more broker/dealers that have chosen to "make a market" in that stock. To illustrate, assume Mr. Burt bought 100 shares of JMC on the initial offering. He paid $10 per share, and would like to sell it for $13 per share. So he calls his stockbroker and says he would like to sell his 100 shares of JMC for $13 per share. Since the stock has just become public, there is not yet a market for it. What usually happens in this case is that the investment banker who brought the issue public says it will "make a market." This means that after the stock is declared free to trade, someone at the firm, in our example Stodge Brothers, will sit by the telephone and buy or sell the stock as orders come in from other brokers for their customers. The person who makes the market is called a trader. There may be more than one firm making a market in a given stock. Any firm registered with the National Association of Securities Dealers (NASD) can make a market in any stock that is traded over-the-counter.

When a stock initially comes public, typically between one and five firms let it be known that they are making a market in that stock. If the offering was large—500,000 shares or more—more firms are likely to make a market since they expect a lot of trading. A thin stock—say 100,000 shares—might only have one or two firms making a market. The brokerage firm that Burt used was not making a market in JMC stock, so his stockbroker called all three firms that were making a market and told them he had a customer who wanted to sell 100 shares of JMC at $13. At that point, none of the traders who were making a market wanted to pay $13 for the stock. In the language of Wall Street, none of the traders were willing to bid as high as $13.

The price someone is willing to pay for a stock is called the *bid* price, or just the *bid*. The price at which someone is willing to sell a stock is called the *asked*. In the case of JMC, the traders would only have been willing to bid $13 if they thought they could resell it shortly for more, say $13.50 or $14.00; but since the stock had just been declared free to trade, bids from the public were just beginning to come in and the traders were not sure exactly for how much they could resell the stock. Nevertheless, the traders knew Stodge had underpriced the issue slightly and therefore expected investors to bid up the price. Also, since the issue was fully subscribed, it was likely that some people who wanted the stock but had been unable to get any on the offering would now want to buy it in the over-the-counter market. From the traders' experience with this type of stock they guessed JMC would probably trade up to about $12 or $13. Thus, when Burt's stockbroker called the three houses making markets in JMC, the three traders said they would bid $11.00, $11.00, and $11.25, respectively. So the stockbroker called Burt and told him the best bid he could get was $11.25. Burt said he was not willing to sell that low, so he thanked his broker and hung up.

Another individual, Mr. Byers, called his broker later that morning and said he wanted to buy 100 shares of JMC and asked him to find out how much it would cost. So Byers's broker called all three market makers and asked, "What is the market on JMC?" The first trader replied, "$11 bid, $12 asked." In other words, he (the first trader) was willing to buy at $11 and sell at $12. The second trader responded, "$11.00 bid, $12.25 asked." The third trader said, "$11.25 bid, $12.50 asked." Why are the prices different? Each trader is free to adjust his bid and asked prices as he wishes, and will do so depending on how anxious he is to buy or sell the stock. In practice, prices never vary by much between market makers because, for example, if one were bidding lower than the others on a stock, he would never make any purchases and quickly discover the reason why by calling the other market makers and asking what their "market" was. He would then have to adjust his "market" accordingly.

When a market maker gives an *asked*, it means she is obligated to sell at least 100 shares at that price. Of course she can sell more if she chooses. She can sell the stock at her *asked* price whether or not she owns it. If she does not own any, she would "sell" it to Byers, anyway, with the expectation that she could buy it later from someone else at a lower price and use that stock to deliver to Byers.

Byers was willing to pay $12. In fact he was willing to pay up to $13 or $14 if necessary, so he told his broker to buy 100 shares "at the market." This meant the broker should call the traders back, ask "what the market was" again, and then buy the stock from whichever trader would sell it for the lowest price. That is exactly what happened. The first trader's *asked* of $12 was still good so the stockbroker said he would take 100 shares at $12 per share. At this point, the transaction was consummated and the first trader's firm owed Byers 100 shares. Actually, they owed Byers's broker 100 shares, who in turn owed Byers 100 shares. Byers owed $1,200 (plus commission) to his stockbroker, who in turn owed $1,200 to the first trader's firm. The first trader's firm now owed 100 shares it did not have. In the language of Wall Street, the firm was "short" 100 shares.

Later that day, Mr. Sellers called his broker and said that he wanted to sell his 100 shares and asked how much he could get for it. Sellers's broker called the three traders and asked "what the market was." He did not say he wanted to sell; otherwise the traders might have lowered their bid price, since they obviously want to buy the stock for themselves for the minimum amount possible. At this point, the first trader said "$11.50 bid, $12.25 asked." The others were both bidding $11.25. The first trader had raised his bid a little because he was "short" the stock (he owed some he did not have) and was anxious to buy so he could pay off what he owed. The broker called back Sellers and told him $11.50 was the best bid. Sellers said to sell at $11.50 but not less. In other words, if, by the time the broker had called back the first trader, that trader had lowered his bid to $11.25 for some reason, the broker was under orders not to sell. As it happened, the trader was still holding his $11.50 bid and the sale was consummated. At this point, the trader had "covered his short." This means he had bought 100 shares (from Sellers), and was now able to deliver the 100 shares he owed to Byers's broker.

This is how over-the-counter markets work. Our example was for a new stock, but the same things apply to stocks that have been traded OTC for years. Suppose for example Mr. Cassens wants to buy 100 shares of XYZ Industries. His broker tells him the current market is "$22 bid, $23 asked." If he thinks the stock is about to go up immediately, he would instruct the broker to buy at the market, which in this case would be $23 (unless the "asked" changed while Cassens was making up his mind). Alternatively, if Cassens is not worried about the stock going up immediately, he might tell his broker to bid $22.50. This way, if someone does come down on his asking price, Cassens will be the first to get it since he has made the highest bid. So, what the broker would do is leave the order to buy at $22.50 with one of the traders. If the broker's own firm is making a market in XYZ Industries, he would probably leave the buy order of $22.50 with his firm. At this point, that trader could then say the market bid is $22.50 with his firm, or that his market is now $22.50, $23.00 asked. Now, if another order comes in from Mr. Teller to sell at $22.50, or at the market, Teller's stock would be sold to Cassens. This is called a *cross*. A cross is when a trader finds a buyer and a seller of the same stock at the same price. Thus, an OTC trader can either buy and sell stock from his own account, as occurred with the JMC stock, or he can cross a buy and a sell order from two customers, as occurred with the XYZ Industries.

Trading on a stock exchange, such as the New York Stock Exchange or the American Stock Exchange, is slightly different in terms of how the price of the purchase or sale is reached. The difference is that, instead of many market makers as in the over-the-counter market, stocks that are listed on a stock exchange are traded primarily in only one place (at the stock exchange) with only one market maker, called the *specialist* in that stock, doing most of the trading. We will return to this in Chapter 14.

PART TWO

Securities other than Common Stock: Bonds and Preferred Stock

8

Bonds

In early 1981, JMC decided to build another new mouse-trap plant. The bigger, more efficient plant that JMC management had in mind, to be designated Plant Number 3, was estimated to cost $20,000 to build and equip. There are four common ways a company can obtain enough money to finance (pay for) a new plant. First, the company can sell new stock, called an equity financing. Second, the company can borrow the money, called a debt financing. These are called external or outside financings. Third, the company can use cash that has built up as a result of profits earned from operations in past years. In this case, we say the company is "financing the plant from retained earnings." This is called an internal financing.

Recall that Retained Earnings is an accounting entry (review the definition, at the end of Chapter 2). It may or may not reflect cash. It is possible that all the cash has been spent and the Cash account is $0. However, it is also possible that some of the cash profits earned in past years were *not* paid out as dividends, nor were they spent on anything else (raw material, wages, new plant or equipment, and the like) and thus were still available as cash to pay for something. So, when we say something is being paid for or being financed from retained earnings, we really mean it is being paid for from available cash that was generated by previous years' profits (retained earnings).

A fourth and less common way to finance a plant would be to sell off existing assets to raise cash. For instance, a company that made paper goods, furniture, and clothing might decide the clothing business was by far the most attractive and should be expanded, and the company might sell off its furniture or paper goods business to raise cash for a new clothing goods plant.

JMC did not have enough extra cash (unused retained earnings) available to build the new plant. Cash (cash and U.S. government securities) at December 31, 1980, was only $15,000, and much of that was needed for the day-to-day operations of the company. JMC could have waited to save up enough cash from future retained earnings, but management anticipated it would take three or four years to do that and they were anxious to get started on the plant now because they saw a lot of new markets for their mousetraps which they wanted to reach before a competitor got there. Thus an external or outside financing was needed. Management decided it was preferable to finance this plant with borrowed money rather than by selling new stock, as in 1979. The reason for this decision will be shown below.

Management felt safe borrowing the money because even if the net profit level did not increase as a result of the new plant, they knew they would be able to repay the loan over time just from the profit earned from already existing plants. As it happens, management's projections showed that, as a result of the newer and more efficient plant, earnings should go up substantially when the new plant was completed.

The $20,000 might have been borrowed from a bank, but management did not want to go to a bank, primarily because they liked to use bank borrowings for short-term needs, such as receivables financing and unexpected needs, which occur from time to time. If they used a major bank borrowing to build the new plant now, banks might be reluctant to lend them more for receivables financing or in an emergency later on. Also, loan agreements with banks are usually very restrictive in terms of financial ratios the company is required to maintain. Management wished to borrow in a way that left them freer than under the typically tight bank agreements. Selling bonds in the public market usually provides such an opportunity for a company in good financial condition. While this kind of borrowing also places restrictions and obligations on the company, these are typically less burdensome than bank arrangements. The debt financing (bond sale) was planned for early spring 1981.

Let us now catch up with the changes at JMC, look at its latest financial statements, and see why management chose to sell bonds rather than new equity (stock). The factors affecting the decision between selling new bonds and selling new stock reveal a lot about the way corporations think, but understanding that is not necessary in order to understand what bonds are. Thus, the reader can skip ahead to the Bond Basics section without missing any necessary information.

On September 1, 1979, JMC's stock issue was sold and $10,000 was received (ignoring commissions). That $10,000 was quickly put to use to build the then-new Plant Number 2, which was completed by December 31, 1979. Thus, in 1980, JMC had the benefit of Plant Number 2 for the whole year in addition to the old Plant Number 1. As a result of this expanded capacity and an increase in the price for which the traps were sold, JMC's sales in 1980 moved up to $125,000. The full-year 1980 income statement looked like this:

JMC
Income Statement
For Year Ending 12/31/80

Sales		$125,000
Expenses:		
CGS....................................	$ 86,000	
Selling, gen. and		
adm. expense..........................	22,000	
Interest charges..........................	3,000	
	111,000	111,000
Pretax profit		14,000
Taxes for the Year...........................		7,000
Net profit after tax..........................		$ 7,000

The balance sheet at the end of 1980 was as follows:

JMC
Balance Sheet
12/31/80

Assets			*Liabilities*		
Current assets:			Current liabilities:		
Cash....................	$ 7,000		Accounts payable	$	8,000
U.S. govt. sec............	8,000		Short-term debt		2,000
Acc't receivable	14,000		Taxes payable		2,000
Inventory:			Sinking-fund payments		
Finished goods.........	25,000		on long-term debt		
Work in progress	7,000		due within one year.......		2,000
Raw materials..........	21,000		Total current liabilities.........		14,000
Total current assets.........	82,000				
			Capitalization:		
Fixed assets:					
Property.................	4,000		Long-term debt:		
Plant....................	15,000		8% Term loan..............		6,000
Equipment...............	51,000		9% First mortgage bonds....		20,000
Total fixed assets...........	70,000				
			Stockholders' Equity		
			Common stock (par value $.10)		
			(authorized 6,250 shares,		
			outstanding 6,250 shares)...		625
			Additional paid-in capital		14,375
			Retained earnings............		97,000
			Total stockholders' equity		112,000
Total assets................	$152,000		Total liabilities and equity......		$152,000

Compare this with the balance sheet of 12/31/78 on page 28. The following changes have occurred:

1. *Common at par* and *Additional paid-in capital* were increased when JMC sold new stock in September 1979. Cash went up at that time, too, but the cash was since spent on new property, plant, and equipment.
2. *Property, plant, and equipment* are up by $1,000, $2,000, and $7,000 respectively, reflecting Plant Number 2 that was built with the money raised on the stock offering. Note that the old plant, Number 1, is still in place and operating. At this point we are assuming that the old plant has not yet begun to wear out or deteriorate, so it is still carried at its original cost.
3. *Accounts receivable* and each of the *Inventory* categories are up. This results from the increased sales level due to the new plant. Obviously, additional *Raw material* is needed to feed the new plant, which in turn results in more *Work in progress* and a higher level of *Finished goods* awaiting sale to the expanded customer list. Since the sales level is higher, the *Accounts receivable* level is also higher.
4. *Cash* is down. This reflects the following: (*a*) money spent to increase the level of inventory; (*b*) money used to reduce accounts payable and short term debt; and (*c*) money spent to meet the sinking-fund obligations under the 8 percent term loan agreement. Notice that the latter declined $2,000 in each of the years 1979 and 1980.
5. *Retained earnings* is up, reflecting both the $5,000 earned in 1979 and the $7,000 earned in 1980.

SELLING BONDS VERSUS SELLING STOCKS

JMC management wanted $20,000 to build the new plant. To decide whether it would be preferable to sell new stock or bonds, it is necessary to project the income statement and balance sheet into the future to see what they would look like under the different assumptions of either a new stock sale or a new bond sale.

Since both plants were operating at full capacity in 1980, we start by assuming that the income statement for 1981 and the next few years would look essentially the same as 1980 if business continued to be good but no new plant capacity was added. Inflation might cause a small increase in costs, but prices could be raised by the same amount, which would result in no significant change in net earnings. Therefore, *Assumption A —no external financing, wait a few years —*results in an income statement that looks like the 1980 income statement. Actually, future earnings under Assumption A would enable JMC to repay some debt, which would result in lower interest payments and therefore produce slightly higher earnings; but this difference is minor, compared to the potential changes resulting from a new stock or bond sale, so we will ignore it.

Assumption B —the sale of $20,000 worth of bonds. Under this assumption, the following factors went into JMC management's income statement projections. First, after discussions with Stodge Brothers (investment bankers), JMC concluded that it would have to pay about 10 percent interest per year. Second, management was now quite experienced in the manufacture of mousetraps and knew how to build a plant that would be more efficient (i.e., produce traps for a lower cost per trap). Finally, management knew that with the JMC sales force and management already in place, *Selling, general, and administrative* expense would not have to go up very much. As a result of detailed calculations, including the above factors, management projected that the income statement would look as follows once the new plant was operating:

	Assumption A —no external financing	Additional yearly sales and expenses from new plant	Assumption B —sell bonds
Sales...............	$125,000	$ 40,000	$165,000
CGS................	86,000	25,000	111,000
SGA	22,000	5,000	27,000
Interest.............	3,000	2,000	5,000
Pretax profit.........	14,000	8,000	22,000
Tax (assume 50%)	7,000	4,000	11,000
Net income	$ 7,000	4,000	$ 11,000
Shares outstanding	6,250		6,250
EPS................	$ 1.12		$ 1.76

Assumptions A and B also produce the following changes on the balance sheet and in certain ratios. Again, under *Assumption A —no external financing,* we simply use the current balance sheet as indicative of the future.

	Assumption A —no external financing	Assumption B —sell bonds
Long-term debt.....	$ 26,000	$ 46,000
Equity.............	112,000	$112,000
$\frac{\text{Long-term debt}}{\text{Total capital}}$ ...	18.8%	29.1%
Interest coverage ...	5.7x	5.4x

By selling bonds to build the new plant, we see that earnings per share, once the plant is up and running, will rise dramatically. On the other hand, interest coverage declines and long-term debt, as a percentage of total capital, moves much higher (i.e., both these ratios deteriorate). Thus, to sell the bonds will so change the ratios that it would be more difficult for JMC to borrow any additional money should the need arise. The effect on earnings, however, is so favorable as to make the bond sale worthwhile despite this potential problem. Furthermore, the higher earnings will enable JMC to pay back its debt faster, which will, in turn, cause a reduction in interest expense. Therefore, the debt-to-total capital ratio would again decline and the interest coverage improve (go higher). Review these ratios in Chapter 4.

Assumption C —the $20,000 is raised by having another offering of new stock. This, of course, may result in earnings dilution (i.e., although the new plant will produce more earnings, the increased number of common shares outstanding may result in a net decline in earnings per share). But it is also possible that the increase in earnings, as a result of the new plant, will be so big that, despite the increased number of common shares outstanding, the EPS figure will increase. This is called negative dilution. In order to find out which is the case, one must go through the dilution calculations shown in Chapter 6.

	Assumption C —sell new stock
Sales...............	$165,000
CGS	111,000
SGA	27,000
Interest............	3,000
Pretax profit.........	24,000
Tax	12,000
Net income	$ 12,000
Shares outstanding ...	?
EPS................	?

JMC stock is currently selling at a price-earnings ratio of 6 times (6x). Thus, it turns out that to raise $20,000, JMC would have to sell 2,425 new shares.

$$\text{EPS} = \frac{\$12,000}{6,250 + 2,425} = \frac{\$12,000}{8,675} = \$1.38 \overset{\text{P-E}}{\times} 6x = \overset{\text{Stock price}}{\$8.28} \times \overset{\text{New shares}}{2425} = \overset{\text{Money raises}}{\$20,079}$$

Old shares ⌐   ⌐New shares

Thus, under *Assumption C —sell new stock,* EPS would look as follows:

	Assumption A —no external financing	Assumption B —sell bonds	Assumption C —sell new stock
Sales...............	$125,000	$165,000	$165,000
CGS................	86,000	111,000	111,000
SGA................	22,000	27,000	27,000
Interest	3,000	5,000	3,000
Pretax profit.........	14,000	22,000	24,000
Tax.................	7,000	11,000	12,000
Net income..........	$ 7,000	$ 11,000	$ 12,000
Shares outstanding...	6,250	6,250	8,675
EPS................	$ 1.12	$ 1.76	$ 1.38

The interest coverage and debt ratios would then look as follows:

	Assumption A —no external financing	Assumption B —sell bonds	Assumption C —sell new stock
Long-term debt	$ 26,000	$ 46,000	$ 26,000
Equity	112,000	112,000	132,000
$\frac{\text{Long-term debt}}{\text{Total capital}}$:	18.8%	29.1%	16.5%
Interest coverage	5.7x	5.4x	9.0x

Selling new stock to raise the $20,000 results in negative dilution—the projected profit from the new plant is so great that it will more than compensate for the increased number of shares outstanding, and earnings will go up from $1.12 to $1.38. However, the resulting increase in EPS is much lower than if bonds are sold. Therefore, since higher earnings should produce a higher stock price, other things being equal, it is in the best interests of the current shareholders for the money to be raised by selling bonds rather than by selling stock even though the bond sale results in a deterioration of the balance sheet.

An interesting exercise is to work through the numbers and see what would be the effect of equity financing (selling new stock) if the price-earnings ratio were 15x or 30x. Answer: If the P-E were 15x, the money could be raised selling 780 new shares. This would result in EPS of $1.71, only slightly below the $1.76 resulting from a bond sale. In this case, it would probably be preferable to raise the money selling stock, because the minor loss in EPS is more than made up for by the stronger balance sheet (i.e., less debt and better interest-coverage protection). If the P-E were 30x, the $20,000 could be raised selling 370 new shares which would result in EPS of $1.81. This is even higher than the EPS resulting from the bond sale and, therefore, it is certainly preferable to sell new stock at 30x earnings rather than bonds because it results not only in higher EPS but also leaves a better balance sheet.

However, with JMC stock selling at 6x earnings, management decided to go ahead with the bond issue. Mr. Jones decided that it was time for his entire management team to learn more about bonds, so Mr. Stodge was asked to come in. He made the following presentation.

BOND BASICS

A *bond* is a contract between a lender (lenders) and a borrower. The bond certificate is a piece of paper that says the owner of this certificate is the lender in the contract and has the right to be paid back on a certain date and to receive a certain amount of interest on certain dates. The certificate gives very little other information. Rather, the certificate refers to an *indenture*, which is the complete detailed agreement between the lender(s) and the borrower. The indenture states all the obligations of the borrower and all the rights of the lender in the event that the borrower fails to live up to the agreement. The *trustee* under the indenture is the party (typically a bank) who looks out for the rights of the bondholders. If, for example, you are a bondholder of Company XYZ and don't receive your interest payment, you would call the trustee, not Company XYZ, which owes you the interest. In fact, most typically, the borrowing company makes the interest payment to the trustee who, in turn, distributes it to the bondholders. If the company fails to make the interest payment, the trustee is obligated to take legal action against the company or to invoke some other right stated in the indenture. The trustee also watches the borrowing company's financial statements to make sure they are maintaining certain financial ratios agreed to in the indenture. Should the company fail to meet these agreements, the trustee is again obligated to act to invoke your rights (discussed later).

A company can have more than one issue of bonds outstanding at one time. In this case, each issue would have its own indenture and its own trustee. The obligations under the various indentures could be similar or totally different. An indenture sometimes precludes the company from having any further bond issues without permission of the existing bondholders under that indenture.

The typical bond features covered in the next few pages concern both nonconvertible bonds and convertible bonds. Convertible bonds, however, also have additional important features, which are covered in Chapter 9. The current discussion refers primarily to corporate bonds (i.e., bonds issued by a corporation). Bonds issued by a government agency or a city or state have many similar features but are not covered here.

Issuing bonds is very similar to issuing new stock—in terms of having to register with the SEC, putting out a prospectus, and the actual selling process through an underwriting or investment banking group. When the bonds are initially registered and sold by the company, it is a primary offering and the money goes to the company. Once registered and initially sold, bonds can be bought and sold on the secondary market, just like stocks, at whatever price the buyer and seller agree upon. Thus the New York Bond Exchange is a market for "secondary" bond purchases and sales, just as the New York Stock Exchange, as we will see later, is a market for "secondary" stock purchases and sales.

BOND FEATURES

Maturity

Final maturity is the date when the bonds must be redeemed if they have not been redeemed or retired earlier under a sinking-fund or call provision (discussed later).

Face value

Face value, also called *face amount* or *par value*,[1] is the amount of money the company must pay back if the bond is redeemed at final maturity. If the bond matures ahead of final maturity, under a call provision (discussed later), then the amount that must be paid to the bondholder may be slightly more than the face value.

Face value for most bonds is $1,000 (i.e., each bond represents a loan of $1,000). Occasionally, a particularly large issue may include some bonds with face values of $5,000 or $10,000. Similarly, one occasionally sees an issue that has bonds with a face value of less than $1,000 (i.e. $500 or $100). These are called "baby bonds." In this chapter we will always be referring to $1,000 bonds.

Most companies issue bonds at par value (i.e., $1,000). Thus, if a company wishes to borrow $60,000, it would issue 60 bonds. In recent years, however, some companies have chosen to issue bonds at less than the face amount. In this case we say the company has issued a bond at a discount from par. Such bonds are sometimes called "original issue discounts" or abbreviated "OID's." For example, a $1,000 bond could be issued at $800 (i.e., sold to the lender for $800). In this case, although the company would have only borrowed $800, it would still have to pay back $1,000 when the bond matured. In this case the company wishing to raise

---

[1] Do not confuse par value of a bond with par value of a common stock. They are unrelated.

$60,000 would have to sell 75 bonds instead of 60 bonds[2] (75 bonds ×
$800 received per bond = $60,000).

Redemption and retirement

These words do not mean exactly the same thing. *Redemption* usually
refers to returning the bond certificate to the company or trustee in
exchange for the amount of money due. If the bond is redeemed at final
maturity, the amount of money due is the face value. If the bond is
redeemed before final maturity (i.e., at an earlier maturity under a
sinking-fund or a call provision), then the amount of money due may be
slightly more or less than face value.

When a bond is redeemed, it is automatically retired forever. It
cannot be reissued, like treasury stock. *Retirement* can happen either
because the bond was redeemed or because the issuing company bought
the bond in the secondary market. When a bond is repurchased in the
secondary market by the issuing company it is automatically retired
forever.

Suppose a company bought one of its bonds in the secondary market
for $984, or for $1,072, or for any other price. The price does not matter.
Once the issuing company has bought back one of its bonds, the interest
and debt repayment obligations on that bond cease to exist. The company cannot owe itself money or interest anymore than you or I can owe
ourselves interest. Of course, if a company has bought back some but not
all of the bonds of a particular issue, it still has its obligations to the
remaining outstanding bondholders. Also, the company remains under
the restrictions of the indenture until all the bonds under that indenture
are retired. A company may buy back its bonds simply because it has
extra cash lying around or because it is obligated to do so under a
sinking-fund provision.

Sinking fund

A *sinking fund* is an obligation to retire a certain amount of bonds on
or before a specified date ahead of final maturity. A bond issue may or
may not have a sinking-fund provision. To illustrate, suppose ABC Company issued $100,000 worth of bonds (100 bonds) on January 1, 1970. The
indenture has a sinking-fund provision, which says the following: "The

---

[2] The reason a company would issue a bond for $800 when it knows it will have to pay
back $1,000 later is that, because the bondholder has a built-in capital gain of $200 when
the bond matures, he would be willing to take a lower annual interest rate than he would
otherwise want in order to be willing to buy the bond. Thus a company that wants to
borrow money but can only afford to pay a limited amount of interest, might choose to sell
(issue) bonds at a discount (i.e., below face value).

bond's final maturity is on December 31, 1990, except that at least $5,000 worth of face value (5 bonds) must be retired each year by December 31, beginning in 1982." Thus, the sinking fund is $5,000 per year in each of the years 1982 to 1989, for a total of $40,000. The remaining outstanding $60,000 would then be redeemed for face value at the final maturity date, December 31, 1990. The repayment at final maturity, if it is larger than the annual sinking-fund requirement, is called a *balloon* payment. A bond issue that has no sinking-fund payment and is completely redeemed at final maturity is called a *term bond* or a *bullet*. While term bonds need not be retired before final maturity, there is no reason why the company cannot earlier buy some (or all) back on the secondary market if they are available. A bond may have no balloon and, rather, be redeemed in equal sinking-fund installments. For example, the indenture for a $100,000 issue may specify a $10,000 sinking fund for each of the last 10 years up to and including the final maturity.

A company may meet its sinking-fund obligations in a number of ways. One way is simply to buy the necessary amount of bonds on the secondary market prior to the specified date and retire them. Although ABC Company in the above example is required to retire at least $5,000 face value prior to December 31, 1982, it is allowed to retire more. It is common to see a company try to get one or two years ahead of the required sinking-fund schedule, so if, in a given year, it is unable to buy any bonds back, it will have already met its contractual obligation.

The purpose of the sinking fund is to help assure that the bond issue will be retired at final maturity. If there were no sinking fund, ABC Company would have to come up with $100,000 at final maturity. By having a sinking fund, there is less to retire at final maturity, and also it forces the company to start planning its finances early to meet these obligations. If the company gets ahead of the sinking-fund schedule, it makes it that much easier to meet the remaining redemption obligation at final maturity. Of course, the company's wishing to buy back bonds ahead of schedule, or even according to schedule, does not obligate anyone to sell them.

Thus, the indenture usually provides an alternative mechanism for the company to meet its sinking-fund obligation by a random selection, called a *lottery*. Since each bond has a serial number, the trustee will draw numbers at random to select bonds for the required sinking-fund redemption. The bonds that have been selected will then mature perhaps one month later—to give the bondholder time to get the bond out of the bank vault and mail it in to the trustee. Since this bond has now matured early under the sinking-fund lottery selection procedure, it no longer earns interest after the sinking-fund redemption date and thus the bondholder would have nothing to gain by not surrendering it.

Whether the company meets sinking-fund obligations by buying bonds in the secondary market or by using the lottery procedure is usually up to the company. For example, if the company can buy a $1,000 face value bond at $940 in the market, that is obviously preferable to redeeming it at the full $1,000 because the company saves $60. If the bonds are selling at more than face value, or if there are none available to be purchased in the market, then the company invokes the lottery procedure.

A third way sinking-fund obligations are met is through serial redemption. When serial bonds are initially issued, it is specified that certain serial numbers will be retired in certain years, thereby constituting the sinking fund. Serial bonds are common today with state and local agencies, but are rare in corporate bonds, except in equipment trusts. An *equipment trust* is a bond issued for a particular purpose, such as an airline borrowing money to buy an airplane or a railroad buying railroad cars. Equipment trust bonds always specify that, if the company fails to meet its obligations under the indenture, the equipment trust bondholders get to take possession of the specified equipment, which they can then sell in order to get their money back.

Interest payment

Most bonds require the company to pay interest semiannually. If it is a *registered bond* in your name, you will get a check in the mail for the specified amount. A registered bond belongs to the person in whose name it is registered and there is no risk if it is lost. On the other hand, a *bearer bond* belongs to the person who possesses it. It is not registered. Bearer bonds have attached coupons for each interest payment, and, when a given payment date is approaching, the bearer simply clips off the coupon with that date on it and presents it or mails it to the trustee and gets the interest payment by return mail.

Whether a bond pays interest annually, semiannually, quarterly, or monthly, the amount is almost always fixed. A few newer bonds specify a variable interest payment based on certain other market interest rates, such as six-month U.S. treasury bills, but these exceptions are few and will be ignored in this book.

The interest payment required by a bond is called its *coupon*. For example, a $1,000 face value bond might have a specified coupon of $50 semiannually for a total of $100 per year. In this case we would say the *coupon rate* is $100 divided by $1,000, or 10 percent:

$$\text{Coupon rate} = \frac{\text{Coupon}}{\text{Face amount}} = \frac{\$100}{\$1,000} = 10 \text{ Percent}$$

Note that the coupon is fixed in dollars. The coupon rate is also fixed. It is the dollar coupon per year (fixed) divided by the dollar face value or par (also fixed). Thus, the coupon rate is fixed. The price the bond sells for in the secondary market may vary above or below $1,000, but the coupon rate is always a fixed percentage *of face value*, which does not vary.

Current yield and coupon yield

The coupon rate is sometimes called the *coupon yield*. Coupon yield (which is fixed) should not be confused with current yield (which varies with price). The *current yield* is the dollar coupon (fixed) divided by the current price of the bond in the secondary market (which varies). For example:

			Current yield (percent)	Coupon yield (percent)
A.	$\dfrac{\text{Coupon}}{\text{Face amount}}$	$\dfrac{\$\ \ 100}{\$1,000}$	?%	10%
B.	$\dfrac{\text{Coupon}}{\text{Current price}}$	$\dfrac{\$\ \ 100}{\$\ \ 833}$	12	10
C.	$\dfrac{\text{Coupon}}{\text{Current price}}$	$\dfrac{\$\ \ 100}{\$\ \ 943}$	10.6	10
D.	$\dfrac{\text{Coupon}}{\text{Current price}}$	$\dfrac{\$\ \ 100}{\$1,000}$	10	10
E.	$\dfrac{\text{Coupon}}{\text{Current price}}$	$\dfrac{\$\ \ 100}{\$1,086}$	9.2	10

When a $1,000 par value or face value bond is selling at more than par (i.e., more than $1,000, as in case E above), we say it is selling at a premium (to par). In this case, its current yield will always be less than the coupon yield. When a bond is selling below par, as in cases B and C above, we say it is selling at a discount (from par). In this case, its current yield will always be greater than the coupon yield.

Notice in cases B, C, D, and E that, as the bond price increases, current yield decreases. Conversely, as price decreases, current yield increases. From the other point of view, a declining yield implies a rising price. A rising yield implies a declining price. This inverse relationship between current yield and bond price is always initially confusing. If you become confused thinking about it, you can always refer back to this example, or, if you have a calculator handy, make up your own example.

Coupon yield and current yield are not to be confused with *yield to maturity*. This is something else and is discussed later.

Bond ratings

Bonds are rated according to their safety. Safety means the probability that all future interest payments as well as repayment of the principal (face amount) will be met. Nonpayment of any of these is called default. There are three independent agencies that establish and publish ratings, Moody's Investors Service, Inc., Standard & Poor's Corporation, and Fitch Investors Service. The bonds or companies deemed to be the most safe (i.e., have the highest probability of meeting all future payments), get the highest rating. The ratings for Moody and Standard & Poor's, the two most widely used services, are as follows:

	Moody's	S&P	
Safest	Aaa	AAA	High-grade bonds, considered very safe.
	Aa	AA	
	A	A	Medium grade.
	Baa	BBB	
	Ba	BB	Lower grade—containing some degree of speculation as to eventual payment of future interest and principal repayment obligations.
	B	B	
	Caa	CCC	Highly speculative as to payment of interest and principal. Lowest ratings include bonds already in default.
	Ca	CC	
Least safe	C	C	

The ratings are based on a number of financial ratios. Standard & Poor's recently published[3] certain three-year average financial ratios for each rating category. Included in those were the following:

	AAA	AA	A	BBB	BB	B
Pretax interest coverage	12.82x	9.50x	6.65x	4.41x	3.14x	2.13x
$\frac{\text{Long-term debt}}{\text{Capitalization}}$	17.11x	21.66	27.70x	33.94x	45.16x	56.17x

In addition to these and many other financial ratios, subjective factors also enter into the rating determination. If a company has good ratios but

---

[3] These figures are taken from Standard & Poor's "Credit Week," Nov. 30, 1981, with permission.

the trend has been deteriorating, or if a rating agency has good reason to believe the ratios and financial security will change, they may alter the rating accordingly.

The majority of bonds get the same level of rating from each agency. Sometimes one agency rates a particular bond one notch higher or lower than the other agency. This is called a split rating. Most often, all the bond issues of a company have the same rating, but sometimes different bond issues in a company will have different ratings. When this occurs, the bond that gets paid first in the event of bankruptcy almost always gets the higher rating. However, just because one bond in a company has this priority does not mean it will necessarily have a higher rating.

The lower a company's bond rating, the greater the risk that the company will default on some future interest, sinking fund, or final maturity payment, according to the judgment of the rating agency. Potential bond buyers demand a higher yield to compensate them for the higher risk of default on lower-rated bonds. Bond yields, then, are directly related to the market's perception of the bond's risk. Thus, bonds trading on the market will rise or fall in price to adjust the yield to changing perceptions of risk.[4] Similarly, when a company is issuing new bonds, it usually has to offer an interest rate comparable to the interest rates of similarly rated bonds already on the market. In fact, a company selling new bonds usually has to offer an interest rate slightly higher than similar bonds already in the market in order to induce potential investors to sell their old bonds and buy the new ones with which the investors are less familiar.

Most bonds' perceived risk is accurately reflected by the agency's ratings, but sometimes the market evaluates a bond's risk as being greater than or less than the ratings suggest. For instance a given bond may be rated AA, but the market (i.e., most investors) may feel it is more risky and should only be rated A. In this case the bond would be likely to sell at a similar yield as other A-rated bonds. Thus the market does not always agree with the rating agencies. In fact, it often happens that the rating agencies raise or lower their ratings after the market has already reflected such a change. For the majority of bonds, however, the market usually agrees with the rating agencies and thus, for these bonds, yields at any given time are directly related to their ratings. For example, on December 11, 1981, new long-term industrial bonds with the following ratings typically had the accompanying yields:[5]

---

[4] Bond prices also will rise or fall in the market to adjust the yield to changes in interest rates caused by economic or government policy factors, rather than reasons related to changing perceptions of the risk of an individual company.

[5] These figures taken from Salomon Brothers, Inc., "Bond Market Roundup"—"Week Ending December 11, 1981," with permission.

```
AAA. . . . . . .   14.75%
AA . . . . . . . .   15.25
A . . . . . . . . .   15.88
BBB. . . . . . .   16.63
```

It is harder to identify a typical rate for lower-rated bonds since they vary more widely, but new long-term industrial BB-rated bonds were yielding approximately 17.20 percent and B-rated bonds were closer to 18 percent at that date.

This does not mean that all A-rated bonds had exactly a 15.88 percent yield. Other factors—such as sinking-fund provisions, call features, time to maturity, as well as individual investors' judgments about risk—would cause the yields to vary slightly around the 15.88 percent. If interest rates in the economy in general changed, say, upward, the interest rate for each rating class would move upward. While the rates would all move upward they might move up slightly different amounts so the yield difference between two ratings, called the *yield spread*, will vary. The following example shows the spreads on new long-term industrial bonds in late January 1981 and at the end of May 1981 for bonds with different ratings:[6]

1/23/81	Spread	5/29/81	Spread
AAA. . .13.00%		13.75%	
	.63%		.50%
AA 13.63		14.25	
	.75		.63
A 14.38		14.88	
	1.12		.87
BBB. . .15.50		15.75	

The table above shows that yields rose in all categories from January to May 1981, but the spreads between them narrowed. What causes overall interest rates to change and why the spreads between the ratings change is a very complex subject and beyond the scope of this book. But the relative positions always remain the same (i.e., a triple-A bond will always yield less than a double-A bond, which will always yield less than a single-A bond, and so on, except where the market disagrees with ratings or when comparing very different kinds of bonds). Bonds of industrial manufacturing companies, for example, may have somewhat different yields than bonds of utilities, such as electric power companies.

When a company wants to raise money by issuing bonds, it obviously

---

[6] These figures are taken from Salomon Brothers, Inc., "Bond Market Roundup"—"Week Ending January 23, 1981" and "Week Ending May 29, 1981" with permission.

wants to issue them at the lowest possible interest rate (given its rating). It also wants to have maximum flexibility on how and when it pays back the loan, and have the fewest possible restrictions of any sort in the indenture. Conversely, the buyer of a bond wants the highest possible interest and the greatest possible protection. The features and restrictions discussed next will have a bearing on what interest rate is actually necessary to sell the bonds.

Call feature and refunding

A bond indenture may specify that the bond is callable. When a bond is callable, it means that the issuing company has the right, at its option, to redeem the bond early, rather than wait until final maturity, and the bondholders have no choice. A company wants the right to call the bonds for a number of reasons. First, the company may have extra cash around and simply want to pay off the bonds so it will not have to make interest payments. Second, suppose the bonds were issued with a 13 percent coupon (i.e., $130 interest per year on a $1,000 face value bond) and, since that time, interest rates on similarly rated bonds have fallen to 10 percent. In that case, the company would obviously like to issue new bonds with a 10 percent coupon ($100) and use the money to redeem the old bonds with the 13 percent ($130) coupon and thereby save $30 interest per bond. The third reason the company might want to call the bonds (redeem them immediately) is that the bond indenture may have restrictions (i.e., regarding financial ratios, that are preventing the company from doing something it wants, such as issuing new debt). By calling and redeeming the bonds, the restrictive indenture ceases to exist and the company once again has its flexibility. From the bond-holders' point of view, the call feature is undesirable. The bondholder who bought the bond with a 13 percent coupon would certainly not want to give it up when he or she could only reinvest the money at 10 percent.

Thus, other things being equal, if a bond were callable, a potential buyer would demand a higher initial interest rate to compensate for the risk that the bond might be called away just when it was most attractive. For example, if there is no call feature, a bond may be able to be sold when initially issued at, say, 13 percent. If the company wants a highly flexible call feature, it might have to pay 13½ percent. If the company is willing to settle for a somewhat restricted call feature, it may be able to sell the bonds at 13¼ percent.

This is typical of the factors that go into determining whether a bond will be attractive to a buyer at a given interest rate. Given the company's desire to have the flexibility of calling the bond, and the bondholders' aversion to it, the call feature usually represents a compromise. Using the example of the ABC bonds issued in 1970 and due in 1990, a typical call feature may begin as follows:

"These bonds are callable at the option of the company *but not before 1975*. In the event they are called in 1975, the company will pay a 5 percent premium above par (i.e., an additional $50). If they are called in 1976, the company will pay a 4 percent premium. If they are called in 1977, the company will pay a 3 percent premium, etcetera . . ."

In this case, the bondholder is protected against having the bond called away from him for the first five years after issue, and if the bonds are called away sometime between the fifth and tenth years the bondholder will get some extra money, referred to as a *call premium*, to compensate him. With this type of compromise, the bonds would still look attractive to the initial buyer in 1970, but would add some flexibility for the company in the later years.

The call feature in the indenture also frequently says, "Although these bonds are callable from (date) to maturity, and with a (specified) premium, they may not *be refunded.*" This means that it is okay for the company to call the bonds if it is because the company has extra money available, *but it is not permitted to call the bonds if the money used to redeem them is obtained by issuing new bonds at a lower interest rate.*

DEFINITION

Refunding   Refers to the process just described, where a company issues new bonds at a low interest rate to pay back old bonds that have a higher interest rate.

Refunding, then, is something that may be done by the company, if permitted under the indenture. The term does not refer to the processes whereby the bondholder returns the bond to the company to get his money back. That is redemption.

Thus, a given bond may be "callable but not refundable." This would be a lot more acceptable to a potential bond buyer than a bond that was callable for any reason. Obviously, it would be even better from the buyer's point of view if the bond were not callable for any reason. If a bond is callable, the buyer would obviously desire that the call provision have a limited number of years, a high "call premium," and limitations on the reasons for which it may be called, such as non-refundability. Any or all of these features are called *call protection*. If the potential buyer does not like the call features, he does not have to buy the bond. Most bonds issued today are callable at any time but are non-refundable for a number of years. Bonds of industrial companies are typically protected against refunding for ten years from date of issue, and bonds of utilities are typically protected from refunding for five years. The call features can vary substantially from bond to bond and should be checked closely by potential buyers.

Covenants and negative covenants

The bond indenture usually contains a number of covenants or promises by the borrowing company regarding financial ratios, such as "The company will maintain a current ratio of at least 4 to 1" or "The company will maintain interest coverage of at least 4.0 times." It is the trustee's job to watch the company and make sure the covenants are met. If they are violated, the trustee informs the bondholders and then they, as a group, have to decide if they will excuse the violation or if they wish to invoke some right which is specified in the indenture. Such rights (which only become effective if a covenant is violated) may include a penalty payment, but most typically allow the bondholders to demand immediate redemption of the bonds. In the real world, when a company violates a covenant, the bondholders usually waive their right to immediate redemption. Most often, they waive it because the covenant violation was minor and will be corrected shortly without any effect on the likelihood of payment of interest or principal by the company. Should the company be facing difficult times, however, the covenant violation may be more serious and reflect a real risk of nonpayment of interest or principal by the company. In this case, it is still common for the bondholders to waive their right because often, when a company is in trouble, it would do the bondholders no good to demand their money since it would result in the company's going into bankruptcy. In that case, employees, taxes, banks, and perhaps other creditors get paid off first, and quite probably there would be little or no money left for the bondholders. Thus, the right of immediate redemption is seldom invoked.

Negative covenants are also restrictions on the issuing company's flexibility, usually phrased as a negative. A negative convenant may say, "The company may not pay a common dividend if (a certain financial ratio) falls below (a specified level)." Another common negative covenant is, "The company may not issue any further bonds or allow bank debt to build up beyond $ (an amount) without permission of these bondholders." Similarly, "The company may not sell any division with sales of over $ (an amount) or acquire any company for more than $ (an amount) without our permission."

These restrictions—covenants and negative covenants—provide extra protection for the bondholder and therefore make the issue more attractive (i.e., sellable at a lower interest rate) to potential buyers. Conversely, this type of restriction may be exactly what management wants to get out from under by calling the bond ahead of maturity. To use the example of Company ABC's 20-year bonds issued in 1970, it may be that the company badly needed the money from the bond issue in 1970, and thus agreed to a covenant against acquiring any other company; but by 1986 fortunes had improved, cash had built up well beyond immediate needs, and ABC wanted to acquire another company. By calling the bond issue and retiring it, the company would be free from the indenture's restriction against acquiring another firm. Alternatively, the company could simply ask the bondholders to waive the covenant and offer something in return, such as small increases in the coupon (interest) payable on the bond.

Interest rates

There are many different interest rates in the money and capital markets. *Interest rates* include four commonly discussed types: (1) bond rates—the yield to bondholders. (2) bank rates—what banks charge customers for loans. The prime rate is what they charge their safest customers (i.e., what they might call their AAA customers). Their riskier customers get charged more. Bank rates also include what banks pay to depositors on passbook accounts or on time certificates of deposit. (3) discount rate—what the Federal Reserve charges when it lends money to banks. (4) federal funds rate—the rate banks charge when they lend money for a day or two to other banks to help them meet reserve requirements. There are other interest rates too numerous to mention: the rate on government treasury bills, government agency bonds, and city and state bonds are but a few.

When interest rates are rising, it is normally the case that each of these is rising, although perhaps by different amounts and for different reasons. The same holds true when interest rates are falling. Interest rates rise and fall for reasons too complex to discuss here. There are whole books and courses about the factors which influence interest rates. Even if we listed, discussed, and became experts on all the apparently influencing factors, it would still be very difficult to predict whether interest rates would be rising or falling in the near and distant future. Even the experts are in substantial disagreement on what factors cause interest rates to change, and how. In sum, interest rates reflect in some complicated and perhaps unknowable way the entire economic outlook of the marketplace (i.e., the anonymous result each person's influence on each of the factors which enter into the determination of interest rates). Because interest rates have a very powerful effect on the economy,[7] certain rates, such as the discount rate, are fixed by the Federal Reserve at what it feels is best for the economy. These changes tend to have an effect on most of the other interest rates in the capital markets.

---

[7] The question of whether interest rates determine the level and direction of economic activity, or whether the economy determines the level and direction of interest rates, is like asking which came first, the chicken or the egg.

Yield to maturity

When a $1,000 face value bond is selling at $1,000 and has a coupon of $100, its coupon yield and current yield are obviously both 10 percent. However, if the bond price falls to $943, for example, the yield is not so obvious. The coupon yield is still 10 percent and the current yield is easy to calculate, and as shown on page 81 is 10.6 percent. However, when the bond is selling at $943, the person who buys it not only gets a $100 coupon each year, for a current yield of 10.6 percent, but also gets a capital gain of $57 when the bond matures at $1,000. Thus, the yield is somewhat higher than the current yield. Current yield reflects only the interest one receives and ignores the capital gain. The yield to maturity is a yield figure which mathematically takes into account both the current yield and the capital gain at maturity. Unfortunately, the calculation that gives the yield to maturity is more complex than it looks and cannot be done accurately on a simple calculator. As a result, tables have been published in which one can look up the yield to maturity for a bond with a given price, a given coupon, and a given time to maturity. Here, we can only say with certainty that, as long as the bond is selling below par (below $1,000), its yield to maturity will be greater than its current yield. Similarly, if the bond is selling at a premium (more than par), the yield to maturity will be less than the current yield because, in addition to the annual interest payments received, the buyer of the bond will incur a capital *loss* when the bond is redeemed at par at maturity.

Example.   For a bond with a $70 coupon and 12 years to maturity:

Price	Coupon yield	Current yield	Yield to maturity
$1,150......	7.0%	6.1%	5.3%
1,100......	7.0	6.4	5.8
1,050......	7.0	6.7	6.4
1,000......	7.0	7.0	7.0
950......	7.0	7.4	7.6
850......	7.0	8.2	9.1

For most investors the yield to maturity is the more meaningful because it takes everything into account. However, individual investors have different investment requirements. Look, for example, at the following bonds of three similarly rated companies. Each matures 12 years from now, but because they were issued at different times they have different coupons. Bond A was issued at a time when AAs were yielding four percent, so its coupon payment is $40. Bond B was issued when AAs were yielding seven percent, so its coupon is $70. And Bond C was issued when AAs were yielding 10 percent, so its coupon is $100. Assume that AA rated issues today are yielding 7 percent.

	Annual coupon	Coupon yield	Today's price	Current yield	Yield to maturity	Yearly interest	Capital gain (or loss) at maturity
Bond A....$	40	4%	$ 759	5.3%	7.0%	$ 40	$241
Bond B....	70	7	1000	7.0	7.0	70	none
Bond C....	100	10	1241	8.1	7.0	100	(241)

Notice that all three bonds are so priced that their yield to maturity is the same. Thus, a bond buyer who has no tax to worry about, and does not need the money until after 12 years, would be indifferent to which bond he bought. If the bond buyer was a retired person who needed current income to live on, and was in a low tax bracket, he would prefer Bond C. A wealthy person in a high tax bracket would prefer Bond A because Bond A pays relatively little interest, which for him would be taxed at a high rate, but gives a big capital gain at the end, and capital gains are taxed at a much lower rate. Thus, individual tax considerations and financial requirements may make one bond more attractive than another; but for the person not paying tax and not needing the money before the bond matures, the yield to maturity of 7 percent for each bond makes him indifferent to which he owns.

How bond yields change

Let's say Bond A was issued in 1970. The bonds mature in 1990 and there is no sinking fund or call privilege. Assume it is now 1978, so there are 12 years to maturity. The bonds have a coupon rate of $40, or 4 percent of the face value of $1,000 per bond. The bonds are rated Aa by Moody and AA by Standard & Poor's. The bonds were initially issued by the company to their first owners (a primary offering) on January 3, 1970. At that time, presume all AA-rated bonds were yielding 4 percent, so these bonds were sold for exactly $1,000. Mr. Smith purchased one of the bonds by paying $1,000 to the company (through his broker). Thus, his coupon yield was 4 percent, his current yield was 4 percent, and his yield to maturity was 4 percent. Bond rates did not change at all during 1970. So, when Smith sold the bond to Mr. Wood on December 31, 1970 (a secondary offering), he received $1,000. Wood paid $1,000 for the bond, so his coupon yield, current yield, and yield to maturity were also 4 percent. Wood intended to hold the bond until maturity in 1990.

In January 1971, the general level of interest rates began to rise. This means bond prices began to fall. On January 20, 1971, Wood looked in the newspaper and saw that his bonds were selling at $975. At $975, the current yield is 4.1 percent and the yield to maturity is 4.2 percent.

$$\text{Current yield} = \frac{\text{Coupon}}{\text{Current price}} = \frac{\$40}{\$975} = 4.1 \text{ Percent}$$

$$\text{Yield to maturity (from tables)} = 4.2 \text{ Percent}$$

Notice that the current yield and yield to maturity always relate to the current price. From Wood's point of view nothing has changed, since he does not intend to sell the bond. He still gets $40 interest payments each year and $1,000 at maturity. He is still getting a 4 percent yield *on his original investment of $1,000.* But when we talk about bond yields we are not talking about some individual's yield based on a price he paid sometime in the past. We usually talk about the yield you would get beginning today if you bought the bond today.

Why did the bond price fall? Or the interest rate rise? It did *not* do so because some government agency said that all AA bonds would now sell at $975 or would now have a yield to maturity of 4.2 percent. Rather, what happened is this. Ms. D, Mr. E, and Mr. F were holders of Bond A and were sophisticated students of the bond market and interest rates. They had observed upward changes in other interest rates, such as the prime rate, and had been watching Federal Reserve moves in the markets and they, independently, concluded that interest rates were about to go up. If interest rates went up on AA-rated bonds to, say 4.1 percent, that would mean that another company about to issue new bonds, Company XYZ for instance, would have to pay a coupon of $41 per $1,000 bond. If Companies A and XYZ had the same rating and other features of the bond were similar, and if Bond A were still selling at $1,000 and yielding 4 percent exactly, it would obviously be preferable to hold the bonds of XYZ and get the higher coupon. Anticipating this, Ms. D decided to sell her bonds in early January and use the money to buy the bonds of XYZ. Because the bonds she was selling were just one of many AA issues on the market, she had to lower her price a little to make her bond more attractive to a buyer. Thus, the price was forced downward, say to $997. Messrs. E and F were bond speculators and did not particularly care whether they bought the XYZ bonds or not; but because they expected interest rates to go up, they therefore (automatically) expected prices to go down. Therefore, they wanted to sell their bonds, too. In the process of selling, they forced the price down even further. By January 20, the price had fallen to $975. Since each sale has a buyer and a seller, the $975 price and 4.1 percent current yield and 4.2 percent yield to maturity obviously reflected the balance that day of those who wanted to sell because they thought the bond was going lower, and those who wanted to buy because they thought the price had reached bottom and would stay there or move higher. Thus, yield to maturity on double-A-rated bonds has now moved up to 4.2 percent. The price moved down and the yield moved up responding to many investors' decisions to buy and sell, which in turn reflected their anticipations of market changes and how best to invest their money.

Markets always anticipate the future. The price of a bond or stock (or many other items for that matter) on a given day always represents the "market's opinion" (i.e., the balance of myriad investors' transactions that reflect differing opinions on whether the price is going up or down in the future).

Changes in interest rates and yields are often quoted in terms of *basis points*. A basis point is 0.01 percent, or one one-hundredth of a percentage point. For example, if interest rates went from 11 percent to 12 percent, we would say they went up by 100 basis points or one full percentage point. If the rate then declined from 12.00 percent to 11.90 percent, we would say the rate declined by 10 basis points. Since interest rate changes are often small and gradual, investors who work with these numbers every day find it easier to talk about changes in interest rates in terms of basis points rather than saying, "The rate was down by 20 one-hundredths of a percent, or one-fifth of a percent."

In the example of Bond A, we saw how bond prices fall and yields rise. Let's now look at Bond C and see why bonds can sell at a premium to par (i.e., at over $1,000). When Bond C was initially issued at 10 percent, it sold at par. As rates dropped and new similarly rated bonds were issued, which yielded only 9 percent or $90 per coupon, Bond C suddenly became very attractive with its $100 coupon. Therefore, investors began to buy it and were willing to pay a premium to get it because, even though they would ultimately incur a capital loss at maturity, the extra current income each year (above the $90 they could get on new bonds) made up for it. Up to what price would potential buyers pay for this bond? The answer is up to a price where its yield to maturity is the same as the yield to maturity of a new similarly rated bond being issued today at par at today's interest rate. The yield to maturity tells you exactly where the capital loss is offset by the extra current income. Thus, if new AA-rated bonds were yielding 7.0 percent and Bond C was selling at $1,232 for a yield to maturity of 7.1 percent, the yield to maturity is telling you that at the current price, Bond C is more attractive than the new issue. The extra current income more than offsets the capital loss at maturity, so that the yield to the investor from Bond C is better than the yield from the new bond at 7 percent. Thus, buyers would still prefer to buy Bond C and, in fact, would be willing to pay up to $1,241, at which point its yield to maturity would be exactly 7 percent, just in line with new similarly rated bonds.

Bond titles

When you look at the balance sheet in the annual report of a company you will usually see each of the bond issues listed separately. A balance sheet with many bond issues may look like this:

Bonds:

10.00%	Equipment trust certificates due 1998
5.60	Mortgage bonds due 1993
7.10	Sinking-fund debentures due 1988
6.25	Notes due 1985
10½	Senior subordinated debentures due 1990
9.40	Subordinated debentures due 1999
14.25	Junior subordinated debentures due 2003
10.00	Convertible subordinated debentures due 1993

Each of these issues is a separate contract with a separate indenture. The order in which they appear is usually their priority in being paid off in the event of bankruptcy. That order is not necessarily (in fact, usually not) the order in which they were issued or the order in which they mature. A company is not obligated to print them in any particular order and often one has to refer to the footnotes or directly to the indentures to figure out the priorities. *Moody's Industrial Manual* or *Standard & Poor's Corporation Records* are also helpful in this regard. These books are published yearly by Moody's Investors Services and by Standard & Poor's, Inc. They provide a lot of basic data on almost all publicly traded stock and bond issues of public companies. The bond titles usually relate to their priority in bankruptcy. Let's look at each to see what the words mean.

5.60% Mortgage bonds due 1993. This bond has a coupon rate of 5.60 percent and final maturity is in 1993. There may or may not be a sinking-fund provision. The bond title does not tell us. The title, mortgage bonds, means there is one or more specific pieces of property, usually buildings or plants, which are "pledged" to the bondholders. Thus, in the event that the company cannot meet its obligations to the bondholders, the pledged property becomes the property of the bondholders, who can then sell it off to get their money back.

10.0% Equipment trust certificates due 1998. These are much like mortgage bonds except that the pledged property is usually a piece of transportation equipment, such as an airplane or a railroad car.

7.10% Sinking-fund debentures due 1988. Not all bonds have a specific piece of property pledged to them. Bonds that do not are usually called "debentures." Debentures are backed by the "full faith and credit" of the company. This means that, if the company is unable to meet its obligations to the debenture holders, the debenture holders do not get possession of a specific asset but must go to court and ask that the company be declared bankrupt, and have its assets sold off so that the debt holders can be paid off. In this case, the debenture holders get in line with everyone else and get paid off after all debt holders with priority rights get paid off. The words *sinking fund* in the title give you the additional information that there is a sinking fund. Even if the title does not say sinking fund, there may be one. If there were not a sinking fund, the title of these bonds would simply have been "7.10% Debentures due 1988." Since there is a sinking fund and those words are included in the title, the title might be abbreviated "7.10 SFD's 1988."

6.25% Notes due 1985.   Notes are exactly like bonds or debentures, but usually are issued with shorter maturity dates ranging from 1 to 10 years. Longer maturities are normally called bonds or debentures.

9.40% Subordinated debentures due 1999.   This title gives the information that the rights of the holders of these debentures are in some way subordinated to the rights of other debenture holders. Most probably, it means that the other debenture holders get paid off first in the event of bankruptcy. Subordinated debentures can arise in two ways. First, suppose the 7.10% Sinking-fund debentures (SFD) were issued in 1972. In the 7.10% SFD indenture it said that if the company issued any new debt, the new debt would have to have lower priority in bankruptcy than the 7.10% SFDs. Thus, when the company wanted to issue some more debt in 1974, it had to be subordinated to the 7.10% SFDs. Thus, the 9.40s of 1999 get the title "9.40 Subordinated debentures due 1999." They are often abbreviated "9.40% Sub. debs. of '99." Subordination can also arise another way, described under the 10½% Senior subordinated debentures.

10½% Senior subordinated debentures due 1990.   This title tells you that these bonds are subordinated in some way to some other bonds (it does not tell you which, although it appears that they are subordinated to the 7.10% SFDs). It also tells you that these bonds are senior to some other subordinated debentures, probably the 9.40s, the 10.0% Convertibles, and the 14.25s. *Senior* just means priority in some rights, again usually the right of prior payment in the event of bankruptcy.

When the 9.40s were issued in 1974, the company had a lot of debt outstanding; and in order to make the issue attractive enough to be sold, the company not only had to pay this high 9.4 percent interest rate, but also had to agree in the indenture not to issue any further bonds. However, in the 1974–75 recession, things got so bad that the company was faced with bankruptcy if it could not raise some more money quickly. The stock market was such that it was almost impossible to sell new stock, and banks refused to make any further loans to the company. Thus, the company knew it would have to issue more bonds even though it had agreed not to in the indenture under the 9.40% Sub. debs. Thus, the company's management wrote a letter to the bondholders (and the trustee) explaining how bad the situation was and asked the bondholders to waive this agreement and allow the company to issue some new bonds. The letter further explained that if the company did not raise new money, bankruptcy was inevitable.

The letter also pointed out that, in the event of bankruptcy, the holders of the 9.40s were the last people to be paid off and that it was unlikely that they would get all, if any, of their money back. Further, the case might be in the bankruptcy court for years, and during that time they would not even get interest. Thus, it became apparent that it was in the best interests of the 9.40 Sub. deb. holders to waive their rights and allow the company to issue new bonds and then hope that the company could pull out of trouble and could continue to make good its interest and ultimate redemption obligations. The company's investment bankers also told it that, even with permission of the bondholders, it would be almost impossible to sell new bonds since they would be so risky. In order to make the new bonds attractive enough to sell, the investment bankers not only suggested a 10½ percent interest rate, but also suggested that they be given priority to the 9.40s in the event of bankruptcy. Once again, the 9.40% bondholders were approached and told that if they did not subordinate their rights under bankruptcy to the new bonds, that it was unlikely that the new bonds could be sold and, again, bankruptcy was inevitable.

The 9.40% bondholders said they would give permission for the new bonds and allow the new bonds to be senior to them, but, although they made an exception this time, they still retained all their rights under the indenture and would refuse any further permission for new bonds.

Thus the Senior subordinated debentures were issued in 1975 and were "senior" to the 9.40% Sub. Debs. in bankruptcy rights, but were still "junior" to all other debt in bankruptcy rights.

14.25% Junior subordinated debentures due 2003. In 1978 the company once again needed to borrow money to avoid bankruptcy. Again the holders of the 9.40% sub. debs. (as well as the other debt holders whose indentures prohibited the company from further borrowing) were asked for their permission to allow the company to issue new debt. The 9.40% sub. deb. holders again granted their permission for the new debt, but this time they refused to subordinate their rights in the event of bankruptcy. Thus the company's new debt issue was to be junior to even the 9.40%s of 1999. As a result of this lowest priority in the event of bankruptcy, the new debentures were titled "junior subordinated debentures." Also, being given the lowest priority in a company that was clearly near bankruptcy, the company had to offer a coupon rate of 14.25

percent, which seemed outrageously high at that time, in order to induce people to buy them.

The words *senior, junior,* and *subordinated,* then, just refer to the relative priorities of bonds in the event of bankruptcy. Note also that neither the date of maturity nor the date of issue is an indication of priority rights in bankruptcy.

10.00% Convertible subordinated debentures due 1993.   Convertible debentures are almost always the most junior issues in a company's debt structure, although one occasionally sees a convertible bond which is backed by a specific piece of property, like a mortgage bond. In the case of these 10.00% Convertible subordinated debentures of 1993 (abbreviated 10% CSD's of '93), although we are not specifically told that they are junior to the 14.25%'s of '03, that is a good assumption. The conversion feature is discussed in the next chapter.

9

Convertible bonds

Convertible bonds are just like other bonds, but they have one additional important feature. They can be converted into stock. To demonstrate, suppose BCD Corporation issued $100,000 worth of convertible bonds on January 2, 1970. The bonds have a 20-year life and therefore mature in 1990. The conversion feature of the convertible bond may say something like this:

Each bond may be converted into 20 shares of common stock of the company at the option of the bondholder anytime after January 1, 1975.

This means that if the bondholder decides to convert, she mails her bond certificate to the company (or trustee) and by return mail she gets a certificate for 20 shares of common stock of BCD Corp. Notice that this bond cannot be converted during the first five years of its life. Sometimes the indenture specifies that the bond is only convertible after a specified period (like this one). Sometimes the indenture may also specify that the bond *cannot* be convertible after a specified time. For example, a convertible bond may be convertible only for the first 10 years of its life. Another 20-year bond may be convertible only after the fourth year but before the 18th year. Other convertible bonds may be convertible anytime during their life.

Sometimes the conversion feature reads like this:

This bond may be converted into common stock of the company at $50 per share.

This does *not* mean that the bondholder has to pay $50 per share. Although it is not clear from the wording, it means that *$50 worth of face value* of the bond may be exchanged for one share of common stock. Since the bond has a face value of $1,000, it therefore converts into 20 shares of common stock:

$$\frac{\text{Face value}}{\text{Conversion "price"}} = \frac{\$1,000}{\$50} = 20 \text{ Shares}$$

One cannot partially convert a bond. If you decide to convert a bond, you convert it entirely, in this case into 20 shares of common. However, if you own more than one bond you may convert only some, but not all, of your bonds. Note that this bond converts into 20 shares regardless of the price you paid for the bond. *The conversion rate is based on face value, not the current price.* So even if the price of the bond falls to $894, or rises to $1,150, or any other price, it still converts into exactly 20 shares.

Although the conversion rate (number of shares a bond converts into) is fixed for the vast majority of bonds, one occasionally sees a bond that has a variable conversion rate. The conversion feature of such a bond may say:

> This bond converts into 30 shares of common stock anytime prior to December 31, 1984, into 35 shares of common stock between January 1, 1985 and December 31, 1988, and into 40 shares of common stock thereafter.

Such bonds are unusual, and for the remainder of this book it is assumed that a convertible bond's conversion rate is fixed.

The price of a convertible bond sometimes behaves differently from a nonconvertible bond. The price of a nonconvertible bond moves up or down primarily reflecting the changes in yield to maturity of other bonds of similar rating, coupon, and time to maturity. The price of a convertible bond, however, may move higher than a similar nonconvertible bond, depending on the market price of the underlying common stock (the stock into which the bond converts).

To illustrate, let's look at the convertible bonds of BCD Corporation. The bonds have a 5 percent coupon, are rated A, have eight years left to maturity, and convert into 20 shares of common stock (at $50 of face value of bond per common share). Suppose the underlying common stock is selling at $60/share. What would the bond sell for? Since each bond converts into 20 shares and each share is worth $60, the bond is obviously worth $1,200 because anyone owning the bond could convert it into 20 shares and sell them on the market for $60 each for a total of $1,200.

Number of common shares per bond		*Market price per common share*		*Value to bondholder if converted*
20	×	$60	=	$1,200

Thus, if the bond were selling for anything less than $1,200, say $1,150, someone would buy it, convert it, and sell the stock for $1,200 and keep the $50 profit. Thus, the price of a convertible bond will usually move up in line with the underlying common stock. Suppose the stock moved up to $70/share. Then the bond price would move up to $1,400.

$$\underset{20}{\underline{Number\ of\ shares}} \times \underset{\$70}{\underline{\substack{Market\ value \\ per\ share}}} = \underset{\$1,400}{\underline{Converted\ value}}$$

As long as the market price of the stock is above the conversion "price" of the bond, the bond price will move up in line with the stock price, as shown in the following table.

Common stock price	Bond price	Yields for a 5 percent coupon with 8 years to maturity		
		Coupon yield	Current yield	Yield to maturity
$70	$1,400	5.0%	3.6%	Negative
65	1,300	5.0	3.8	1.08%
60	1,200	5.0	4.2	2.25
55	1,100	5.0	4.5	3.55
50	1,000	5.0	5.0	5.00

Notice that as the stock price moves higher (and hence the bond price moves higher), the current yield and yield to maturity move lower and therefore obviously have little influence on the decision to buy or not to buy the bond. At this point the decision to buy or sell the bond is based on its relationship to the stock price and the investor's outlook for changes in the stock price.

Suppose the price of the stock falls to $30 per share. The converted value of the bond then falls to $600.

$$\underset{20}{\underline{Number\ of\ shares}} \times \underset{\$30}{\underline{\substack{Market\ value \\ per\ share}}} = \underset{\$600}{\underline{Converted\ value}}$$

Does the bond price then fall to $600? Not likely. The price of this bond will only fall to the price where its yield to maturity is equal to that of similar 8-year, A-rated bonds, convertible or nonconvertible. Assume similar 8-year, A-rated bonds are currently selling at a yield to maturity of 6.6 percent. According to the tables, an 8-year bond with a 5 percent coupon would sell at $900 in order to yield 6.6 percent. Thus, the price of the BCD bond would be unlikely to fall below $900.

Suppose the price of the stock now rose to $45. At that price the converted value is exactly $900 (20 shares × $45/share = $900). So, for any stock price under $45, the bond will sell for about $900. As the stock price rises above $45, the bond price will begin to move up with it. In reality, even if the stock price was slightly under $45, it is probable that the bond would sell for slightly more than $900, because the conversion feature, which gives it the possibility of unlimited gains in the future, would cause some investors to be willing to pay a little more for it than they would for an otherwise similar nonconvertible bond.

Advantage of a convertible bond from the bondholder's point of view

We can now see the advantage of a convertible bond from the bondholder's point of view: It has the best features of both bonds and stock. If the stock price is low, relative to the conversion price, the bond has "downside protection" in that its price will behave like any other similar nonconvertible bond and won't go below a level reflecting the appropriate yield. But if the stock price moves up above the conversion price, the bond price will behave like the stock price, and there is no limit to how high it can go. For nonconvertible bonds, the bond price will always reflect only the appropriate yield. Nonconvertible bonds will not "participate" in the movement of the stock price.

Stock price	Bond price	Coupon yield	Current yield	Yield to maturity[*]
$80	$1,600	5.0%	3.1%	Negative
70	1,400	5.0	3.6	Negative
60	1,200	5.0	4.2	2.3%
55	1,100	5.0	4.5	3.6
50	1,000	5.0	5.0	5.0
45	900	5.0	5.6	6.6
40	900	5.0	5.6	6.6
30	900	5.0	5.6	6.6
20	900	5.0	5.6	6.6

[*] Based on 8-year maturity.

Note that common stock alone does not have the downside protection of a convertible bond. If things look bad for a company, its stock can keep going lower even if there is a dividend, because there is always the possibility that the dividend will be cut, whereas the bond interest is a legal obligation and must be paid as long as the company is able.

Advantage of convertible bonds from issuing company's point of view

Since the conversion feature adds a possibility of unlimited price appreciation, which nonconvertible bonds lack, a convertible bond is obviously more attractive to the bondholder, other things being equal. Thus, if a company is willing to sell convertible bonds, it may be able to sell the bonds with a lower interest rate than if it were selling nonconvertible bonds. How much lower the coupon would be is related to how attractive the conversion feature is. Suppose, for example, CDE Company has an A rating and its stock is selling at $40. If CDE sells nonconvertible bonds it would have to pay the current interest rate on similar A-rated bonds, which is 9 percent (i.e., each $1,000 bond would have a $90 coupon). If the bond is convertible and converts at $40/share (i.e., into 25 shares), the bond would be very attractive because any upward movement in the stock would immediately cause an upward movement in the price of the bond. Thus, the bond might be able to be sold with a 5 percent yield, or a $50 coupon instead of the $90 coupon. On the other hand, if the bond only converted into 20 shares (at $50 per share), it would not be quite as attractive. In this case, the converted value of the bond is 20 shares × $40/share market price = $800, and the stock would have to move up to about $50 before the bond began to move with it. In this case, the "conversion feature" is less attractive, but it is still there and may be quite rewarding at some time in the life of the bond. Thus, the coupon necessary to sell this bond would be greater than the 5 percent necessary with the more attractive conversion feature, but still less than the 9 percent without the conversion feature. Perhaps it would be 7 percent. Thus, the more attractive the conversion feature the lower interest the company will have to pay. While paying a lower interest rate is an obvious advantage to the company, the related disadvantage is that, if the bonds are converted, the more shares they convert into, the more potential dilution to earnings per share.

Another important advantage to the company is that sometimes, if a company is in trouble and needs money badly, nobody would want the bonds except at an interest rate that was so high the company could probably not afford to pay it. In this case, an attractive conversion feature would enable the company to sell the bonds with a coupon rate it could afford to pay.

Premium and discount to conversion

Let us look again at the bonds of BCD Company (see table on page 99). Assuming BCD's stock is selling at $60, it is possible—in fact it is probable—that the bond will not sell at exactly its converted value of $1,200. Suppose the bond is selling at $1,224. In that case, we could say it is selling at a $24 "premium to conversion" (i.e., $24 above its converted value). Normally, however, the premium is expressed as a percent of the converted value, and we would say it is "selling at a 2 percent premium to conversion." In other words, it is selling for a price 2 percent higher than its converted value.

$$\frac{\text{Premium above converted value}}{\text{Converted value}} = \frac{\$24}{\$1,200}$$

$$= .02 \text{ (i.e., 2\% Premium to \$1,200)}$$

Similarly, if the bond is selling at less than its converted value, it is selling at a discount to conversion. Suppose the bond is selling at $1,182. That represents an $18 discount from converted value, or a 1½ percent discount.

$$\frac{\text{Dollar discount from converted value}}{\text{Converted value}} = \frac{\$1,200 - 1,182}{\$1,200} = \frac{\$18}{\$1,200}$$

$$= .015 = 1\frac{1}{2}\% \text{ Discount to conversion}$$

One reason a bond sells at a discount to conversion is that if one wanted to buy the bond, convert it, and sell the common stock to keep the difference, he or she would have to pay commissions for buying the bond and selling the stock, and thus the bond is actually "worth" slightly less than its converted value. One reason a bond may sell at a premium to conversion is as follows. Suppose you expect a stock to go up, but very little of that stock is traded in a day. Thus, if you try to buy a lot of it, you may force the price up past what you want to pay for it. So you might want to buy the convertible bond instead of the stock. But if other investors are thinking the same thing, you may have to bid up the bond price to a slight premium to conversion in order to acquire all the bonds you want. You can do this and still, in effect, be "buying the stock" at a lower price than if you bought it directly. Another reason a bond may sell at premium is that the bond's interest would make the bond more attractive than the stock if the stock paid no dividend or only a small dividend. You might have the same capital gain from either the stock or the convertible bond if the stock goes up, so why not buy the bond and also get the higher yield while you are waiting? Furthermore, suppose you are wrong and the stock goes down. By buying the bond instead of the stock, you at least have some protection against an extreme decline.

Do not confuse premium and discount to conversion (converted value) with premium and discount to par. When we say a bond is selling at a premium or a discount, one usually knows by the context whether the statement is referring to par or conversion. Assume the bonds of BCD Company are selling at $927. The stock is selling at $45 so the converted value of the bond is $900 (20 shares × $45/share = $900). With the bond priced at $927, it is selling at a 3 percent premium to conversion and a 7.3 percent discount to par. If the bond were selling at $990, it would be selling at a 10 percent premium to conversion and a 1 percent discount from par.

Call rights and sinking fund

A convertible bond may be callable or have a sinking fund the same as a nonconvertible bond, or both. If the company calls the bond, or if it is about to be redeemed under a sinking-fund provision, the bond-holder almost always has the opportunity to convert if he so chooses. In this way, the company can sometimes force people to convert if the bond is selling above par. Suppose BCD's bonds are selling at $1,200, reflecting the underlying stock price of $60 per share. If the company wants to force conversion, it simply exercises its right to call the bonds. The bonds are callable at par plus some call premium (review in Chapter 8) of, say, $40 per bond. So the bondholder has a choice. He can either let the bond be called and receive $1,040, or convert it and receive $1,200. Obviously, he would choose the latter.

Effect of convertible bonds on earnings per share

We have said that the price one should be willing to pay for a share of stock is related to its current and expected future earnings per share (because that is an indication of possible future dividends). Forecasting future earnings is always a difficult task, and the presence of a convertible bond further complicates the forecast, because *if* some or all of the bonds are converted, it will result in more shares outstanding (which would lower EPS) and less interest expense (which, of course, would raise EPS). The change in EPS as a result of conversion of a convertible bond may be large and is always considered by professional investors when estimating future EPS. We will not go through the mechanics of converting a bond here, because most readers will never have occasion to do it, but we will discuss the effects of it.

Let's assume BCD Company is estimated to have earnings per share of $4.00 assuming *none* of its convertible bonds are converted, and $2.80 if *all* the bonds are converted. Assuming the stock is thought to merit a price-earnings ratio of 10x, what is the stock worth?

| | | Stock |
EPS	P-E	Value
$4.00 × 10x =		$40.00

or

| $2.80 × 10x = | | $28.00 |

Since the bonds have not in fact been converted, the actual EPS is $4, but would you want to pay $40 for the stock knowing that bondholders might convert with the resulting decline in EPS?

One answer is to be conservative and assume conversion. Since most investors hate to lose money, why take chances? The most conservative investor would always use the lowest EPS, and thus, in this case, he would make his determination of the value of the stock based on EPS of $2.80. If he believes the stock is worth 10 times earnings, he would be willing to pay up to $28 for the stock but not higher. If other investors bid the stock up higher, the conservative investor would simply avoid this stock and look for other stocks.

On the other hand, what if the bond is never converted and simply gets redeemed at maturity? In that case, the stock might be attractive up to $40 per share, and therefore very attractive around $30 per share. So which EPS figure does one use? The accounting profession has come up with a decision rule which tells companies when to assume conversion and when not to in calculating the EPS figures they publish in their annual reports. The rule is based on the likelihood, at the time of issue, that the bonds will at sometime be converted. The effect of the rule is to create two definitions of earnings per share, called *primary earnings per share* and *fully diluted earnings per share*. Again, the mechanics of using the decision rule are less important than the results, because companies are required to report both primary and fully diluted EPS, and thus most investors will never need to go through the conversion process.

DEFINITIONS

Primary earnings per share   The earnings per share figure that results from converting all convertible issues which, according to a detailed decision rule, are likely to be converted to stock at some time.

Fully diluted earnings per share   The earnings per share figure that results from converting all convertible issues, whether or not they are likely to ever be converted.[1]

The definitions above are correct as far as they go but are not complete. Both primary and fully diluted EPS calculations consider a number of factors in addition to convertible bonds. These include convertible preferred stocks (discussed in Chapter 10), and warrants, rights, and stock options.[2] The latter three items are usually far less significant than convertible bonds or convertible preferreds and will not be covered. Suffice it to say, these items are all included in the primary and fully diluted EPS figures reported to the public.

---

[1] If all a company's convertible issues are likely, as defined by the decision rule, to be converted, then primary earnings per share would be the same as fully diluted earnings per share.

[2] Stock options in this case refers to options given by a company to its employees to buy company stock from the company. It has nothing to do with the put and call options you can buy through your stockbroker on the options exchanges. These latter kinds of options have no effect on company earnings.

From the discussions so far, it is still not clear whether it is best to use primary or fully diluted EPS. While primary EPS was intended to be the single best figure, mechanical decision rules are never perfect and thus there is no absolute answer to the question. Some investors and institutions choose to use primary and some fully diluted.

While we can say with a high degree of confidence that primary EPS is better than a calculated EPS figure which does not even consider the potential dilution effect of convertible issues, we cannot say that either primary EPS or fully diluted EPS is absolutely better than the other. It comes down to a matter of personal preference. When discussing stocks with your stockbroker, be sure to ask if his or her earnings estimates are primary or fully diluted.

When investors talk about a company's earnings without specifying primary or fully diluted, it is often because the company has no convertible issues and, therefore, there is only one EPS figure. This is the case for Polaroid, which is discussed at length in Chapter 18.

10

Preferred stock

When JMC raised $20,000 in 1981 to build a new plant, the company chose to sell bonds, a debt financing. The company considered selling common stock, an equity financing, but found debt financing to be the more attractive alternative. Another alternative, not considered by JMC at that time, was to sell preferred stock. When a company sells preferred stock it is also an equity financing, although preferred stock is in some ways quite different from common stock. In fact, preferred stock has some of the characteristics of common stock and some of the characteristics of bonds.

The treasurer of JMC decided he had better learn more about preferred stock so the next time JMC wanted to raise money, the company would be better able to consider all the alternatives. He went to Mr. Stodge and asked for an explanation of preferred stock. Stodge made the following points.

Overview of preferred stock

Preferred stock is often initially confusing, because at first glance it seems to be more like a bond than like common stock. This is because the dividend on a preferred stock is generally fixed, like the interest on a bond. In addition, some preferred issues are redeemable, may have a sinking fund, and may be callable—again, characteristics more typical of bonds than common stock. Finally, some preferreds are convertible into common stock, yet another characteristic of bonds.

Despite this bondlike appearance, preferred stock is equity, not debt. Perhaps the primary distinction here is that the interest paid on a bond is a legal obligation of the company and, if it is not paid, bondholders have the right to demand that the entire bond issue be paid back immediately, and if it is not, they can go to court and have the company declared bankrupt. However, if the preferred dividend is not paid, the preferred shareholders have no right to immediate repayment and no right to have the company declared bankrupt in court. More typically, preferred stocks usually provide that if the preferred dividend has not been paid for a specified number of quarters, typically four or six quarters, then the preferred stockholders will have the right to elect two directors of their choosing to the board.

Preferreds that are not convertible are called *straight* preferreds. Straight preferreds will be covered first because their characteristics almost always apply to convertible preferreds also.

Preferred stocks are also sometimes called preference stocks. Usually, if a company has issues of both preferred stocks and preference stocks, the different titles are primarily to help distinguish them. The possible minor difference between them is discussed later.

The preferred dividend

The first major difference between a common stock and a preferred stock is the dividend it receives. Whereas dividends paid on a common stock, called the common dividend, tend to change frequently depending on the success of the company, the dividend on a preferred stock, called the preferred dividend, is usually fixed. Most preferred stocks specify a quarterly dividend, but some pay a semiannual or only an annual dividend. The title of a preferred stock usually states the actual dollar dividend, unlike a bond where the title specifies the interest as a percent of the face amount. Thus, a typical preferred stock might be called the $3.60 Preferred. This tells you that each outstanding share of this preferred stock issue is entitled to receive an annual dividend of $3.60 per share. So if the dividend is paid quarterly, the holder of this preferred stock would receive $.90 per quarter.

Not all preferreds have a fixed dividend. A few preferreds specify that the dividend automatically goes up or down after a certain year, or if a certain profit level is reached by the company, or if some other specified circumstance is met; but even in these cases the new amount of the dividend is usually specified. Those rare preferred issues where the dividend can vary with the common dividend are called *participating preferreds*. There is no limit to the complexity of some preferred stocks, but such variable dividend preferreds are rare, and in this discussion we assume the dividend is always fixed.

In contrast to the fixed dividends of a preferred, recall that common dividends are frequently increased or decreased at the discretion of the board of directors, and, over the long run, the common dividend's growth or decline is usually related to the profit growth or decline of the company. Thus, if a company's earnings per common share[1] grows, its common stock price will most likely move up in anticipation of increases in the common dividend, or higher eventual dividends if the company is not currently paying a dividend. However, since the preferred dividend is fixed regardless of the earnings of the company, the price of a preferred stock will not move up like a common stock. Rather, the price of a preferred stock tends to behave like the price of a bond, moving up or down to keep its yield in line with other similar preferred stocks.

Although the preferred dividend is fixed, as is the interest on a bond, the preferred dividend should not be confused with an interest payment. Whereas the interest on a bond is a legal liability and is always due on time, a preferred dividend is just one of the things the board of directors may choose to do with the company's profit. The preferred dividend then, must be voted on by the board of directors each time it is due. Thus when a preferred stock is initially issued, the directors are in effect, stating that they intend the payment of the preferred dividend to be an extremely high priority use of the company's future profits and cash for as long as the preferred stock is outstanding, which may be forever. The board is usually neither legally nor contractually required to pay the preferred dividend, but they almost always do, unless the company's earnings in that quarter were not enough to pay the dividend, and even then they often choose to pay it anyway.

The importance of paying the preferred dividend is that investors who buy preferred stock generally do so with the idea that the dividend has a very high probability of being paid if the company is able to do so. Thus if the directors failed to vote to pay a preferred dividend payment when the company was able to pay it, investors would be very unlikely to buy preferred stock of that company again, and thus, the company would lose that option next time they wanted to do a financing. Therefore the directors want to build a reputation for always paying a preferred dividend even when it is difficult for the company to do so.[2]

---

[1] Until now we have always used the term *earnings per share* to mean earnings per common share. This is as it should be. As we will see shortly, preferred shares are never added to common shares when calculating earnings per share. Therefore, the term earnings per share will always mean *earnings per common share* (EPS).

[2] The same thing is true to a lesser extent for the common dividend. The dividend on a common stock, while less important to investors than that on a preferred stock, is nevertheless an important consideration in buying a stock. A company that has a reputation

Another difference between an interest payment and a preferred (and/or common) dividend is that an interest payment is an expense and is deducted from sales in order to get profit before tax. A dividend, common or preferred, is *not* an expense. Again, it is something directors may choose to do with the aftertax profit of the company.

Preferred stocks always provide, however, that if the preferred dividend is not paid in a given quarter, then no common dividend can be paid that quarter. If the company earns enough to pay the preferred dividend but not the common dividend, it usually pays the preferred dividend. When a dividend is not paid, we say it is "omitted." After paying the preferred dividend, the board then has to decide how much of the remaining profit it wishes to pay as a common dividend and how much it wishes to retain in the company.

A preferred stock can be either *cumulative* or *noncumulative*. A noncumulative preferred stock specifies that as long as the preferred dividend is not paid, the common dividend cannot be paid. But once the preferred dividend has been resumed (i.e., the company starts to pay it again), then the company may declare whatever common dividend it wants. A cumulative preferred specifies further that if the preferred dividend has been omitted for one or more quarters, no common dividend can be paid until *all* the omitted preferred dividends from the past are paid up. When a preferred dividend has been omitted for one or more quarters, we say the preferred is "in arrears." When all the arrearages have been paid, the company is once again free to declare any common dividend it wants. Thus the first reason for the word *preferred* is that preferred stock has a prior right to dividends ahead of common stock.

Issuing preferred stock

Issuing preferred stock is just like issuing common stock in that, first, it has to be approved by the shareholders, and then, if it is going to be sold to the public, it must be registered with the Securities and Exchange Commission. Like common stock or bonds, preferred stock is also usually sold through investment bankers, who may or may not underwrite the issue. Recall that underwriting means that investment bankers have guaranteed to sell all the shares being issued or to buy the unsold shares themselves. If the entire issue of preferred stock is being sold privately (i.e., "to less than a small number of sophisticated investors") then it need not be registered with the SEC.

---

of paying its common dividend through thick and thin is likely to attract a wider group of investors and, therefore, possibly sustain a higher common stock price than it might have if the common dividend were reduced or omitted.

There is no limit to the number of issues of preferred stock that a company can have outstanding. Nor is there a limit to the number of shares each issue can have. Each issue and its number of shares, however, must first be authorized by the stockholders. Each issue of preferred stock may have different characteristics or the same characteristics. They may have different dividends. One or more may be cumulative, while others are noncumulative. One or more may be convertible, while others are not.

The most common reason a company issues preferred stock is that it wants to raise money, but it already has a lot of debt outstanding and does not want any more, and it does not want to issue common stock because this would cause too much dilution of earnings per share. Preferred stock represents a compromise. It is not exactly debt because if the preferred dividend is not paid due to lack of profits, the preferred stockholders cannot ask the court to declare the company bankrupt. Yet preferred stock is not exactly common stock because the dividend it receives does not go up with the success of the company.

Another common reason for preferred stock to be issued is in exchange for acquiring a company. Suppose JMC wanted to acquire the Smith Rattrap Company (SRC). Assume SRC is a private company owned by Mr. Smith and his eight investors. If JMC did not have enough cash to pay for SRC, and did not want to give common stock because of the dilution, JMC might offer a preferred stock. If Smith and his investors were willing to take a preferred, JMC and Smith could then negotiate what dividend and how many shares would be agreeable to both parties. Note that since only nine people are getting this issue, it would be a private sale of stock and therefore not have to be registered with the SEC. Later on, of course, if Smith or any of his eight investors wanted to sell the preferred to the public, it would first have to be registered.

Companies that issue preferred stocks often have more than one issue of preferred outstanding, because each time that the company wanted to issue preferred stock it was necessary to have different dividends and other characteristics in order to sell the stock. Thus the capitalization section of a company's balance sheet might look something like this:

Long-term debt:
10% Mortgage bonds .... $ 1,000,000
Other bonds .... —

Equity:
$2.40 Noncumulative preferred (authorized 60,000 shares,
issued and outstanding 55,200 shares) .... $?

$3.20 Cumulative preferred Series A (authorized 40,000
shares, outstanding 16,020 shares) .... ?

Equity —cont.

$4.20 Cumulative preferred Series B (authorized 40,000 shares, outstanding 34,000 shares)	?
$9.50 Cumulative preferred Series C (authorized 100,000 shares, none issued)	—
$7.75 Cumulative convertible preferred (authorized 30,000 shares, outstanding 6,312 shares)	?
Common at par $2 (authorized: 2,000,000 shares, issued 1,000,000, outstanding 1,000,000 shares)................	2,000,000
Additional paid-in capital	17,650,000
Retained earnings..	33,473,000
Total equity	$53,123,000

The words *Series A* and *Series B* and the like have no meaning by themselves, but are just titles to distinguish the different issues. Notice that the Series C has been authorized by the shareholders, but as yet none has been issued. The Series A and Series B information does not tell you how many shares were originally issued, but in both series there are fewer shares outstanding than were authorized. There is no way to tell from the information given if more of the Series A and B were issued and outstanding at one time. The company also has a convertible preferred; this also has fewer shares outstanding than authorized, and there is no way to tell from this information if the currently outstanding 6,312 shares were all that were ever issued, or if more were issued but some were converted or bought back by the company and retired.

Notice also the question marks where the dollar figures should be, next to the preferred issues. Different companies use different dollar figures. Some companies will use the amount of money the preferred was sold for, or the value of the preferred if it was exchanged when acquiring a company. Other companies will use the liquidating value (discussed below). Other companies will only use part of the amount of money the preferred was sold for and put the rest in Additional paid-in capital. Since the dollar figure beside the preferred stock can represent any of a number of things, this book has used question marks to indicate the confusion that may exist. Regardless of the figure put there, preferred stock is classified as equity, although, as will be seen below, in some cases it is questionable whether this is appropriate.

A preferred stock can be sold for whatever price the buyer and seller agree on. Many preferred issues are initially sold at $100 per share, but it is getting more common to see a preferred that is issued at $40 or $25 or some other figure. When a preferred is initially issued by a company (sold for cash or exchanged for another company or other asset), it is a primary offering. When any individual who owns the stock sells it to another individual, it is a secondary offering, just as with bonds or common stock. The amount of money (or value) a preferred stock is initially sold for (exchanged for) is often declared to be its par value or stated value. However, many companies treat preferred stock the same as common stock and declare only a small par value and put the rest of the amount it was sold or exchanged for into Additional paid-in capital. The par or stated value of a preferred stock, like a common stock, has little or no investment significance.

Effect of preferred stock on earnings per share

The term *earnings per share* (EPS) means earnings per common share. The reason is as follows. Earnings per share is calculated to give the common stock investor an indication of the possible dividend per common share, and it is ultimately the current and potential future dividends per common share that determine what a common stock is worth. Thus, when we calculate or project future earnings per share, we are really asking how much earnings will be available to pay to common shareholders. The earnings available to pay to common shareholders is equal to the net earnings after tax *less the preferred dividend.* This is because the preferred dividend must always be paid before any common dividend can be paid. Thus, the portion of earnings that must be paid as preferred dividends can never be available to be paid as common dividends, and, therefore, the correct calculation of earnings per common share (shown below) always uses only earnings available for common dividends, which, again, is net earnings minus all preferred dividends.

Similarly, the correct calculations of earnings per share uses only the number of *common* shares outstanding, *not* common shares plus preferred shares. This is because after the preferred shares have received their fixed dividend, they do not get to take advantage of any growth in profit available for common. For example, let's look at ABC Company which has two issues of stock outstanding.

Issue	Shares Outstanding	Required dividend per share	Total required dividend
Preferred	40	$2	$80
Common.....	100		

Company ABC's income statement is shown in Column A and the calculation of earnings per share is shown in Column B.

	Income statement (A)	Calculation of earnings per share (B)
Sales......................	$1,000	$1,000
Cost of goods sold	− 400	400
Selling and admin. expense ...	− 150	150
Interest expense	− 50	50
Pretax profit	400	400
Taxes (assuming 50% rate) ...	− 200	200
Net profit....................	$ 200	$ 200
Less: Preferred dividend		80
Equals: Profit available for common		$ 120

$$\frac{\text{Profit available for common}}{\text{Common shares outstanding}} = \frac{\$120}{100} = \$1.20/\text{Share}$$

For another example let's look at XYZ Company, which has the following stock issues outstanding.

Issue	Shares outstanding	Required dividend per share	Total required dividend
Series A preferred	200	$5	$1000
Series B preferred	100	6	600
Common stock	1,000		

Income Statement
and Calculation of Earnings per Share

Sales	$100,000
Less: Cost of goods sold	60,000
General and admin. expense	18,000
Interest expense	2,000
Earnings before income tax.........	20,000
Income tax......................	10,000
Net earnings	10,000
Less: Total preferred dividend.....	1,600
Equals: Earnings available for common....................	$ 8,400

$$\frac{\text{Earnings for common}}{\text{Common shares outstanding}} = \frac{\$8,400}{1,000} = \$8.40/\text{Share}$$

In the calculation above, the entire preferred dividend of both pre-ferred issues was subtracted to get earnings available for common. The *Earnings for common* is then divided by only the common shares out-standing. If one had incorrectly used net earnings of $10,000, and also incorrectly used the combined common and preferred shares out-standing, the calculated EPS would be: $10,000 divided by 1,300 shares = $7.69/share. This is a meaningless number.

To repeat an earlier statement, the term *EPS* or *earnings per share* always means per *common* share.

Question: What is the net earnings of XYZ Company? Answer: $10,000. Do not confuse the net earnings of a company with the earnings available for common. The difference, the preferred dividend, is one of the things the directors choose to do with company profit. In XYZ Com-pany, the board chose a long time ago, when the Series A and Series B preferreds were issued, to use some of future profits to pay preferred dividends. Note that XYZ may or may not pay a common dividend, but it is not required and therefore does not enter into the calculation.

Life of a preferred stock

Some preferred stock issues, like common stock, may be outstanding forever unless the company buys it back on the secondary market and retires it. Other preferreds are more like bonds, in that they have a fixed life and maturity date. Such a preferred, like a bond, may have a sinking fund or may be left outstanding until the guaranteed redemption date, which is the same thing as final maturity on a bond (i.e., the day the company must buy back all the outstanding stock or bonds). Some pre-ferreds are also similar to bonds in that they may have call features and nonrefunding provisions (review call and refunding features in Chapter 8).

When a bond has a guaranteed redemption date, it would seem more appropriate to treat it as long-term debt rather than an equity item. Debt is generally thought of as money put into the company that will be paid back eventually. Equity is generally thought of as money put into the company permanently. Perhaps the reason that a preferred with a guar-anteed redemption date is thought of as equity is that, if the company is unable to pay the preferred dividend, the preferred stockholders cannot have the company declared bankrupt; whereas, if the company is unable to pay a bond's interest, the bondholder may be able to have the com-pany declared bankrupt.

A company issuing a preferred would like the flexibility to call it, either to refund it at a lower dividend, or simply because the company has excess cash available and, by calling and retiring the preferred stock, the company no longer has to pay the preferred dividend. The advantage of refunding is this. Suppose the company issued 1,000,000 shares of a preferred stock with a dividend of $8.00 per share. Assuming the preferred was sold at $100/share, it would have had an initial yield of 8.0 percent. Now, suppose interest rates for similar preferreds fell to 7 percent. If the company had the right to call the preferred for refunding, it would be able to sell a new 1,000,000 share issue of preferred at $100 per share, but with a $7 dividend, and use the proceeds to call and pay back (redeem) the $8 preferred. Thus, the company could lower its preferred dividend payments from $8,000,000 per year to $7,000,000 per year. While the company would obviously like this flexibility, the buyer of the $8 preferred stock would just as obviously not want to have his $8 preferred (which is yielding him 8 percent on his initial purchase price) called away when he could only reinvest his money at the current market rate, which is 7 percent.

Liquidating preference

The second way in which a preferred stock has priority over a common stock is in its right to receive money in the event the company liquidates. Recall that when a company liquidates, either voluntarily or in the event of bankruptcy, first it sells off all its assets and then pays off all its liabilities, and then any left-over money goes to the common stockholders. However, if there is any preferred stock outstanding, the preferred shareholders get a certain amount of money before the common shareholders get anything. The amount of money each preferred share gets is called its *liquidating preference* or *liquidating value*. Each share of preferred stock outstanding in a given issue has the same liquidating preference (i.e., gets the same amount of money in the event of liquidation). But different issues of preferred stock may have different liquidating preferences. The liquidating preference is set when the preferred is initially issued and, like the preferred dividend, rarely ever changes except in the case of a few unusual preferreds. A preferred issue's liquidating preference may be unrelated to how much the preferred was initially sold for.

A typical preferred stock portion of a balance sheet of a company with preferred stock outstanding may look as follows:

Equity

$3.75 Noncumulative preferred Series A (authorized 60,000 shares, outstanding 10,000 shares) (liquidating preference $50 per share)...........................

$6.00 Cumulative preferred Series B (authorized 10,000 shares, outstanding 8,000 shares) (liquidating value $20 per share) ....

$5.00 Cumulative convertible preferred Series C (authorized 40,000 shares, issued and outstanding 1,500 shares) (liquidating value $10 per share)..................

If this company were liquidated, the following amount of money would be paid to the preferred shareholders, assuming there was enough available after all the other liabilities had been paid off.

	Shares out		*Liquidating preference*	Total
Series A:	10,000	×	$50	= $ 500,000
Series B:	8,000	×	$20	= $ 160,000
Series C:	1,500	×	$10	= $ 15,000
Total liquidating value				= $ 675,000

Then, after the $675,000 was paid to the preferred shareholders, any remaining money would be split up among the common shareholders.

If there was some money, but not the full $675,000 available, then there might be a predetermined priority among each series as to which gets paid first, or they may all have equal priority, in which case each series would get a portion of its liquidating value. When there is a priority of one preferred over another in the event of liquidation, the one with the lower priority is sometimes called a preference stock instead of a preferred. In many cases, however, the term *preference* stock just refers to older issues of preferred when "preference" was popular.

To review liquidating priorities, first the current liabilities and then the long-term liabilities get paid off. Then, if there is money left over, preferred stock gets paid off, followed by preference stock. Finally, if there is still some money left over, it is split up among the common stockholders. These are the formal priorities. Nevertheless, as mentioned earlier, in the event of a liquidation due to bankruptcy, the courts have not always followed these priorities precisely. In such cases, however, the distribution of funds has usually been close to the formal priorities.

Book value per common share

In Chapter 4, book value per common share was defined as total assets less total liabilities divided by the number of common shares outstanding. Now that definition must be modified to consider the liquidating value of the preferred. The new definition of book value per common share is:

DEFINITION

Book value per common share   Total assets, less total liabilities, less liquidating value of preferred (if any), divided by common shares outstanding.

We will not go through the actual calculation of book value since the number is usually available from many financial sources, which your stockbroker has.

Convertible preferred

Some preferred stocks, like some bonds, are convertible into common stock. Convertible preferreds have all the features of straight preferreds described thus far in this chapter, but have the added feature that they may be converted into common stock. Convertible preferreds are usually convertible at any time at the option of the holder, although in some cases they may only be convertible before or after a specified date. Most convertible preferreds convert into a fixed number of common shares, but, like convertible bonds, there are a few convertible preferreds where the conversion ratio changes over time, or depending on the company's profit level or some other factor. For example, an unusual convertible preferred might say the following:

> This convertible preferred may not be converted before January 1, 1984. After that date, the owner of these shares may convert them, at his option, at the rate of 2 common shares for each share of convertible preferred, up until December 31, 1986. Beginning January 1, 1987, the convertible preferred shares may be converted into common stock at the ratio of 2.4 shares for every share of convertible preferred.

Effect on EPS of converting preferred stock

Calculating earnings per share for a company, with a convertible preferred, presents the same problem as a company with a convertible bond (i.e., do you calculate EPS assuming conversion or not assuming conversion). The answer is that the same procedures that apply to convertible bonds also apply to convertible preferreds. Therefore, the presence of one or more convertible preferreds, like convertible bonds, may give rise to both a primary EPS figure and a fully diluted EPS figure, and the investor must choose the figure he prefers.

PART THREE

Accounting for Assets

11

Fixed assets and depreciation

Thus far, the only long-term assets we have discussed in this book are property, plant, and equipment, and we have always carried these on the balance sheet at original cost. In fact, most assets, except for land, wear out and are eventually disposed of. In this chapter we will see how to account for wear and deterioration and disposal of plant and equipment and how it affects a company's earnings and, hence, stock price.

When we looked at the balance sheet of JMC Corporation in Chapter 3, the *Fixed assets* section appeared as:

Fixed assets:
Property .... $ 3,000
Buildings.......... 13,000
Equipment 44,000
Total fixed assets 60,000

The figures beside property, buildings, and equipment reflect the initial cost of these assets. With the passage of time, however, these assets change in value from what they originally cost. Buildings and equipment deteriorate. A plant becomes old and inefficient in terms of the current needs of the corporation. It must be rebuilt or replaced. A machine tool wears out in time, or better manufacturing techniques are developed and the old machine tool becomes obsolete and worthless. Land (property), on the other hand, frequently increases in value.

When buildings or equipment wear out and become worth less than their original cost, the company has obviously lost something of value. This loss to the company must be reflected on the financial statements. Suppose, for example, the company bought a machine tool for $10,000. At the time of purchase $10,000 is added to the Equipment account. From experience, the company knows the tool will last about 10 years before it is worn out and must be replaced. The company could carry the tool on the books (in the Equipment account) at $10,000 for 10 years, and then, when the tool is disposed of, reflect the loss as an expense of $10,000 in the income statement. But in reality the tool wears out gradually over the 10 years, and thus it would be more reasonable to gradually reflect the loss in value of the tool over the 10 years. Let us assume the machine wears out evenly over the 10 years. Using that assumption, since it cost $10,000 and is expected to last 10 years, we can say it is losing its original value at the rate of $1,000 per year, or, in the language of Wall Street, it is *depreciating* by $1,000 per year. How do we show this depreciation on the financial statements?

For simplicity, let us assume this is the only asset of Company ABC and that it was acquired January 1, 1979. Thus, at the time the asset was acquired the *Fixed assets* account would appear as follows:

COMPANY ABC
Part of January 1, 1979, Balance Sheet

Fixed assets:
    Plant and equipment. $10,000

At the end of the year the tool would be depreciated by $1,000, so the *Fixed asset* account would look like this:

COMPANY ABC
Part of December 31, 1979, Balance Sheet

Fixed assets
    Gross plant and equipment $10,000
        Less: Accumulated depreciation   1,000
    Net plant and equipment   9,000

DEFINITIONS

Gross plant and equipment   Gross refers to initial cost. As long as a company owns an asset, that asset's *original* cost appears under *Gross plant and equipment*, regardless of how much it has been depreciated.

Accumulated depreciation   The total amount by which all the assets in the *Gross plant and equipment* account have been depreciated down through the years. One can also talk about the accumulated depreciation of *one* piece of equipment, which is the total amount by which *that* asset has been depreciated down through the years. Here, the company has only one asset, so the accumulated depreciation of that asset is equal to accumulated depreciation of the company—in this case, $1,000.

Net plant and equipment This is simply Gross plant and equipment less Accumulated depreciation. When computing the book value of the company, it is the net plant and equipment that is used, not the gross. Similarly, the book value of a *single piece of equipment* is equal to the original cost of *that piece of equipment* less the accumulated depreciation of *that piece* of equipment. Thus, the book value of Company ABC's machine tool was $9,000 at December 31, 1979.

The $1,000 of depreciation taken on the machine tool also appears as an expense on the income statement for 1979.

COMPANY ABC
Income Statement from
January 1 to December 31, 1979

Sales		$10,000
Expenses:		
Costs of goods sold	$4,000	
SG&A.................	1,500	
Interest expense	500	
Depreciation expense ...	1,000	
Total expenses...........	7,000	7,000
Profit before taxes........		3,000
Tax expense.............		1,500
Profit after taxes..........		$ 1,500

Most companies list depreciation as a separate expense as in the example above, but some companies include it in *Cost of goods sold* or in *Selling, general, and administrative expense* (SG&A), or both, such as shown below.

COMPANY ABC
Income Statement from
January 1 to December 31, 1979

Sales		$10,000
Expenses:		
Costs of goods sold	$4,600	
SG&A.................	1,900	
Interest expense	500	
Total expenses...........	7,000	7,000
Profit before taxes........		3,000
Tax expense.............		1,500
Profit after taxes..........		$ 1,500

In this income statement, $600 of depreciation expense has been included in *Cost of goods sold,* and $400 of depreciation expense has been included in the SG&A account. In a real company, there would be no way to know how much of the depreciation expense was in each category.

Assume there was still only the one fixed asset in Company ABC in 1980. The asset is now depreciated by another $1,000, so the *Fixed assets* portion of the balance sheet would look like this:

COMPANY ABC
Part of the December 31, 1980, Balance Sheet

Fixed assets:
Gross plant and equipment $10,000
Less: Accumulated depreciation   2,000
Net plant and equipment   8,000

Note that accumulated depreciation *on the balance sheet* is the total of all the depreciation for this year and past years. On the other hand, the depreciation expense *on the 1980 income statement* would still be only $1,000. The depreciation expense *on a given year's income statement* is only *that year's* depreciation.

At the end of 10 years the *Fixed assets* would appear as follows:

COMPANY ABC
Part of the December 31, 1989, Balance Sheet

Fixed assets:
Gross plant and equipment $10,000
Less: Accumulated depreciation   10,000
Net plant and equipment   0

What happens if the machine tool is still working? The answer is nothing changes. Since the asset has been depreciated down to $0, it cannot be depreciated further. Thus, in each succeeding year the Fixed Assets portion of the balance sheet would remain identical to 1989 until the machine tool was sold or thrown away and was no longer the property of the company. Then all its numbers are taken off the balance sheet.

In a real company, of course, there would be many assets. In some companies they are all lumped together into one category—*Property, plant, and equipment.* More frequently, companies categorize their assets into the three separate accounts of *Property, Plant,* and *Equipment.* For example, it is common to see a *Fixed assets* portion of a balance sheet that looks like this:

XYZ CORPORATION
Part of the December 31, 1978, Balance Sheet

Fixed assets:
Gross property . . . . $ 5,000
Gross plant and equipment
Plant . . . . $ 50,000
Equipment   100,000
                                                                          150,000
Less: Accumulated depreciation   60,000
Net plant and equipment   90,000   90,000
Net property, plant, and equipment   95,000

Notice that *Property* (land) is recorded separately and not depreciated. This is because property does not wear out, in the usual sense, and in fact its value frequently increases over time. No account is kept on the balance sheet to reflect this increase. Land is almost always carried on the books at initial cost until it is sold.

Depreciation's impact on company earnings

Understanding depreciation and watching the annual changes in a company's depreciation expense is important to investors as it can give hints about upcoming changes in company earnings. This, in turn, can directly impact the price of the company's stock. Look for example at High Flying Airlines Corporation (HFA). HFA's income statement for the past four years looks as follows. HFA has 100 shares of common stock outstanding.

HFA
Income Statements for 1979–1982

	1979	1980	1981	1982
Sales..................	$10,000	$11,000	$12,000	$10,000
Cost of goods sold....	5,000	5,500	6,000	5,000
SG&A	1,000	1,100	1,200	1,000
Depreciation.........	3,000	3,000	2,800	2,400
Total expense	9,000	9,600	10,000	8,400
Pretax profit	1,000	1,400	2,000	1,600
Tax (assume 50%)......	500	700	1,000	800
Net income............	$ 500	$ 700	$ 1,000	$ 800
EPS..................	$ 5	$ 7	$ 10	$ 8

From 1979 to 1981 the company's sales and earnings grew. In 1982 however, a recession year, sales and earnings fell. Looking at the individual expense numbers, however, we see some interesting differences, which can help the investor project future results.

Notice that the Cost of goods sold in each year increased by the same percent as the sales increased. Thus the cost of goods sold remains at a constant 50 percent of sales. Similarly, the Selling, general, and administrative expense also went up by the same amount as Sales each year, and therefore remained at a constant 10 percent of sales each year. But depreciation expense from 1979 to 1980 did not go up. And in 1981 and 1982 depreciation expense began declining by increasing amounts. What this almost certainly indicates is that an increasing number of the company's airplanes are becoming fully depreciated, and therefore no further depreciation is being taken on them. Thus, as investors, if we read the annual report and other company releases carefully and see that HFA is not currently planning any major new purchases of airplanes, we can reasonably conclude that depreciation expense should continue to fall. Thus, if we assume that the country will recover from the recession in 1983 and that HFA's sales will recover to the 1981 level, and if we further assume that Cost of goods sold and SG&A will continue to be about the same percentage of sales, we could come up with the following earnings estimate for 1983.

	1982 Actual	1983 Estimated earnings
Sales...................	$10,000	$12,000
Cost of goods sold	5,000	6,000
SG&A	1,000	1,200
Depreciation..........	2,400	2,200
Total expense	8,400	9,400
Pretax profit	1,600	2,600
Tax (assume 50%)......	800	1,300
Net income.............	$ 800	$1,300
EPS...................	$ 8	$ 13

Of course, we don't know for certain by how much depreciation will decline, or for that matter, do we know for certain that sales will recover in 1983. But each of the assumptions in the 1983 estimated earnings appears reasonable, based on past trends. Thus, as investment analysts, we can foresee that HFA's earnings per share could jump substantially in 1983 to a new high level, considerably above the previous peak in 1981. This could be a great opportunity to buy the stock.

However, suppose the company had announced that it was planning to completely change over its fleet of airplanes to a new generation of equipment. Then we might be safer to assume that depreciation of the new aircraft would increase substantially and that earnings would go down. (In addition, interest expense might also go up sharply as money might have to be borrowed in order to buy the new airplanes. Interest expense was not included in the above example; but even if it had been, it would not have changed the point being made about depreciation expense.)

In sum, an investor should always watch changes in a company's depreciation to see what impact it may have on future reported earnings. As we have said before, and will say again, stock performance is generally tied very closely to changes in actual earnings and forecasted earnings.

Selling off an asset

When a piece of equipment is sold or thrown out, its gross cost, accumulated depreciation, and net book value are all removed from the balance sheet. Look at the following changes compared to the balance sheet on the bottom of page 124.

1. XYZ Corporation had no new purchases of property, plant, or equipment in 1979.

2. Depreciation for 1979 was $5,000.
3. A piece of equipment, which had cost $20,000 and had been depreciated down to a book value of $6,000, was sold for $7,000 cash.

To reflect these events, the following accounting changes would occur:

Gross plant and equipment at 12/31/78	$150,000
Less: Initial cost of equipment sold	20,000
Gross plant and equipment at 12/31/79	130,000
Accumulated depreciation at 12/31/78	60,000
Less: Accumulated depreciation of equip. sold off	14,000
	46,000
Plus: Depreciation for 1979.........................	5,000
Accumulated depreciation at 12/31/79	51,000
Net plant and equipment at 12/31/78	90,000
Less: Book value of equipment sold off	6,000
	84,000
Less: Accumulated depreciation expense for 1979	5,000
Net plant and equipment at 12/31/79	79,000

Thus, at the end of 1979, the *Fixed assets* portion of the balance sheet would appear as follows:

XYZ CORPORATION
Part of the December 31, 1979, Balance Sheet

Fixed assets:		
Gross property		$ 5,000
Gross plant and equipment		
Plant............................	$ 50,000	
Equipment......................	80,000	
	130,000	
Less: Accumulated depreciation ..	51,000	
Net plant and equipment	$ 79,000	79,000
Net property, plant, and equipment		$84,000

In addition to these fixed assets changes, there are also some other changes on the financial statements. Since the piece of equipment was sold for $7,000 and had a *book value* of $6,000, a profit of $1,000 must be recorded on the income statement. Had the equipment been sold for $2,000, a loss of $4,000 would have been recorded. The *price* for which the equipment is sold has no effect on the *Fixed assets* portion of the balance sheet, although it does, of course, get added to the *Cash* account under *Current assets*. The amount of profit or loss recorded in selling off used equipment is usually very small compared to the overall profit or loss of the corporation. Unfortunately, there is often no way to tell from the financial statement how much this profit or loss was. If it were large it could give a false impression of the company's earnings growth, but the company would probably be required to note it in a footnote.

Frequently, when an asset wears out or becomes obsolete before it is fully depreciated (down to $0 or near $0), it cannot be sold and must be thrown out or "retired." In this case the accounting would be the same as if the asset were sold for $0. This is sometimes called writing-off an asset. For example, if XYZ Corporation had a piece of equipment costing $5,000, which had been depreciated to $2,000, and had become worthless, the company would *write-off* the remaining $2,000 (i.e., bring $2,000 to the income statement as an expense and add $2,000 to *Accumulated depreciation* to bring the asset's net book value to $0).

When the piece of equipment is actually thrown out, or otherwise disposed of, the $5,000 would be removed from both the *Gross PP&E* and the *Accumulated depreciation* accounts. It is possible that a piece of equipment can be written-off or written-down to $0, even though it is not actually being disposed of. This might occur when an old machine tool is not being used but the company wants to keep it around, just in case it should be needed in a time of unexpectedly strong demand for the company's products. We will return later to the subject of write-offs.

METHODS OF DEPRECIATION

Depreciation, we have said, reflects the declining value of an asset to the company. In ABC Company earlier, we assumed the machine tool in question depreciated evenly over a period of 10 years. This is not necessarily a valid assumption. Often it is not possible to say how rapidly the value of an asset deteriorates. In the case of a company car, for example, as long as the car can get a salesman from one place to another it might be said that the value of the car to the company has not depreciated at all. But as the car gets older it is worth less in the used car market if the company decides to sell it. Further, since the car is older, it is more likely to break down and become worthless all at once. How does a company decide how quickly to depreciate an asset? Should depreciation be taken evenly over the estimated life of an asset, as in ABC's machine tool? Or should more depreciation be taken in the early years and less in the later years? Or less in the early years and more in the later years? The first two methods are both commonly used and the third almost never.

When an asset is depreciated evenly over its estimated useful life, it is called *straight-line depreciation*. When it is depreciated more in the early years and less in the later years, it is called *accelerated depreciation*. The rationale for using accelerated depreciation is that: (1) equipment frequently wears out sooner than expected; (2) resale value generally declines at a more rapid rate in the early years; and (3) equipment often becomes obsolete sooner than expected, possibly because a better piece of equipment comes along to replace it, or possibly because the company may stop making the product the equipment was used for.

Another, perhaps more important reason for using accelerated depreciation is the tax advantage it gives, which will be explained shortly.

Three of the more common methods of computing depreciation are: (1) straight-line, (2) double-declining-balance, and (3) sum-of-the-years'-digits. The latter two are different methods of accelerated depreciation. To compare these methods, let's look at BCD Corporation, which bought a machine tool costing $10,000 at the beginning of 1980. The expected life of the tool is five years. Therefore, if straight-line depreciation is used, the tool would be depreciated by $2,000 each year, or 20 percent per year.

The computation of double-declining-balance and sum-of-the-years'-digits depreciation can be found in any good accounting text and will not be shown here. Rather, we will just show their results in the following comparative table.

Depreciation comparison table

	Straight-line depreciation		Accelerated depreciation			
			Double-declining-balance		Sum-of-the-years'-digits	
Original cost	$10,000		$10,000		$10,000	
Depreciation yr. 1.............		$2,000		$4,000		$3,333
Book value (end of yr. 1)	8,000		6,000		6,667	
Depreciation yr. 2.............		2,000		2,400		2,667
Book value (end of yr. 2)	6,000		3,600		4,000	
Depreciation yr. 3.............		2,000		1,440		2,000
Book value (end of yr. 3)	4,000		2,160		2,000	
Depreciation yr. 4.............		2,000		864		1,333
Book value (end of yr. 4)	2,000		1,296		667	
Depreciation yr. 5.............		2,000		518		667
Book value (end of yr. 5)	0		778		0	

Note the difference between straight-line and accelerated depreciation. Using either method of accelerated depreciation, the depreciation charge (expense) in the early years is greater than what it would be using straight-line depreciation. Conversely, in the later years, accelerated depreciation is less than straight-line. For the remainder of the discussion we will use only double-declining balance for comparison of the effects of accelerated and straight-line depreciation.

There are unlimited other ways of calculating depreciation. In fact, any method that appears "reasonable" to the Internal Revenue Service and the company's accountants is acceptable. For a company that wants to depreciate assets as rapidly as possible, the IRS publishes a set of guidelines, which gives the maximum allowed depreciation rate (i.e., the minimum expected life for every type of asset: cars, tools, buildings, electric generators, office furniture, and so on). Use of the guidelines for maximum depreciation is quite common among corporations, thereby eliminating the need of long philosophical discussions with the IRS and the company's accountants.

Note that at the end of the fifth year, the double-declining-balance method of depreciation has not fully depreciated the asset to $0, but rather has left a small book value of $778. This is called a *residual value*. These residual values are sufficiently small that they do not affect the company's decision to use straight-line or accelerated depreciation.

Why should a company choose straight-line rather than accelerated depreciation, or vice versa? Consider the following case. In 1980, BCD Corporation has sales of $40,000. Its combined cost of goods, SG&A, and interest expense were $20,000. Since none of these will be affected by the choice of depreciation method, we will lump them together in the income statements below. The company has 1,000 shares of stock outstanding. BCD's income statement, depending on whether it chose straight-line or accelerated-depreciation would be as follows:

BCD CORPORATION
Income Statement for 1980

	Straight line	Accelerated
Sales.................................	$40,000	$40,000
CGS + SGA + Interest expense	20,000	20,000
Profit before depreciation and taxes.....	20,000	20,000
Depreciation	2,000	4,000
Profit before taxes	18,000	16,000
Taxes (at 50%).......................	9,000	8,000
Profit after taxes.....................	$ 9,000	$ 8,000
Earnings per share...................	$ 9	$ 8

If BCD wants to show the highest possible earnings per share, it would use straight-line depreciation, but it would have to pay higher taxes. If it wanted to pay the lowest possible taxes, it would use accelerated depreciation. Since both these alternatives are desirable, what does the company do? The answer is both. When filing its income tax return, the company uses accelerated depreciation. When reporting to the public, in the company's annual report, it uses straight-line depreciation. But the annual report then would show taxes of $9,000 when, in fact, the legal tax liability that year was only $8,000. This is reconciled by setting up a new balance sheet liability account in the stockholders' report (annual report) called *Deferred taxes.*

Thus, by using accelerated depreciation for tax purposes only, BCD ends up paying lower taxes in the early years (compared to what it would have paid if it used straight line) but will make up for this by paying higher taxes in the later years. In effect, then, by choosing to pay taxes using accelerated depreciation, BCD is simply deferring the time when it actually has to pay the tax, compared to when the income statement shows the taxes under straight-line depreciation.

The deferred taxes then, will be "paid off" in the third, fourth, and fifth years, when accelerated depreciation becomes less than straight-line depreciation (See Depreciation Comparison Table earlier in this chapter). The deferred tax account is classified as long-term debt, since it is going to be "paid off" later than one year out. Thus, the capitalization part of the balance sheet of BCD might look like this:

Capitalization:

Long-term debt:	
6% Mortgage bonds	$20,000
7% Bonds	4,000
Deferred taxes	1,000
Stockholders' equity:	
Common stock ($2 par)	
(authorized 2,500 shares;	
outstanding 1000 shares) . . .	2,000
Additional paid-in capital	14,000
Retained earnings	40,000
Total stockholders' equity	$56,000

To review, the *Deferred tax* account in the capitalization portion of the balance sheet arises on the stockholders' reports because the company has chosen to use a different method of accounting when preparing its tax return for the IRS. The actual legal tax liability for the current year would be in *Taxes payable* under current liabilities.

From an investment point of view, the important point here is that a company can have a large degree of control over its earnings when choosing or changing its method of depreciation. Thus, a company that has always used accelerated depreciation for both tax and shareholders' report purposes might be able to mask a decline in earnings per share in a bad year by changing its depreciation method for shareholders to straight-line, and thus show an earnings increase.

Identifying this type of accounting change, which can distort the reported earnings per share and thus give a misleading impression of a company's growth, is an important task for any investor. Fortunately, accounting rules require that a change in the method of depreciation (or any other accounting change) that produces a "significant distortion" in earnings, must be explained in the footnotes to the financial statements. While a "significant distortion" has not been precisely defined, it is usually taken to mean a change which affects earnings by over 5 percent or 10 percent of the reported figure.

Of course, a company cannot keep changing accounting techniques back and forth to suit its needs. One of the basic principles of accounting is that a company, having once selected a method of accounting, must apply it consistently over the years. Occasional changes are acceptable, however, and it is this occasional change that must be watched closely because a company may do it in a year when things are going badly and the company wants to cover it up.

Of the two methods of calculating depreciation, accelerated is considered the more conservative. In general, when choosing among accounting options, the more conservative method is the one that shows lower earnings in the current year, even though allowing higher potential earnings in future years. The opposite of conservative accounting is called liberal accounting. Companies that use liberal accounting techniques will show maximum possible earnings in the current year, which to some extent, will result in lower earnings in future years. Other things being equal, companies with conservative accounting generally tend to get higher price-earnings ratios than companies with liberal accounting.

Recall that in the example of High Flying Airlines earlier in the chapter, it was not stated whether HFA used accelerated or straight-line depreciation. For that example, however, it made no difference. HFA's depreciation was declining for "fundamental" reasons (i.e., its airplanes were becoming fully depreciated). Had the company's depreciation been declining only because of a change in accounting technique (which would probably have been stated in a footnote), then our assumption about HFA's 1983 depreciation expense would not have been valid.

12

Cost versus expense, other long-term assets, and write-offs

The topics covered in this chapter are not the kinds of things that are generally heard in investment discussions at cocktail parties. In fact, these topics may seem more like accounting issues than investment-related concerns. We will see, however, both from examples in this chapter and again in Chapter 18, that these are indeed investment issues. But we must learn how accountants present them in the financial statements in order to understand them. Also, these topics are covered in a generalized manner, so the reader will be better able to understand the wide variety of specific issues that are certain to be encountered in most companies' financial statements. The prudent investor must know when something is, in fact, simply an accounting detail, and when it may have an impact on company earnings and hence investment results.

The difference between a "cost" and an "expense"

In general conversation, the words *cost* and *expense* mean about the same thing. In an accounting sense, they have very precise and different meanings. Nevertheless, even Wall Streeters use the words loosely and often use one when they mean the other. When you understand clearly the difference between a cost and an expense, two things will happen. First, a great deal of accounting begins to make more sense, and second, you can use the words interchangeably because you will usually know from context which is meant.

The following definitions of cost and expense often initially create confusion in the mind. Following the definitions, examples are given to further clarify this distinction, and finally a specific company example, SFC Corporation, is presented to show the investment importance.

DEFINITIONS

Cost   A cost is incurred when a company becomes obligated to pay for something, whether or not the money is actually paid out at the same time.

For example, when a company buys something, it may pay cash or it may incur an account payable (which of course must be paid off later). Whether cash is paid or an account payable is incurred, the cost has definitely been incurred.

Another example of a cost is when a company declares a cash dividend. The cash might not actually be paid for three weeks, but the company has placed this obligation upon itself and therefore has incurred a cost. Note that we say the cost is incurred when the dividend is declared, not when it is actually paid out three weeks later.

When a cost is incurred, it may or may not also be an expense.

Expense   An expense is any and all dollar figures that are deducted from sales to reach net profit. An expense always reflects a cost, but the cost may not have occurred in the same year. It may have occurred in a prior year, or it may be expected to occur in a future year.

Let's look at some examples. When Jones Mousetrap buys some wood to use to make mousetraps, the price of the wood is put in *Inventory*. Since JMC is obligated to pay for that wood, whether paid in cash now or later, the purchase of inventory is definitely a cost. It is not an expense because nothing has to be brought to the income statement to be deducted from sales. That does not happen until the finished goods in inventory are sold. Then the dollar value of the finished goods that were sold becomes Cost of goods sold expense, but not until then. Since inventory is usually converted to finished goods and sold within one year, some people think of an inventory purchase as an expense as well as a cost, but this is not accurate.

An easier example is the payment of interest. When interest is paid, it is both a cost and an expense. It is a cost because the company becomes obligated to pay it when it is due. It is an expense because it is deducted immediately from sales in order to calculate profit.

What about the wage earned by an employee? If it is paid for building mousetraps that have not yet been sold, it is a cost but not yet an expense. If it is paid for building mousetraps which have been sold, then it is both a cost and an expense. If wages are paid for general and administrative work, such as a portion of the wages paid to Mr. Arbetter in the example in Chapter 1, then it is both a cost and an expense. It is an expense because it is brought directly to the income statement and deducted from sales at the time (or in the period) it was paid.

When a company buys a machine tool, a cost is incurred. Since the machine tool will be used for many years, the cost of the machine tool is put under *Fixed assets* on the balance sheet. This cost will *not* be deducted from sales that year in deriving net profit. Hence, when a fixed asset is purchased, a cost is incurred but *not* an expense. In the language of Wall Street, the cost of the machine tool is *capitalized*, not *expensed*.

When an asset is capitalized (i.e., its cost is put on the balance sheet as a fixed asset), it must be depreciated (except in the case of land). The depreciation taken in any given year *is* an expense, but *not* a cost. The depreciation is an expense because it is deducted from sales in deriving net profit. Depreciation is not a cost because there is no obligation to pay for something. The obligation to pay for the machine tool was incurred in a prior year. Thus, when an asset is capitalized and then depreciated in later years, what has really happened from an accounting point of view is that *the expensing of the cost has been deferred*. Practically all costs ultimately have to be expensed. Exceptions are: (1) the purchase of land, (2) the declaration of a dividend, and (3) repayment of the principal portion of a debt obligation.

The rationale for capitalizing the machine tool and expensing it gradually over a period of time is that, since the machine tool is going to be used to help generate profit over a period of years, it would seem fair to account for its "cost" over the same period of years. The way this is done is by reflecting its cost, through depreciation expense, over a period of years. In the previous chapter we said an asset is depreciated because it wears out. While that is true, it is more accurate from an accounting viewpoint to say that an asset is depreciated because its cost is being expensed over a period of years, which perhaps equals the estimated time it takes to wear out.

Thus, any capitalized asset may be thought of as causing a deferred expense. In fact, many balance sheets contain an asset category called *Deferred expense*. This title does not tell you much. It only tells you that a cost was incurred for something that has not yet been expensed.

Sometimes a balance sheet will use the title "Deferred costs" or "Deferred charges" instead of "Deferred expenses." They mean the same thing, although we now know that the best term is *Deferred expense*. *Charge* is a loose word, which can mean a lot of things depending on context, but usually means "expenses." If the conceptual difference between cost and expense is understood, one can usually tell from context what is meant by charge, cost, or expense.

Deciding whether to capitalize an asset or expense is not always as clear cut as one might assume. A machine tool will last for years, but certain parts, such as the cutting edges, have to be replaced monthly, or even daily. If we buy a large supply at one time, should its cost be capitalized or expensed? What about the tires on a company truck that might last 6 months or 18 months, depending on usage and whether they are retreaded? Without trying to answer these questions, it should be apparent that there is some discretion involved in making the decision. Here again is an opportunity for management to control earnings. A conservative company would expense all these discretionary items (i.e., deduct them from sales in the current year, either as CGS or SGA) and show a lower profit. A company with liberal accounting might capitalize such items and depreciate (expense) them over a period of years. Hence, the company with liberal accounting would show higher earnings in the initial year because they only expensed a small portion of the discretionary items (through depreciation), but would show lower earnings in the later years because they would have to continue deducting the depreciation expense (which the conservative company had fully expensed or written off in the first year).

The term *written off*, therefore, simply means "expensed." A write-off usually refers to expensing the full amount of an asset, as in the discretionary items above. But it would be equally correct to say "20 percent of a machine tool was written-off in one year," meaning the machine tool was depreciated by 20 percent in that year. For example, assume the machine tool cost $10,000 and was depreciated on a straight-line basis over five years. All the following sentences say the same thing:

1. The tool is being depreciated by $2,000 per year.
2. The tool is being written off by 20 percent, or $2,000 per year.
3. The capitalized value of the tool is being charged to earnings at the rate of $2,000 per year.
4. The initial cost of the tool is being deferred, and expensed evenly over a five-year period.

Capitalizing a piece of plant or equipment is not the only thing that can create a deferred expense or deferred charge. Two other common examples of deferred expenses or deferred charges are as follows.

A specific example: Deferred research and development

To understand the investment significance of capitalizing a cost, as opposed to expensing it, let us look at the specific example of research and development costs at Super Fast Computer Corporation (SFC). When SFC spends money on research and development (R&D) of new products, should the cost be capitalized or expensed? The cost, of course, is incurred now, but the benefits of the R&D may not be realized until many years later when the products that were being developed are actually sold. Therefore, would it not be most reasonable to recognize the "cost" (i.e., do the expensing at the same time that the profits are recognized)? But what if the products being developed are never successfully sold? How does one decide how much of the R&D cost was actually spent developing successful products and how much spent developing unsuccessful products? Further, how do you know in advance which products will be successful and which will not, and for how long a period of time will the successful products be successful? If you capitalize R&D, over what period of time do you expense it? Since these questions are usually unanswerable, it is common practice to write off R&D as incurred (i.e., expense the cost in the year it was incurred).

When a company does capitalize R&D (liberal accounting), the expense it takes in later years is called *amortization*, rather than depreciation. Depreciation usually refers to writing off the cost of hard assets, such as plant and equipment, which are deteriorating in value. R&D is not a hard asset, and, in fact, may increase in value as new improvements are built into old products. Amortization does not imply a deterioration, but just refers to deferred expensing of a cost incurred in an earlier year. Thus, depreciation may be thought of as one kind of amortization. The distinction is minor.

An example of where a company might capitalize R&D is in the case of a small, high-technology company that was formed to develop a particular product and has little or no other sales yet. Super Fast Computer Corporation, for example, was formed in 1981 by three bright engineers who all quit a large computer company because they thought they could manufacture a better computer, and by having their own company they would make more money. During 1981 SFC spent $100,000 on R&D on the new computer. Also that year, the company manufactured some small components at a cost of $30,000, which it sold for $40,000 to raise some cash. If the $100,000 R&D cost had been capitalized, the company would have shown a profit and the simplified financial statements of SFC would appear as follows:

SFC Corp.
Income Statement 1981

Sales	$ 40,000
Expenses......................	30,000
Profit before tax...............	10,000
Tax...........................	5,000
Net profit	5,000

Long-term Assets Portion of Balance Sheet
12/31/81

Plant and equipment...........	$ 50,000
Deferred R&D..................	100,000
Total long-term assets	$150,000

Had R&D been expensed, the same simplified statements would appear as follows:

SFC Corp.
Income Statement 1981

Sales	$ 40,000
Expense......................	130,000
Net *loss*	(90,000)

Long-term Assets Portion of Balance Sheet
12/31/81

Plant and equipment............	$ 50,000
Total long-term assets	$ 50,000

Note the convention of putting the loss in parentheses.

There are no real benefits of capitalizing R&D to show a profit. Potential investors should know that SFC is actually spending far more than it is taking in. If it does not begin making a "real" profit soon—rather than the "accounting" profit of 1981—the company will soon run out of money and either have to raise more or go out of business. Such a stock is an extremely risky venture.

In the *Long-term Assets* portion of the balance sheet, *Deferred R&D* might have been called "Deferred charges," or "Deferred costs," or even "Deferred assets." Obviously, Deferred R&D is the most descriptive because it tells what kind of "asset" is having its expensing deferred. Deferred R&D might also be called an "Intangible asset." Although the information or knowhow learned as a result of the R&D cost is definitely an asset, it is not clear when and how much of it will eventually be converted to products.

The important point here is that the sudden appearance on a balance sheet or a sharp increase on the balance sheet, of a "deferred" asset account, whether in the form of *intangible assets* or *deferred charges* or *deferred R&D* and the like, is a flag to the investor warning that even though earnings might be increasing, there might be some large outflow of cash that is not yet being reflected (expensed) on the income statement, and therefore the company's financial condition might be much worse than one would gather by just looking at the increasing earnings.

Intangible assets

Intangible assets can also come from other sources, but, like deferred R&D, almost always reflect a deferred charge (i.e., a cost that has not yet been expensed or amortized). An intangible asset might be a patent, a copyright, or just a brand name. Suppose for example, General Drinks, Incorporated (GDI) decided to buy a company that sold instant coffee under a well-established brand name. The book value of the coffee company was $1,000,000, but GDI paid the original owners of the coffee company $1,400,000. What has happened? GDI has purchased $1,000,000 worth of net property, plant, and equipment, but it has also purchased the right to use the coffee company's brand name. The $400,000 of cost above the $1,000,000 worth of net assets (i.e., the cost in excess of the book value of the acquired assets), would be attributed to the value of the brand name, and thus be called an *intangible asset* or *goodwill*, and in this case be equal to $400,000. The $400,000 cost of the brand name must eventually be deducted from sales as an expense, just as the property, plant, and equipment, which were acquired for $1,000,000, will have to be depreciated (expensed). In the case of the PP&E, the depreciation expense can be taken over the estimated lives of the assets. But what is the estimated life of the brand name? In the case of an instant coffee, the brand name might be good for 10 or even 20 or more years, or it might lose its appeal in six months. Thus, a conservative company might "expense" the $400,000 right away and not carry it on the balance sheet at all. A company with liberal accounting policies, which wants to show the highest possible earnings immediately, would want to amortize the cost of the brand name over as many years as possible to have the lowest possible amortization expense each year.

It is up to the company and its accountants to decide over what period of time the brand name, or goodwill, should be amortized. What if the brand name were Coca-Cola? The life expectancy of this brand name is indefinite. It is, however, a generally accepted accounting principle that goodwill should be amortized over a period of no more than 40 years.

DEFINITION

Goodwill   When Company A acquires Company B, and pays more for it than Company B's net book value, the difference between what Company A pays and Company B's net book value is called *goodwill* and goes on Company A's balance sheet. Goodwill is an intangible asset. It is worth something, but you cannot touch it.

Goodwill may be thought of as a deferred charge since its cost— $400,000 in this case—will not be expensed (charged to profit) immediately but will be amortized over a period of years. Goodwill, however, is almost always called *goodwill* rather than *deferred charge*. Only in the case where the dollar value of goodwill is very insignificant might it be lumped together with other things under a heading such as "Deferred assets" or "Deferred charges."

The investment significance of goodwill can be minimal or substantial. While goodwill is carried as an asset on the balance sheet, it may or may not truly reflect something that is actually worth the dollar amount shown on the balance sheet. For example, if the well-established brand name of the instant coffee company acquired by GDI enabled GDI to generate substantial sales and earnings, the intangible asset Goodwill would then be well worth the $400,000 that GDI paid for it. But what if the brand name suddenly lost favor and no more coffee could be sold under that name? The balance sheet would continue to reflect an "asset" of $400,000, but now it would be worthless. Thus the appearance of *Goodwill* on a balance sheet is a flag to the investor that the company's book value might be overstated if, in fact, the value of the item reflected in goodwill has declined. This is important because some investors look at book value per share as a price against which to value the price of the stock. This gives rise to an improved definition of book value called *tangible book value*, which is discussed below.

While the balance sheet term *Deferred charges* may include goodwill, it is more likely to refer to something like an insurance premium that was paid in advance. Suppose for example, GDI Corporation pays an insurance premium of $12,000 for three years of insurance in advance. Since GDI is now insured for three years, it would seem reasonable that the cost of the insurance should be amortized or charged to earnings (expensed) evenly over the three years. Thus, GDI would set up a new asset account on the balance sheet called *Deferred charges* or *Prepaid insurance*, which it would amortize evenly over three years, or $4,000 per year. Thus GDI's balance sheet might look like this:

GDI
Balance Sheet at 12–31–81

Assets		*Liabilities*	
Current assets:		Current liabilities:	
Cash	$ 1,000,000	Short-term debt	$ 500,000
Accts. rec.	3,000,000	Accounts payable	4,000,000
Inventory	4,500,000	Total current liabilities	4,500,000
Total current assets	8,500,000		
		Long-term debt:	
Fixed assets:		7% bonds due 1991	7,000,000
Gross PP&E	21,000,000		
Less: Accum. depr.	7,000,000	*Stockholders' Equity*	
Net PP&E	14,000,000	Equity:	
		Common stock	500,000
Intangible assets:		Additional paid-in	
Goodwill	400,000	capital	4,604,000
Deferred charges	12,000	Retained earnings	6,308,000
	412,000	Total equity	11,412,000
Total assets	$22,912,000	Total liabilities and equity	$22,912,000

Book value and tangible book value

In Chapter 10, book value was defined as: Total assets, less Total liabilities, less Liquidating value of preferred stock. As discussed earlier, when calculating book value it is more prudent to also subtract intangible assets and call the result tangible book value instead of just book value.

DEFINITIONS

Book value   Total assets less total liabilities less liquidating value of preferred stock.

Tangible book value   Total assets *less intangible assets* less total liabilities less liquidating value of preferred stock.

Since GDI does not have any preferred stock, its book value and tangible book value can be calculated as follows:

	Book value	Tangible book value
Total assets	$22,912,000	$22,912,000
Less: Intangible assets		412,000
		22,500,000
Less: Total liabilities	11,500,000	11,500,000
	$11,412,000	$11,000,000

Note that people frequently say "book value" when they mean "tangible book value." Tangible book value is the more conservative calculation. It is preferred by most investors, first, because it is hard to know whether the intangible assets really have any current worth, and second, because intangible assets, such as deferred R&D and goodwill, generally cannot be sold for anything if the company goes bankrupt. This is not always the case, however. If GDI went bankrupt it is possible that the instant coffee brand name they acquired could be sold for a lot of money. In fact, following a period of rapid inflation such as the United States experienced in the 1970s, that brand name might be worth far more than GDI paid for it.

Tangible book value is sometimes called "tangible net worth." Net worth just means equity. Therefore, *tangible net worth* means equity less intangible assets. The terms *book value, net worth,* and *tangible net worth* are often used interchangeably. The tangible book value of GDI of $11,000,000 is very close to its total book value or net worth of $11,412,000. This is frequently the case when there is no preferred stock and few or no intangible assets. Nevertheless, it is not a good idea to assume that the book value equals equity or net worth. It is always safer to calculate it yourself, particularly when there is preferred stock outstanding or a large amount of intangible assets.

Finding "hidden assets" in an inflationary period

Even such tangible assets as property, plant, and equipment might increase in value in an inflationary period. For example, consider a company that owns a hotel built 10 years ago at a cost of $40 million. Although its cost may have been depreciated down to a book value of $30 million, the cost of building a new hotel like it today, as a result of inflation, may be $90 million. Thus the book value of the company, which includes the hotel valued at $30 million, would badly understate what the whole company is worth today if someone wanted to buy it. Wall Street would refer to the hotel as a "hidden asset," not because the company kept the hotel's existence a secret, but because its true value is hidden by the accounting requirement that the hotel's value on the books be carried at original cost less depreciation, rather than at current replacement cost. In a period of inflation, the whole concept of book value, tangible or intangible, must be questioned.

The importance of looking for hidden or undervalued assets is that when the stock market "discovers" them, these stocks often go up. Thus, if you "find" them before other investors, you can buy the stock before it goes up. An excellent example of the discovery of hidden assets is in Hilton Hotels Corporation. Hilton has many hotels that were built before the inflationary period of the 1970s. In addition, the hotels have been depreciated down to even less than their original cost. But since they have been maintained in excellent condition at relatively modest cost, the value of these hotels is very high now. This is important to investors for two reasons. First, because Hilton could sell some of these hotels and realize a lot of money. But more important, since a competitor building a hotel would have to pay the real value, Hilton will have a lower-cost hotel and thus will be able to either charge a lower price for their rooms, and thereby get more customers, or raise the price of its rooms to the same level that new hotels will have to charge. But then Hilton will show higher profits, which, in turn, should push the stock higher. In other words, the increased worth of Hilton's hotels, as the result of inflation and the increased cost of building new hotels, will enable Hilton to show more rapid increases in profits and therefore should result in a higher stock price. Recognizing the value of these hidden assets and the influence it should have on the stock, Hilton began to publish the market value of its hotels in its annual reports beginning in 1977. And in fact, Hilton stock did much better than the market over the following few years.

Extraordinary write-offs

The terms *write-off* or *write-down*, like many other words used in the investment community, have a variety of meanings or connotations depending on how they are used. The normal depreciation of assets, we said, can be thought of as a write-down. This type of write-down is quite regular, in that assets are continuously being depreciated or written down.

Write-off or write-down is used more frequently, however, in a case where an asset has become useless and is being written down to either $0 or scrap value all at once. For example, assume a machine with an expected life of eight years breaks down after five years and the company does not want to repair it since other machines can pick up the load. Since this machine was not yet fully depreciated to $0 or scrap value, the company must write it down to $0 or scrap value since that is all it is now worth. Another example—a company car is only one year old and has a bad accident, which is not covered by insurance. The company could get the car repaired, but decides to replace it with a new car. The old car would have to be written off.

A third example—a furniture company has a large inventory of a certain style of bedroom set, which is not selling well. After trying different advertising approaches without success, management finally decides this style is unlikely to ever sell well and the product is taken off the market to be used for scrap wood. Therefore, its dollar value in the Inventory account must be written down to scrap value.

These three kinds of write-offs are not as regular as depreciation, but most often amount to a small dollar figure relative to the company's overall financial results. In such a case, the company would simply include them in the income statement as part of cost of goods sold, or selling, general, and administrative expense, or depreciation, depending on the company's normal accounting procedures. In practice there are probably a few such small write-offs in every quarter for every company, so their effects may be smoothed out. Typically, however, most companies make more of these adjustments in the fourth quarter. Perhaps it is just human nature for management to put off admitting it made a mistake on that style of bedroom set, in the above example. Or perhaps it is simply human nature to put off making any noncritical decisions until year-end when the accountants force them to. Also, of course, it is possible that management is intentionally delaying such write-offs because they want to get the stock as high as possible early in the year and therefore want to show the maximum possible earnings. This could be done either because management plans to have a stock offering or because they want to sell some of their own personal stock. Of course, it is unethical and illegal to show artificially high earnings for either of these last two reasons.

The point is that fourth quarter earnings can be harder to predict than any of the first three quarters. In the event that such write-offs come to a significant proportion of income, perhaps 5 percent or more, the company should mention it in a footnote. In a case where such write-offs were extremely large, the company would be required by accounting rules to note them separately as extraordinary items. This would typically occur in unusual cases, such as if a fire or explosion destroyed a plant totally and it had to be written-off. It might also occur when a company sells off or closes a division. Such an extraordinary item is sometimes called a "non-recurring item." Since these write-offs can badly distort the progression of a company's earnings, and therefore impact the stock price significantly, it is very important for investors to understand the effects on reported earnings of an extraordinary or nonrecurring write-off.

For an example, let's look at Boom Boom Dynamite Company, which had an explosion in one of its four plants in December of 1981. The plant was not insured.

Without the explosion, the year-end financial statements would have looked like this:

Part of Balance Sheet BBD COMPANY
12/31/81

Fixed assets:

Gross property, plant, and equipment....	$12,000,000
Accumulated depreciation	7,000,000
Net property, plant, and equipment	5,000,000

BBD COMPANY
Income Statement for 1981

Sales.........................		$6,000,000
Expenses:		
Cost of goods sold..........	$2,000,000	
SG&A	500,000	
Depreciation...............	400,000	
Interest	100,000	
Total expense	3,000,000	3,000,000
Profit before tax................		3,000,000
Tax..........................		1,500,000
Net profit.....................		$1,500,000
EPS (500,000 shares outstanding)		$3.00/share

The destroyed plant had an original cost of $5,000,000 and had been depreciated down to a book value of $2,000,000. (That is, the accumulated depreciation on that plant from the time it was built in 1975 until the explosion was $3,000,000.) Since the plant was totally destroyed it had to be removed entirely from the books. Thus the $5,000,000 cost was removed from *Gross PP&E*, the $3,000,000 of *Accumulated depreciation* was removed, and the $2,000,000 of *Net PP&E* was removed. The Fixed assets portion of the balance sheet, then, looked like this:

Fixed assets:

Gross property, plant, and equipment.....	$7,000,000
Accumulated depreciation	4,000,000
Net property, plant, & equipment	3,000,000

Since the net book value of the destroyed plant was $2,000,000, it might be said that the company incurred a $2,000,000 loss. This loss must be written off against earnings. It can either be included in *Cost of goods sold,* or handled separately as an extraordinary item. Both methods will be shown.

BBD COMPANY
Income Statement for 1981 (Plant write-off included in CGS)

Sales		$6,000,000
Expenses:		
Cost of goods sold	$4,000,000	
SG&A	500,000	
Depreciation................	400,000	
Interest	100,000	
	5,000,000	5,000,000
Profit before tax.................		1,000,000
Tax............................		500,000
Net profit......................		$ 500,000
EPS (500,000 shares outstanding)		$1.00/share

By including the plant destruction in *Cost of goods sold,* the reported earnings of $1 per share look a lot worse than the $3 per share the company is capable of earning when it is operating normally. While BBD may not be capable of earning $3 per share next year without the plant, it may be able to earn close to the $3 and at least retain their customers by working more in the remaining plants, and possibly temporarily buying dynamite from competitors to service their customers, until a new plant can be built. Therefore, including the plant write-off in CGS does not give the reader a fair picture of what actually happened and what it implies for the company's future. The presentation below, with the plant write-off handled as an extraordinary or nonrecurring item, would be preferable.

BBD COMPANY
Income Statement for 1981 (Plant write-off handled as extraordinary item)

Sales		$6,000,000
Expenses:		
Cost of goods sold	$2,000,000	
SG&A.....................	500,000	
Depreciation...............	400,000	
Interest	100,000	
	3,000,000	3,000,000
Profit before taxes..............		3,000,000
Taxes........................		1,500,000
Profit before extraordinary item ...		$1,500,000
Extraordinary loss (net of tax at 50%)		$1,000,000
Net profit......................		$ 500,000
EPS (before extraordinary loss)...		$3.00/share
EPS (including extraordinary loss)		$1.00/share

Note how the tax is handled. According to the Internal Revenue Service, the plant write-off is deductible when calculating taxes. As a result, $1,000,000 was saved in taxes. Nevertheless, since the purpose of presenting the extraordinary item separately is to show what the company's results would have been with and without the extraordinary loss, it makes sense to deduct that $1,000,000 tax saving from the extraordinary loss which caused it, rather than from the normal earnings of the company. Thus *Taxes* reads $1,500,000 even though only $500,000 was paid. Similarly, *Extraordinary loss (net of tax)* reads $1,000,000, even though the loss was actually $2,000,000.

Effect on stock price

The important point here is that when an extraordinary or non-recurring event occurs, the investor must attempt to find out what caused it, what temporary or lasting effects it will have on the company's operations, and what financial hardships it may cause the company. If the effect is expected to be temporary, one should try to reconstruct the income statement as it would have been without the extraordinary item, in order to determine what progress the company may have been making in the normal course of business. Thus in the case of BBD, the $3 per share earnings figure may be more representative of the company's future earnings than the $1 per share. Thus, what would probably happen is that, when the news of the plant explosion got out, the stock would go down briefly, as investors were initially uncertain about what long-term effects it would have on the company's ability to generate earnings and dividends. But as investors learned that the company's earnings progress would only be temporarily hurt and not permanently impaired, the stock would probably return to or near its former level.

The extraordinary write-off in the example above resulted from unexpected destruction of plant and equipment. An extraordinary or non-recurring write-off can also occur when a company manufactures a large inventory of a product and then discovers that the product cannot be sold. In such a case, the inventory would have to be written off or written down to scrap value. An example of this was Polaroid's $68 million write-off of its Polavision movie camera and film inventories, discussed in Chapter 18.

13

Inventory accounting—
Impact on company
earnings

We saw in Chapter 1 that when Jones Mousetrap Company sold a mousetrap, the cost of manufacturing the mousetrap was removed from *Finished goods inventory* on the balance sheet and added to *Cost of goods sold* expense on the income statement. In that simple example, we were able to calculate the exact cost of each mousetrap, which was the combination of the raw materials cost plus the labor cost that went into making the trap. In many companies, however, keeping precise track of inventory costs (and hence cost of goods sold expense) is either not practical or not possible, and thus certain assumptions must be made. We will see in this chapter that different but reasonable assumptions can cause reported earnings to be either higher or lower than they otherwise would be. Thus, since stock prices are related to earnings, investors must be aware of how these inventory valuation assumptions may have impacted past reported earnings per share and may yet impact future earnings.

LIFO and FIFO inventory valuation assumptions

When an automobile dealer sells a new car from his inventory in the back lot he can tell exactly how much it cost him by looking at the invoice or the check he used to pay the manufacturer in Detroit. So when a sale is made, the dealer removes the cost of the car, say $5,600, from inventory and adds it to Cost of goods sold expense. Of course he also adds the selling price, perhaps $7,000, to both *sales* and either *cash* or *accounts receivable*. In this easy case, as in the Jones Mousetrap case, the precise value of the inventory is known and no assumptions need be made. Now let's look at a case where it is not possible to know exactly what the cost was, and an assumption must be made. Consider a copper company, which buys raw copper ore, smelts and processes it, and then sells it. In this case the inventory cost is more difficult to compute because new ore is continuously being added to the melting furnace and mixed with the old ore already there.

Assume that on January 1, the Dirty Copper Company (DCC) bought 1,000 pounds of raw copper at $6 per pound and put it into a smelting furnace or vat for processing. On February 1, DCC added another 1,000 pounds of raw copper to the vat but this time DCC paid $7 per pound. On March 1, DCC added another 1,000 pounds at $8 per pound. There were now 3,000 lbs. of copper all mixed up in the vat at a total cost of $21,000.

January 1	1,000 lbs. at $6/lb.	=	$ 6,000
February 1	1,000 lbs. at $7/lb.	=	$ 7,000
March 1	1,000 lbs. at $8/lb.	=	$ 8,000
			$21,000

On March 31, DCC sold 2,500 pounds of finished copper at $10 per pound, for a total sale of $25,000. How much did the 2,500 pounds cost DCC? That is, what cost should be taken out of inventory and added to cost of goods sold? Did DCC sell all of January's $6 copper plus all of February's $7 copper, plus half of March's $8 copper? Or did DCC sell all of March's $8 copper, all of February's $7 copper, and half of January's $6 copper? There is no way to know since all the copper was mixed evenly in the vat. Thus, one of three assumptions must be made. First, it can be assumed that the *first* copper that came in was the first that was sold. Using this assumption, all the January, February, and half of the March copper was sold. This method of inventory accounting is called FIFO—first in, first out. Second, it can be assumed that the *most recent* copper to come in was the first copper to go out. That is, all the March, February, and half the January copper was sold. This method of inventory accounting is called LIFO—last in, first out. Third, it can be assumed that the copper was sold at an average price of the three. While some companies keep inventories on an average-cost basis, this takes quite a bit of paperwork because new raw materials are usually coming in at different prices throughout every working day, and goods are usually being sold throughout every working day. Thus most companies find it more practical to use either the FIFO or the LIFO method. Which of the two methods chosen can have a meaningful effect on reported earnings, as shown below.

FIFO		
Cost of 2,500 lbs.		
1,000 lbs. @ $6/lb.	=	$ 6,000
1,000 lbs. @ $7/lb.	=	$ 7,000
500 lbs. @ $8/lb.	=	$ 4,000
2,500 lbs.		$17,000

LIFO		
Cost of 2,500 lbs.		
500 lbs. @ $6/lb.	=	$ 3,000
1,000 lbs. @ $7/lb.	=	$ 7,000
1,000 lbs. @ $8/lb.	=	$ 8,000
2,500 lbs.		$18,000

Income Statement Using FIFO Inventory Accounting

Sales	$25,000
Cost (FIFO)	17,000
Profit	$ 8,000

Income Statement Using LIFO Inventory Accounting

Sales	$25,000
Cost (LIFO)	18,000
Profit	$ 7,000

Left in Inventory at March 31
500 lbs. @ $8/lb. = $ 4,000

Left in Inventory at March 31
500 lbs. @ $6/lb. = $ 3,000

LIFO accounting results in cost of goods sold being valued at most-recent cost (called *current* cost), whereas FIFO accounting results in cost of goods sold being valued at oldest cost (called *historical* cost). Thus, in a period when the purchase price of raw copper is steadily rising (as in the case above), LIFO results in a higher cost of goods sold, hence leaving a lower profit. Also, LIFO leaves a lower cost of inventory remaining in the company. Conversely, FIFO inventory accounting results in a lower cost of goods sold, hence leaving a higher profit, and also leaves a higher cost of inventory in the company (on the balance sheet). Note that the selling price of the finished copper has nothing to do with the LIFO/FIFO difference. Obviously, the higher the selling price the more profit; but for any given selling price the FIFO cost of goods sold in this example will always be lower than the LIFO cost of goods sold, and therefore, the FIFO profit will always be higher than the LIFO profit for any given selling price.

The statements in the last paragraph are generally true as long as the price of copper is rising. If the purchase price of raw copper were steadily falling, the opposites would be true in the last paragraph (i.e., the words *higher* and *lower* would be reversed). Work this out for yourself by making up an example similar to the one on the top of the page, but with prices steadily falling.

Thus, in a period of rising prices, if an investor is looking at two companies that have the same EPS and stock price, and are similar in every other way except that one uses LIFO and other uses FIFO, the company that uses LIFO would probably be the better stock to buy because, if it decided to change to FIFO, it would suddenly be showing better earnings and the stock might go up. If these two companies were truly similar except for the FIFO/LIFO accounting difference, the company using LIFO would probably sell at a slightly higher price-earnings ratio, reflecting that potential earnings difference.

Adjusting the inventory value at year-end to lower-of-cost-or-market

At the end of the year, if the price for which the inventory can be sold has fallen to a level below the carrying value of the inventory (on the balance sheet), most companies will automatically lower the inventory value of the goods by the difference and charge (add) the same amount to cost of goods sold for the year. This is called adjusting the inventory to lower-of-cost-or-market (LOCOM). *Cost* in this case means what the inventory cost to build, whether using LIFO or FIFO assumptions. *Market* means what the goods can be sold for on the open market today. Of course, if the price for which the goods can be sold is higher than the cost, whether determined by LIFO or FIFO, there is no inventory adjustment to be made.

To illustrate when a LOCOM inventory adjustment might occur, and how big it might be, suppose DCC made no sales or purchases of copper during the year, other than those mentioned above. DCC's inventory accounting policy is to use FIFO and adjust the year-end inventory on a LOCOM basis, if necessary. When the treasurer of DCC was initially putting together the financial statements for the year they looked like this:

Income Statement (1/1/80 to 12/31/80)

Sales		$25,000
Cost of goods sold . . .	$17,000	
SG&A.	3,000	
Depreciation	1,000	
	21,000	21,000
Profit before tax		4,000
Tax.		2,000
Profit after tax.		$ 2,000

Balance Sheet
12/31/80

Assets			Liabilities		
Current assets:			Current liabilities:		
Cash.	$ 1,000		Short-term debt.	$ 4,000	
Inventory	4,000		Taxes payable	1,000	
Accts. receivable	2,000		Total current liabilities	5,000	
Total current assets. . . .	7,000		Long-term debt	None	
Fixed assets:			*Equity*		
Gross PP&E	20,000		Stockholders' equity:		
Accum. depreciation	7,000		Common stock	1,000	
Net PP&E	13,000		Capital surplus	5,000	
			Retained earnings	9,000	
Total assets.	$20,000		Total liabilities & equity	$20,000	

Before these statements were made final, however, the treasurer realized that the price for which the finished copper could be sold had fallen to $7 per pound. But DCC was carrying its inventory at a value of $8 per pound.

Thus the inventory had to be written down to $7 per pound.

$$500 \text{ lbs. @ } \$8/\text{lb.} = \quad \$4,000$$
$$500 \text{ lbs. @ } \$7/\text{lb.} = \quad \underline{\$3,500}$$
$$\text{Inventory write-down } \$\quad 500$$

This $500 is subtracted from *Inventory* to reflect a more realistic value of the inventory, and is taken as an expense on the income statement in the *Cost of goods sold*. The rationale for expensing it is that the lowering of the price of finished copper resulted in a loss of value to the company (i.e., the finished copper was now worth less than when it was processed). Note that had the inventory been carried at the LIFO cost of $6 per pound, there would have been no inventory adjustment, because in that case the inventory would already be valued at the lower of cost ($6) or market ($7).

After the adjustments the new financial statements would appear as follows:

Income Statement (1/1/80 to 12/31/80)

Sales		$25,000
Cost of goods sold . . .	$17,500	
SGA	3,000	
Depreciation	1,000	
	21,500	21,500
Profit before tax		3,500
Tax		1,750
Net profit		$ 1,750

Balance Sheet
12/31/80

Assets			Liabilities	
Current assets:			**Current liabilities:**	
Cash	$ 1,000		Short-term debt	$ 4,000
Inventory	3,500		Taxes payable	750
Accts. receivable	2,000		Total current liabilities	4,750
Total current assets	$ 6,500		Long-term debt	None
Fixed assets:			**Equity**	
Gross P, P&E	20,000		Stockholders' equity:	
Accum. Depreciation	7,000		Common stock	1,000
Net P, P&E	13,000		Capital surplus	5,000
			Retained earnings	8,750
Total assets	$19,500		Total liabilities and equity	$19,500

In addition to the change in *Inventory* , note also the changes in *Taxes payable* and in *Retained earnings*. The $500 inventory write-down was an expense but not a cost. No actual money was spent when the write-down was taken. However, because this write-down was taken, *Profit before taxes* was lower, hence *Taxes* and *Net profits* were also lower. Therefore, *Taxes payable* on the balance sheet is lower, and, since *Net profit* was down, *Retained earnings* is down.

Had the price of copper at the end of the year been $6 per pound (with DCC using FIFO), the inventory write-down would have been $1,000.

$$
\begin{array}{lll}
500 \text{ lbs. @ } \$8/\text{lb.} & = & \$4,000 \\
500 \text{ lbs. @ } \$6/\text{lb.} & = & \underline{\$3,000} \\
\text{Inventory write-down} & & \$1,000
\end{array}
$$

Had this been the case, DCC's inventory value would now be $3,000, or just what it would have been had the company been on LIFO. For industries where prices tend to go up, there is usually no LOCOM inventory adjustment at all.

An important point here is that in an industry where prices have been falling, the investor always has to be aware of the possibility of year-end inventory write-downs. The semiconductor industry provides an excellent example. When transistors were first introduced in the 1950s, prices were very high. As the technology improved, prices came down. This induced more electronic goods manufacturers to use transistors in place of tubes. This larger volume of business enabled the transistor (semiconductor) manufacturers to automate, with the result that further price declines became possible. Through the 1960s and 1970s continuously improved transistors and then integrated circuits were introduced. Each of these new products went through a similar cycle, whereby prices started out high and gradually came down. Since the declining price nature of this business is well known, semiconductor manufacturers try to keep as little inventory on hand as possible; but, of course, there are always some products on hand that cannot be sold. In some periods, the amount of unsold products will be larger than in other periods. To try to smooth out the effects of such write-downs, most manufacturers of these products write down their inventory every quarter if necessary. Thus, the adjustment at the end of the year should be no bigger than the other quarterly adjustments, and a smoother flow of earnings should result.

If the company only adjusted its inventory at the end of the year, it might show high earnings for the first three quarters and then practically nothing, or even a loss in the fourth quarter. The total earnings for the year would be the same whether the write-downs were taken each quarter or only at year-end; but if the entire write-down was done at year-end, it would give a false impression of high profits during the first three quarters. With high profits in the first three quarters, investors might be misled to believe that the company's outlook was better than it really was, and they would bid up the price of the stock. Then, when the disappointing earnings came in the last quarter, the stock would plunge as people saw their mistake. More important, the fear that this may happen again might cause investors to avoid these stocks in the future. Thus, by having an earnings adjustment quarterly, the quarterly stream of earnings would be smoother, bad surprises would be avoided, and more people would be willing to buy the stocks. The stocks, then, over a period of time would probably sell at a higher average price than if bad surprises were continually recurring.

In the case of semiconductors, where prices are continuously falling and the companies make the adjustments regularly, they are seldom noticed. A classic example of where a bad surprise did occur (a large, unexpected write-down) was in the CB radio business. Through most of 1976 prices were more or less steady and demand was rising. Late in the year, however, sales declined sharply, and manufacturers were caught with large inventories they could not sell. The manufacturers stopped making more CB radios and cut prices drastically in order to sell the large inventories they still had. This hurt earnings in two ways. First, the CBs that were sold were sold at a loss, and second, most of the excessive inventory that could not be sold had to be written down to the new low price. Since the inventory was large and the price cut was drastic, the write-down was large. Earnings therefore came through much lower than previously expected, and the stocks fell sharply as a result. Smart investors, however, did not wait for a bad earnings report. As soon as they learned that CB sales were falling, they sold their stock immediately in anticipation of the fact that a write-off might come.

An important lesson that will be repeated many times in this book is that *the stock market anticipates future events*, which really means that smart investors anticipate future events. If the "smart investors" had been wrong and CB sales only dipped temporarily, and then resumed rapid growth, the stocks would probably have gone up. But the smart investor does not wait around to find out, preferring to take the risk of missing a rise in the stock than being caught in a rapid decline.

Another recent example of a large inventory write-down is Polaroid's 1979 write-down of $68 million of its Polavision home movie products after they failed to sell well despite a period of heavy advertising. Polaroid finally recognized they could not be sold at the current price and that their market value was less than their selling price. Thus Polaroid had to "write them down" to expected market value.

Inventory write-downs are almost always taken to the *cost of goods sold* since they occur as part of the normal operations of the business. Sometimes, however, they are recorded as an extraordinary loss. An occasion where this might occur is when a company is closing down a plant or dropping a major line of business. In this case, any inventory left over after the plant closing would probably be sold at distress prices. Since this type of inventory write-down only occurs because the company is dropping the line, it is reasonable to include the inventory loss as part of the extraordinary plant-closing loss. Of course, closing a plant does not necessarily result in a loss. If the inventory was all sold and if the plant was depreciated down to a low figure, it is quite possible that it could be sold at a profit.

To summarize, determining the value of inventory and cost of goods sold is rarely as easy as in the case of Jones Mousetrap or the automobile dealer discussed at the beginning of this chapter. Fluctuating prices of raw materials as well as selling prices of finished goods can combine with LIFO or FIFO accounting techniques and LOCOM inventory write-downs to produce distortions in a company's reported earnings that can be misleading to investors who are trying to determine a company's ability to generate future growth in earnings. This issue is a complicated one, even for accountants and company officers. Therefore, outside investors must pay particularly close attention to footnotes in the financial statements and to management's comments in quarterly or annual reports, which might give a clue on these distortions. While some such distortions must be revealed in footnotes, this is not true in all cases. For stocks where the company's raw materials costs and selling prices are either moving up or down sharply, or are fluctuating substantially, investors should be mindful to ask their stockbrokers if the broker knows of any such influences beyond those reported in company releases.

PART FOUR

Why stocks go up

14

Listing and trading on the stock exchange

When we left JMC in Chapter 7, its stock was being traded over the counter (OTC). At that point there were only 6,250 common shares outstanding. This was an unrealistically low number of shares, but the low number made the examples easy to follow. While there is no minimum number of shares required for a stock to be traded over the counter, even a small company traded OTC is likely to have 100,000 to 500,000 shares outstanding. As a company grows and has more primary offerings or stock splits or stock dividends, or all three, the number of shares increases.

Let's jump ahead and assume JMC now has 900,000 shares of common stock outstanding. This includes 800,000 shares of registered stock held by the public, and 100,000 shares of stock still held by Mr. Jones and JMC's original investors that have never been registered. Note that some of the 800,000 public shares may also be held by Jones and JMC's original investors. Just because they have unregistered shares, there is no reason why they cannot also buy registered shares on the market like anyone else. The unregistered shares, of course, have to be registered before they can be sold, but the registered shares can be sold anytime.

At this point, Mr. Stodge, JMC's advisor on financial matters, pointed out that JMC was now big enough to apply for listing on the American Stock Exchange. Jones, who was still chairman of the board, admitted that he never really understood the difference between OTC trading and

157

stock exchange trading, and he wondered what advantages his company might enjoy by being listed on a stock exchange. So he asked Stodge if he would make a presentation before the board of directors to clarify these matters. Stodge, of course, was quite willing, and started by reviewing some basic points.

Trading on a stock exchange

Stock exchange trading is much like over-the-counter trading. The main difference is that it is almost all done in one place, at the stock exchange. Whereas a brokerage firm selling an OTC-traded stock might have to make five or more phone calls to market makers to find the best price for its customers, the firm would only have to make one call to sell a stock traded on an exchange. A stock exchange is simply a place where buyers and sellers can get together to haggle over price.

The stock exchange itself neither buys nor sells stock, nor does the company whose stock is being traded. There are some exceptions. Companies will frequently buy some of their own stock to give to employees under stock option plans or for other purposes. Also, some companies occasionally buy back a large amount of their own stock to reduce shares outstanding and thus increase earnings per share. For such major purchases a company must announce its intentions in advance. For the most part, however, a company is not a regular factor in the market for its stock. The exchange never buys or sells stock.

When you read that 12,000 shares of IBM were traded yesterday between $55 and $57½ per share, it means that some individuals[1] bought them from some other individuals. All trades (purchases and sales) on a stock exchange or OTC are secondary transactions of registered stock. The company whose stock is being traded, IBM in this case, has nothing to do with it and has no say in the matter. The only time IBM would be involved with the sale of its stock would be if IBM wished to raise some money by selling *new* stock (i.e., have a primary offering). This, of course, is normally done through underwriters, or investment bankers, and would not involve the stock exchange.

Note that the underwriting or investment banking firm may also be a brokerage firm, but in this case the firm is acting as an investment banker or underwriter, not as a broker. Thus, in a primary offering the new shares are delivered from IBM to the initial purchaser via the underwriter, and their purchase price is remitted to IBM via the underwriter. The new shares do not go through the exchange. However, once the new owners receive their shares, they can then sell them on the New York Stock Exchange if they wish. Since IBM is already listed on the NYSE,

---

[1] Or mutual funds, trust funds, and the like.

any new issue of registered IBM stock can also be traded there after IBM files a form called a Listing Application. IBM or any other already listed company usually files the Listing Application early, and thus the new shares are tradeable on the exchange immediately after they are issued. It would not be necessary to first trade the new shares over-the-counter, as was the case with JMC, which was not yet listed on an exchange.

If the relationship between the stock exchange, the company whose stock is being traded, and the buyers and sellers of the stock is not clear, the following analogy to the automobile business should help clarify it.

Automobile business	*Stock brokerage business*
When Mr. Driver buys a new Ford automobile he is buying from Ford Motor Company through a dealer. This is a "primary" transaction. Driver's money goes to Ford, via the dealer.	When Mr. Driver buys some new shares of IBM stock he is buying from IBM Company through an underwriter. This is a "primary" transaction. Driver's money goes to IBM, via the underwriter.
A year or two later, Driver no longer needs his car. Not knowing anyone who wants to buy it, he brings it to a used car dealer, where it is eventually purchased by Ms. Foehle. This is a "secondary" transaction. The money has, in effect, gone from Foehle (buyer) to Driver (seller) with the used car dealer keeping a "commission." Ford Motor Company has nothing to do with this secondary transaction and no say in the matter.	A year or two later, Mr. Driver no longer wants his investment in IBM. Not knowing anyone who wants to buy it, he brings it to a stock exchange (via his broker), where it is eventually purchased by Ms. Foehle. This is a "secondary" transaction. The money has in effect gone from Foehle (buyer) to Driver (seller) with the brokers keeping a commission. IBM has nothing to do with this secondary transaction and no say in the matter.

The analogy is not perfect, but it should serve to clarify the idea that the company whose stock is being traded and the stock exchange are essentially separate. To recapitulate: a stock exchange is simply a place where people come to buy and sell registered stock in secondary transactions.

There are many stock exchanges in the United States, the New York Stock Exchange (NYSE) and the American Stock Exchange (ASE) being the major ones. Public companies from all over the country—and a few foreign companies—have their stock traded at one of these exchanges. Both are located in New York City. Stocks that are traded at one are not traded at the other. In addition to these two exchanges, there are many other smaller or regional exchanges, such as the Pacific Exchange (PCE), the Midwest Stock Exchange (MSE), the Boston Stock Exchange, and so on. The stocks traded on these exchanges include both smaller companies from that particular region of the country and some stocks that are also traded on the New York or American Exchanges. When a company is traded on a stock exchange we say it is "listed" on that exchange. When a stock is traded on more than one exchange we say it has a "multiple listing." Where this multiple listing occurs, the price of the stock is usually the same on both exchanges and is adjusted very quickly if the price on one exchange differs from the other.

When a stock is listed on one or more exchanges, almost all the trading in that stock is done on one or another of these exchanges. Under some circumstances a brokerage firm with a sell order can sell directly to another brokerage firm with a buy order without going through the exchange, but even in these cases the brokerage firms are required to report the trades to the exchange and the transaction is printed on the tape like any other transaction done at the exchange.

A company desiring to have its stock listed on a given exchange must meet the requirements of that exchange. In 1980, for example, the ASE required, among other things, that a company applying for listing must: (1) have at least 400,000 shares publicly held, (2) have had pretax income in the last year of at least $750,000, and (3) have at least 1200 individual stockholders.

The NYSE requirements include: (1) at least 1,000,000 shares publicly held, (2) $2.5 million in pretax income in the latest fiscal year, and (3) at least 2,000 stockholders who hold 100 or more shares. A company fulfilling these requirements is still subject to the approval of the Exchange before it is listed.

If a company that is listed on an exchange falls below the requirements, it is not automatically thrown off the exchange, or "delisted." Usually, it has to be below more than one of these requirements for two or more years before it is delisted. Chrysler Corporation, for example, reported losses two years in a row, in 1978 and 1979, but it has not been delisted by the New York Stock Exchange. The question of when to delist a stock is more subjective than the question of listing.

About 1,560 companies have their common stock traded on the New York Stock Exchange. Since some companies have preferred stocks as well as common stock traded on the NYSE, there are closer to 2,200 issues traded there. Illinois Power, for example, has 10 preferred stock issues, which are traded on the NYSE in addition to the common stock. Illinois Power's preferred stocks are not traded as actively as the common, and frequently one or more of them does not trade at all on a given day. When this occurs, they do not appear in the usual stock market page of the newspaper but in a separate list, which shows the last bid and asked prices.

Mechanics of trading

Each stock listed on the exchange is traded at a particular location on the floor called a trading post. The actual trading of a given stock,

General Motors for instance, is supervised by one person called a specialist in that stock.

The best way to explain what the specialist does is to describe a series of trades actually taking place. Let's assume it is 11:15 in the morning and the stock market is quiet. The specialist in charge of General Motors, Mr. Moore, is standing at his post waiting for orders. The last trade in GM stock occurred four minutes ago at $46¼; that is, some individual bought some GM stock for $46¼ per share (plus commission) from some other individual, who received the $46¼ per share (less the commission his broker kept). At 11:16 A.M., Mr. Sellers in Chicago decides to sell 500 of his shares of GM. He calls his stockbroker, Mr. Gordon, who works for the brokerage firm of Goldman, Sachs & Co. Gordon has a desktop machine, which is wired directly to the stock exchange, and by pressing certain letters on it he can instantly determine that the last price at which GM traded was $46¼. He tells Sellers this and Sellers, in turn, tells him to sell 500 shares "at the market." This means Sellers wants to sell his stock immediately, and, even if the price should fall in the next few minutes while the order is being transmitted to the trading post and executed, it is OK to sell it at the lower price. At this point Gordon writes the sell order on a slip of paper and it is wired to the floor of the exchange. Under current exchange rules, if the order is of 499 shares or less, it is wired directly to the specialist, who executes it.

If the order is for 500 or more shares, it is wired to a Goldman, Sachs representative on the floor of the exchange, who is called a floor broker. In this case, the order was for 500 shares—so the order goes to the floor broker who takes it and walks over to the post where GM is traded. Elapsed time: three to six minutes. At about the same time, Mr. Buyer in Miami decides to buy 500 shares of GM. He calls his broker, Ms. Green, who works for E. F. Hutton, and tells her to buy 500 shares of GM at $46. Buyer likes to buy and sell stocks frequently even if the profits are small, and consequently considers every fraction of a dollar important. He also knows that the stock prices will fluctuate and, even though the stock is selling at $46¼ now, he thinks that the stock will get down to $46 at some point in the day, so he puts in his order to buy at $46 (or lower). Buyer's broker has the order wired to the E.F. Hutton floor broker, who, in turn, carries the order to the same trading post. Again, elapsed time—about three to six minutes (possibly a little longer on a busy day). In this case, both floor brokers, one to buy at $46 and one to sell "at the market," approach the specialist together.

Since there are orders to buy 500 shares at $46 and to sell 500 shares "at the market" (i.e., at the best price available), the specialist simply directs the Goldman, Sachs floor broker to sell his 500 shares of GM to the E.F. Hutton floor broker for $46 per share, and the deal is done. The floor brokers then go back to their booths and wire the stock brokers who, in turn, call their customers (Mr. Buyer and Mr. Sellers) to inform them that their purchase or sale was executed and at what price. Also, immediately after the trade is executed, the specialist notes that 500 shares of GM were traded at $46 and sends the message to the tape room upstairs. Seconds later a symbol like "5s GM 46" crosses the tape. This indicates that 500 shares of GM were traded at $46. If 200 shares were traded, the symbol would be 2s GM 46. If 100 shares were traded, the symbol would be simply GM 46. Since 100 shares is thought of as the basic unit traded on the exchange, there is no need to say "100 GM 46." When less than 100 shares is traded, it is called an odd lot. Some brokerage firms buy or sell odd lots directly from or for their customers separately from the exchange and nothing appears on the tape. In fact, even when an odd lot is traded on the exchange by the specialist it is not noted on the tape. The tape is situated high above the trading floor in such a position that it can be seen from anywhere on the floor. Simultaneously, it appears on ticker tapes and on display machines in brokerage firm offices throughout the country.

The biggest difference between the stock exchanges and the over-the-counter markets is that every time a trade is executed on a stock exchange, it becomes public information immediately as it crosses the tape. When a trade is executed over the counter the only people who know immediately are the buyer and the seller. Consequently, a person who put in an order to buy stock "at the market" on a listed exchange might feel more confident that his purchase was at a fair price than a buyer "at the market" of shares of an over-the-counter stock. At the end of the day, however, over-the-counter traders (who are members of the National Association of Securities Dealers, NASD), report all their trades of major over-the-counter stocks to the NASD, where records are kept.

Also, more information about listed stocks is readily available in the newspapers. If you look in the stock market section of any newspaper, you will see an over-the-counter section, a NYSE section, and an ASE section. In many of these sections you will see the volume of each stock (i.e., how many shares were traded during the previous day). On the "listed" exchanges, however, you can also read the highest price at which the stock sold during the day, as well as the lowest price and the final price. In the OTC section, you will find only a "bid" and "asked" price. These represent an average of the bid and asked prices at the end of the day of some or all of the OTC traders who happen to make a market in that stock; but it does not tell you how high or low the stock actually traded during that day. You only know the average price at which market makers were willing to buy (bid) or sell (asked) at the end of the day.

Another advantage of being listed on an exchange is that the stock will attract more day traders and thus increase liquidity. "Day traders" are investors who like to trade stocks actively; that is, they may buy and sell a stock in a day or hour, or even minutes. By sitting in their broker's office and watching the tape, they can see all the trading activity on the exchange. Some people say they can get the pulse of the market by watching the tape and know when to buy and sell. Thus, these investors usually prefer to trade "listed" stocks, where they can watch the tape, rather than trade unlisted over-the-counter stocks for which there is no tape and it is more difficult to get the pulse of the trading activity. Having these day traders increases the liquidity, or total volume traded, in a stock, and therefore increases its "marketability" (i.e., how much stock can be easily bought or sold without pushing the stock way up or down). Good marketability—a high trading volume or high liquidity—is desirable because there are many large investors (especially banks, other financial institutions, and many overseas investors) who won't buy a stock unless it meets certain high liquidity requirements. Thus, since a highly liquid stock is likely to attract more buyers, many companies think their stock may sell at a higher price than if it were less liquid as a result of being unlisted. This is another reason that most large companies prefer to have their stock traded on an exchange, and apply for listing as soon as they qualify. In addition, there is a prestige factor to having a company listed on an exchange, especially the NYSE, or "big board" as it is called. Whether this really helps the price of the stock, however, is uncertain.

At this point, let us return to the discussion of the specialist. Suppose Mr. Sellers decides to sell another 500 shares of GM a few minutes later. He calls his stockbroker again; but this time, he places a price limit on his sale, telling his broker to sell at $46 at the lowest. In other words, if the price should fall to $45⅞, Sellers would rather not sell. Once again the floor broker carries the order to the trading post, but this time there is no one there who wants to buy GM. The specialist now has a choice. Either he can buy it for himself, and then sell it later when a buyer comes along, or he can tell the floor broker there is no buyer around—but he (the specialist) will hold the order until a buyer comes along. When the specialist is holding an order waiting to be executed, he writes it in his "book." So he would write "Sell 500 GM at $46 or better." (Obviously, Sellers would be perfectly happy if he got more than $46 for his stock.) Now suppose Buyers decides he wants to buy another 500 shares of GM. His broker tells him that the last trade was at $46. Once again Buyers decides to put his order in at a lower price, with the hope that the market will fluctuate downward. So he tells his broker to buy at $45¾ or less, and the order is transmitted to the specialist in the usual fashion. At this point, however, there is no one willing to sell at $45¾, so again the specialist writes the order in his book and holds it until a seller comes along who is willing to sell at $45¾.

At this point Ms. Fischer in Kansas City decides to sell her 500 shares of GM to help pay for a new house. She calls her broker, Mr. Teller, who tells Fischer that he has been watching the tape all morning and he has seen GM trade from $46¼ down to $46. Being afraid that it might continue to fall during the day, Fischer wants to sell immediately and tells the broker to sell "at the market." When the order arrives at the trading post, the specialist, Mr. Moore, immediately sells Ms. Fischer's stock to Buyers at $45¾. Sellers had put his order in first but he wasn't willing to sell as low as $45¾, consequently his order remains in the book until someone comes along who is willing to buy at his selling price of $46. In actuality, the specialist's book is usually filled with orders to buy and sell various amounts of stocks at different prices, and whenever he can match a buy and a sell, he does.

The specialist is also charged with the responsibility of "maintaining a fair and orderly market." This means the following. Suppose a large number of sell orders came in at the same time at the current market price and there were few available buyers at that price. The specialist would then have to substantially lower the price of the stock to reach the buy prices of orders in the book and to attract more buyers. Seeing this happen, other holders might panic and sell their stock "at the market," forcing the stock price to fall even further. Then suddenly the stock might look so "cheap" that people would rush in and buy it and probably bid the price right back up to near where it started. Similarly, suppose a flood of buy orders came in at another point during the day. This might produce a sharp but temporary upward movement. This excessive volatility is considered undesirable, because it can result in stock prices that, for short periods, in no way reflect the underlying value of the company. Similarly, it allows manipulators to come in and intentionally produce such fluctuations to their own ends. Therefore, the specialist is charged with the responsibility of preventing such activity. In this case, Mr. Moore does this by buying for his own account, when there is an excess of sellers, and selling from his own account, when there is an excess of buyers. Of course, if some bad news should come out about a company that would make the stock worth substantially less, the specialist will let the stock fall to its own level. But the possibility of wild fluctuations—caused simply by the fact that sellers coincidentally chose to sell at one point during the day and buyers coincidentally chose to buy at another point—can easily be prevented. Obviously, the specialist is in a position where he can manipulate the market for his own benefit; but the stock exchanges have rules to prevent this. The activity and profits of the specialist are monitored by the exchange and by the Securities and Exchange Commission.

The stock market averages

On any given day some stocks go up and some go down. So what exactly is meant when someone says the "market was up" or the "market was down"? Most people are referring to one of a number of common averages, such as the Dow Jones Industrial Average or the Standard & Poor's 500 Stock Average. The Dow Jones Industrial Average is an index made up of 30 of the largest industrial companies in the United States. But it is not a simple average of the prices of the 30 stocks. In fact, none of the common averages are simple averages because there are some surprisingly difficult problems in constructing an average which truly reflects the market's behavior. For example, if a stock moves up one point from $50 to $51, should that count as much as a stock that moves up one point from $10 to $11? The one-point gain in the $50 stock was a 2 percent gain. The one-point gain in the $10 stock was a 10 percent gain. Also, should a one-point move in Polaroid, which has 33 million shares outstanding, have the same importance in the average as a one-point move in much-larger General Motors, which has 290 million shares outstanding? How do you adjust the average if one of the companies has a stock split? As a result of these problems, all of the common averages or indexes are more complicated than they look and, rather than try to understand them precisely, it is preferable to just watch them and become familiar with them.

The most commonly quoted average is the Dow Jones Industrial Average, abbreviated DJIA. The 30 stocks in the DJIA are all traded on the New York Stock Exchange. When the DJIA is up strongly, usually well over half of the other stocks on the NYSE are up, also. When the DJIA is down strongly, usually well over half of the other stocks on the NYSE are down. Thus, the DJIA is generally a good indicator of the direction of the market. The following table will help the reader interpret the moves in the DJIA, but there is no substitute for watching it in the newspaper every day, along with your favorite stocks.

Change in DJIA	Interpretation
Up more than $16	Unusually strong gain
Up $10 to $16	Sharp gain
Up $5 to $10	Good gain
Up $2 to $5	Modest gain
Up $2 to down $2	Essentially unchanged
Down $2 to $5	Modest decline
Down $5 to $10	Very weak
Down $10 to $16	Off sharply
Down more than $16	Major decline

Other Dow Jones averages include: the Dow Jones Transportation Average, which consists of 20 stocks of railroads, truckers, and airlines; the Dow Jones Utility Average, which consists of 15 stocks of electric power companies and natural gas companies; and the Dow Jones Composite, which consists of all the 65 stocks in the Industrial, Transportation, and Utility averages.

Standard & Poor's Corporation calculates indexes of industrials, transportations, utilities, and financial stocks (such as banks and insurance companies), as well as a composite. Its indexes use many more stocks than the Dow Jones indexes, and some people think they are a truer representation of the market. For example, the Standard & Poor's (S&P) Industrial Average consists of 400 stocks, and the S&P Composite contains 500 stocks. The latter is commonly called the S&P 500. The New York Stock Exchange also computes its own average, which includes all stocks on the exchange.

Other common averages include the American Stock Exchange Market Value Index, which consists of all stocks traded on the American Stock Exchange, and the over-the-counter averages compiled by NASDAQ, which stands for National Association of Securities Dealers Automated Quotation. Close followers of the stock market, as opposed to individual stocks, tend to watch many or all of these averages and the relationships between them. Market technicians try to predict the market's behavior by watching those and other relationships. For example, if the DJIA was up but the Dow Jones Transportation Average was down, it might indicate something different than if both were up.

Another common way to watch the market is to watch the advance/decline line. The *advance/decline line* is the ratio of the number of stocks that were up for the day divided by the number that were down for the day. Those numbers are published in most major newspapers.

Thus, when someone says the "market is up," he can be referring either to one of the averages or to the advance/decline line. Look for example at the following statistics:

	Wednesday	Thursday	Friday
Advances	1,084	802	758
Declines	372	699	718
Unchanged.............	388	379	395
Dow Jones Industrials	Up $7.23	Up $8.51	Off $1.06

Was the market up more Wednesday or Thursday? Wednesday's DJIA was up less than Thursday's, but the advance/decline line was much stronger on Wednesday. Was the market up or down on Friday?

If you watch these statistics regularly, it will help you understand both the market in general, and your favorite stocks in relation to the market.

15

Price-earnings ratios— When is a stock "low" or "high"?

The discussion in the last chapter centered around the mechanics of trading and to some extent the causes of day-to-day or intraday fluctuations. But these price fluctuations are invariably minor compared to the average price movement, up or down, that a stock experiences over a period of weeks or months. And even these trends often appear minor compared to long-term—year or more—movements that stocks make. Consequently, trying to purchase a stock at the lowest price on a given day becomes far less important than trying to correctly forecast the intermediate (perhaps one to nine months) and longer-term direction and extent of stock moves.

This chapter will discuss the price-to-earnings ratio, probably the most important single tool used by investors to determine whether a stock price is high or low. As discussed in Chapter 4, the price of a share of stock of a company is most often related to the actual or potential dividends of that company. Since the best measure of the ability of a company to pay dividends in the long run is earnings, one might properly relate the price he would pay for a share of a company's stock to the earnings-per-share of that company. That is why we talk about a company's earnings on a per-share basis. One seldom hears investment people say "Polaroid earned $67,710,000." Rather, we divide it by the number of common shares outstanding and say, "Polaroid earned $2/share."

In determining whether the price of a stock is high or low, what is important is not the absolute price per share, but rather the relationship between the price per share and the earnings per share, called the price-earnings ratio. This ratio is so basic to Wall Street language that it is commonly abbreviated as "P.E.R." or "P/E" or just "P-E." If Polaroid were selling at $50 and had earnings per share (EPS) of $2, we would say it is selling at 25x. The phrase "is selling at 25x" is read "is selling at 25 times earnings per share." To see why the P-E should be used as the measure of how "high" a stock price is, consider the following example. Company A and Company B are both in the same business, have approximately the same growth rate of earnings, and pay out 50 percent of earnings as dividends.

	Earnings per share	Price/ earnings ratio	Price of stock	Dividend per share at 50 percent of earnings	Yield to investor per share of stock
Company A....	$10	10x	$100	$5	5.0%
Company B....	2	25	50	1	2.0

An investor with $100 could buy one share of Company A and get a yield of 5 percent on the money.

$$\frac{\$5 \text{ Dividend}}{\$100 \text{ Investment}} = 5\%$$

If the same $100 were used to buy two shares of Company B, the investor would receive $2 in dividends ($1 per share), or a 2 percent yield on the investment.

$$\frac{\$2 \text{ Dividend}}{\$100 \text{ Investment}} = 2\%$$

Consequently, a share of Company A, although twice as expensive as a share of Company B in actual dollars, is the lower-priced stock in terms of dividends received per dollar of investment. Therefore, we could say Company A is the cheaper stock, and this is reflected by its lower price-earnings ratio. To see this clearly, look again at the comparison of Company A and Company B, but this time assume that Company B's price-earnings ratio has fallen from 25x to 10x, to equal that of Company A.

	Earnings per share	Stock price	Price/ earnings ratio
Company A....	$10	$100	10x
Company B....	2	20	10x

Both companies still have the same EPS, but since investors are now only willing to pay 10x earnings for Company B, its stock has fallen to $20. Now let's see how much dividend the investor can get for a $100 investment in Company A or Company B.

	Earnings per share	Dividend per share at 50 percent of earnings	Price of stock	Yield to investors per share
Company A.........	$10	$5	$100	5%
Company B.........	2	1	20	5

Now, an investor with $100 could still buy one share of Company A and therefore get one dividend of $5, for a yield of 5 percent.

$$\frac{\$5 \text{ Dividend}}{\$100 \text{ Investment}} = 5\%$$

Or, with Company B's stock price having declined to $20, the investor could now buy five shares of Company B, and, since each share of B pays a dividend of $1, the investor would now receive $5 in dividends, also a yield of 5 percent on the investment.

$$\frac{\$5 \text{ Dividend}}{\$100 \text{ Investment}} = 5\%$$

What has happened is that the lower P-E resulted in a lower stock price, which enabled the investor to buy more shares of stock and hence receive more dividends. Now, with the P-Es the same, a $100 investment in either company yields the same amount of dividends, and hence we could say that both stocks, Company A and Company B, are "equally priced" in terms of dividends per dollar of investment. Note that this is reflected in their equal P-Es, although one stock still sells at a much higher actual price than the other stock ($100 versus $20).

Of course, the price of a stock today not only reflects the current yield (this year's dividend) but the dividends (smaller or larger) that are anticipated in the future. While the purchaser of the stock today may not expect to hold the stock long enough to receive any future years' dividends, the person to whom she sells the stock at some time in the future may expect to receive them, and consequently the latter's purchase price will reflect more directly the expected future dividends. Thus, if the earnings of a company were in an uptrend and expected to continue upward, carrying with them the possibility of increasing dividends, one should be willing to pay more (a higher P-E) for that company's stock than one would pay for the stock of a company whose earnings were expected to decline.

Similarly, if two companies were both expected to increase earnings, investors should pay a higher P-E for the company that was expected to grow (increase earnings) at a faster rate. If two companies were expected to grow at the same rate, one would pay a higher P-E for the company which appeared more certain to continue to grow at that rate. The P-E of a given stock, then, is directly related to two unknowns: (1) the expected growth rate of the company's earnings per share (because of the potential growth in dividends per share), and (2) the degree of confidence that the expectation will be met.

In the above example of Company A and Company B, the P-Es and yields worked out neatly because both companies were growing at the same rate and had the same dividend payout ratio. If two companies were growing at different rates, the P-E is still the best way to measure whether a stock is expensive or cheap, but now there is no easy basis of comparison. For example, let us compare Company A from the above example to companies that are growing at a much faster rate than Company A.

	EPS	Stock price	P-E	Earnings growth/year
Company A	$10	$100	10x	10%
Company E	10	120	12	30
Company F	10	200	20	30
Company G	5	100	20	30

Company E is selling for a higher price and has a higher P-E than Company A, but its growth rate is substantially greater. Therefore, other things being equal, perhaps Company E is the cheaper stock because, although its growth rate is much higher than Company A, its P-E is only slightly higher. But what if Company E were selling at $150 per share, or 15x earnings? Would it still be cheaper than Company A? What if Company E were selling at $250, or 25x earnings? Unfortunately, there is no precise way to compare P-Es of companies with different growth rates. Also, of course, other things never are equal, and thus attempts to determine exactly what a stock should be worth, either in actual dollars or compared to another stock, are difficult at best. Only by watching the prices, earnings, and P-Es of a group of stocks over a period of time will you develop a feel for how they behave, both individually and compared to each other.

This is a key lesson for successful investing. Investors seeking a formula to determine exactly what price or P-E a given stock can be expected to sell at are doomed to failure. Market conditions change too quickly. By analogy, there is no formula that tells you exactly how fast to drive on a given road. Road conditions change too quickly. But the taxi driver who has driven that road many times before in a variety of traffic and road conditions will be best able to travel that road at the fastest and safest speed.

In the above example, a comparison of Company E to either Company F or Company G may be more valid because they are all growing at the same rate. Since Company E is selling at a lower P-E than Company F or G and has a similar growth rate (30 percent), we can say, other things being equal, that Company E is the cheaper of the three stocks. Finally, other things being equal, Companies F and G should be thought of as essentially identically priced.

P-Es are also related to many other factors. Two of the more important factors are the company's return on equity (see Chapter 4) and interest rates in the economy in general. Companies with a high return on equity generally have higher P-Es than companies with a low return on equity. This will be seen in the history of Polaroid's stock in Chapter 18. Regarding interest rates, P-Es of most stocks tend to be low when interest rates are high. When interest rates are low, P-Es tend to be relatively high. Therefore, when interest rates are rising, P-Es and hence stock prices frequently fall. Conversely, when interest rates are falling, P-Es and hence stock prices usually rise. [1] While these observations are generally true, they are not always so. The inverse correlation between interest rates and stock prices is a good one, but not a perfect one. Again, there simply are no perfect relationships between stock prices and other economic or company factors. But the thoughtful investor who regularly watches stock price behavior in relationship to interest rates and other economic factors, as well as company results, will increase substantially his or her odds of being successful.

Unfortunately, predicting changes in interest rates can be just as difficult or even more difficult than predicting other factors that determine stock prices (such as a company's current earnings per share, expected growth rate of earnings per share, return on equity, and so on). Thus, even if interest rates were readily predictable, they would only partially explain the price behavior of stocks. The easiest way to watch interest rate changes is to watch the business section of any newspaper for changes in the banks' prime rates. Changes in the prime rate usually make the business headlines or lead articles. The interest rates on U.S. Treasury bonds also appear in most newspapers.

In sum, there is no absolute measure of what P-E one should pay for a stock. There have been many studies attempting to determine what P-E should be paid for a given growth rate of earnings or dividends, and a given level of interest rates, but in this writer's opinion there have

---

[1] The reasons why this is so include: (1) the relationship of interest rates to the general level of economic activity and hence companies' near-term earnings and dividend outlook; (2) investors' willingness to borrow money to use to invest in the stock market, called *margin* (see Appendix Two), and many other factors. The literature of the financial community is filled with studies of the relationship between interest rates and stock prices.

always been too many "other" factors for such studies to be useful. In the late 1960s a broad rule of thumb was that the P-E should be twice the expected growth rate of earnings per share if there was a high degree of confidence that this growth rate would continue. For example, if Company C had been growing at 10 percent per year, a P-E of 20x might have been considered "reasonable." In the late 1970s, however, most companies sold for a P-E of less than their growth rate. Thus if Company C had been growing at 10 percent per year in the late 1970s, a P-E of 6x to 9x might have been considered reasonable. Entering the early 1980s, P-Es for stocks in general seemed to be increasing again relative to their growth rates, particularly for small companies in high technology fields with good growth prospects.

When looking at a company's growth rate, investors should be interested in the future expected growth rate, not the past growth rate. Nevertheless, assuming there has been no important change in the company's circumstances, looking at the past growth rate is probably the best first assumption about the future growth rate. Let's look at Company C and Company D, which are small high-technology companies, and, unlike most stocks in the late 1970s, tended to sell at P-Es much greater than their growth rates.

Company C	Earnings per share	Percent increase over previous year
1977	$ .91	—
1978	1.00	10%
1979	1.10	10
1980	1.21	10
1981	1.33	10
		10% Average growth

Company C is an unrealistic example, of course, because no company is likely to grow by exactly 10 percent per year. More realistically a company's growth record might appear as follows:

Company D	Earnings per share	Percent increase over previous year
1977	$ .91	
1978	.96	5.5%
1979	1.11	15.5
1980	1.25	12.8
1981	1.33	6.4
		10.0% Average increase*

---

* Actually, the average growth rate is 10.05 percent per year. To be mathematically correct, it is the *compound* growth rate that is exactly 10 percent per year. Compound

Company D's growth has "averaged" 10 percent, and let's assume one investor thought it should sell for about 20x earnings. Another investor looking only at the period from 1978 to 1981 would see a higher average growth rate, close to 11 percent, and might be willing to pay 22x earnings for the stock. Yet another investor would look at the period from 1978 to 1981 and realize that although the average growth rate was slightly over 11 percent, the rate of growth was slowing down, and if whatever caused this slowdown continued, the company might experience an earnings decline or even a loss in succeeding years. As a result, he would surely not want to pay 22x earnings for the stock unless he were confident that the slowdown in growth was ending and a more rapid growth rate could be safely predicted for the immediate future. Each investor then would have a different assessment of what the stock is worth.

Let us presume, however, that all investors are agreed that the longer-term growth rate will average about 10 percent per year and that a P-E of about 20x is "reasonable" for this company. Then, assuming it is February, the question arises: Should one pay 20x earnings of the recently completed year, or 20x his estimate of the earnings of the year currently in progress? Or if it is December, does one pay 20x the earnings estimated for the year about to be completed, or 20x estimated earnings for the following year?

Assume it is early December 1981, and the stock of Company D is currently selling for $27 per share. The earnings estimate[2] for the full year ended December 31, 1981, is $1.35,[3] and the estimate for 1982 is $1.60.

	Estimated EPS	Stock price	P-E
1981.....	$1.35	$27	20.0x
1982.....	1.60	27	16.9x

---

growth rate is defined as the growth rate which would be necessary so that *if* the company grew at exactly the same percentage rate each year, it would grow from a specified level ($.91 in 1977 in this case) to another specified level ($1.33 in 1981 in this case). The compound growth rate is not concerned with the earnings levels in the middle years. They could be anything. The compound growth rate for Company D, then, is exactly 10 percent, which we can see by looking at Company C. Unfortunately, there is no simple way to calculate a compound growth rate, so if you don't have a special calculator that can do it, it is usually good enough to calculate an "average" growth rate by adding up the growth rates for each year and dividing the total by the number of years.

[2] A brief discussion of the derivation of earnings estimates is presented in Chapter 17. Making earnings estimates is part of the profession of security analysts. Most major brokerage firms have a staff of analysts who keep estimates on a large number of stocks. You can usually get earnings estimates from either your broker or from published services, such as *Value Line*.

[3] This estimate turned out to be too high, because earnings for 1981 came in at $1.33.

Looking at 1981 earnings, the stock is selling at a P-E of 20x, a "reasonable" level. But the investor who buys now (December 1981) is really looking ahead and asking what the price of the stock will be perhaps six months from now, in June 1982, when she may want to sell it. By then, of course, the 1982 earnings estimate will be more important because people buying the stock then will be looking ahead another six months to December 1982. Consequently, the buyer of the stock today, December 1981, is really concerned with the 1982 estimate. Assuming that in June 1982 the $1.60 estimate still appears reasonable, if the stock were still selling at $27 per share, it would be selling at only 16.9x estimated earnings and would appear low relative to its "expected" level of 20x earnings. Consequently, the stock might be expected to go up between December 1981, and June 1982, to a point where it is selling at closer to 20x the 1982 estimated earnings. This would result in a price of 20x × $1.60 = $32 per share. With the stock selling at $27 and expected to rise to $32, we would say the "upside potential" is $5. A $5 gain on a $27 stock is about an 18½ percent increase.

The "reasonable" or "expected" P-E of 20x was chosen simply by looking at the stock's past P-Es. In practice, most investors do not try to derive a reasonable P-E, but rather they simply look at the historical P-Es, what they have been in past years, and use that as a starting point when forecasting a stock's possible moves. Then, they try to determine what might happen to cause that P-E to rise or decline (i.e., what could happen to the company or its industry or in the economy in general to cause an acceleration or deceleration in the company's earnings growth rate), or what might happen to increase investors' confidence that a forecast growth rate can be attained. Or finally, what might happen that will call more attention to this stock to cause new investors to come in and push the price and P-E of the stock up, even though the earnings growth rate might not change at all.

Let's return to Company D and see if the stock looks attractive to purchase at the current price. To begin, let's look at the historical record of the stock price and earnings and the future earnings estimates.

Company D—Historical record and future estimates

	1977	1978	1979	1980	Estimates 1981	Estimates 1982
EPS..........	$ .91	$ .96	$1.11	$1.25	$1.35	$1.60
High price.....	22¾	26⅞	27¾	33¾		
Low price	12¾	15⅜	16⅝	20		
High P-E......	25x	28x	25x	27x		
Low P-E	14	16	15	16		

In 1979 Company D earned $1.11 per share. The lowest and highest stock prices that year were $16⅝ and $27¾; therefore, the low and high

P-Es were 15x and 25x. In 1980, the company earned $1.25 and sold between $20 and $33¾, the low and high P-Es therefore being 16x and 27x. Looking at years prior to 1979 also reveals that the stock usually sold as low as 16x earnings every year and at least as high as 25x. This does not necessarily mean it will every year, nor does it mean that the P-E may not exceed that range considerably on either the high side or the low side in any given year. With the stock selling at $27 in December 1981, however, it looks "low" at 16.9x estimated 1982 earnings.

Further, unless the stock market is depressed all through 1982—or unless there is an important decline in the company's expected growth rate, or in stock market P-Es in general—it is reasonable to assume, based on prior history, that at some point during the year the stock price will get up to 25x earnings or more.

$$\frac{\text{1982 Earnings estimate}}{\$1.60} \times \frac{\text{Assumed P-E}}{25\text{x}} = \frac{\text{Expected stock price}}{\$40}$$

With the stock currently selling at $27, and a good probability that it will reach $40 or more within the year, the stock has an "upside potential" of 48 percent. The risk, though, is that it might be selling at only 16x earnings in six months.

$$\frac{\text{1982 Earnings estimate}}{\$1.60} \times \frac{\text{Assumed P-E}}{16\text{x}} = \frac{\text{Expected stock price}}{\$25\frac{1}{2}}$$

Thus, at $27, an investor today sees a 48 percent "upside potential" and only a 6 percent "downside risk." He should probably buy the stock.

Now let's assume the stock has appreciated to $33 by March 1982. The 1981 earnings per share came in at $1.33, slightly below the estimate, and the $1.60 estimate for 1982 remains unchanged. At this point, then, the stock is selling at about 21x estimated 1982 earnings, midway in its average range of 16x and 25x. The appreciation potential now appears to be about $7, from $33 to $40, and the downside risk is also about $7, from $33 to $26. One might say the stock now is "fairly valued." If the market as a whole were expected to fall, Company D would probably fall with it and the stock should be sold. But if the market was expected to move up, the stock should be held, and possibly even more purchased, for in a real bull market stocks frequently go to the upper end of their historical P-E ranges or even set new high levels, even if there is no change in the company's expected growth rate.[4]

By August the stock reached $41. The estimate of $1.60 still looked good, so the stock was selling at 25.6x earnings, the high end of its usual range, although in some years it has gone higher. But at this point, even if the stock went to 28x earnings, or $45 per share, the upside potential would only be $4 per share, whereas the downside risk from $41 could

---

[4] A *bull* market refers to a rising market. A *bear* market is a falling market.

be about $15 per share ($41 − $26 = $15) or 37 percent if a bear market occurred or if there were some unexpected bad news about the company. The likelihood of a decline all the way to $26 is not too great, however, since late in the summer or early fall, investors are already beginning to project 1983 earnings, which if higher, will make the P-Es look lower.

	EPS	Price	P-E
1982 Estimate......	$1.60	$41	25.6x
1983 Projection.....	1.75	41	23.4x

Another risk is that the company's earnings might be disappointing. That is, they might fall short of the estimate of $1.60. If the 1982 earnings came to only $1.47, the stock would, in fact, already be selling at 28x earnings and look extremely high, and could be expected to fall. Of course, there is no way of knowing what the final earnings figure will be, and the P-E during the year is based only on estimates. However, it is now August and the results of the first two quarters have already been reported, so investors can see the progress the company is making and have more confidence in their estimates.

In the case of Company D, the first two quarters were in line with expectations, and most investors continued to estimate $1.60/share for all of 1982. Nevertheless, with the stock at $41 per share, 25.6x estimated earnings, the downside risk (whether due to a bear market or disappointing earnings) was far greater than the upside potential, and the stock could well be considered high or "overpriced" and should be sold.

We will now define, with qualifications, "low" and "high."

DEFINITIONS

Low   When a stock is selling at the lower end of its normal P-E range (or below) it is *low* or *undervalued*, or *underpriced*.

High   When a stock is selling at the high end of its normal P-E range (or above), it is *high*, or *overvalued*, or *overpriced*.

In the middle of the range it is *fairly valued.*

The qualifications are these. The historical P-E range of a stock can only be considered a reasonable guide to the future P-E range if: (1) the growth rate of earnings is expected to remain the same as it was; (2) nothing has changed in the company or industry to affect one's confidence in his earnings estimates; and (3) the whole market's evaluation of P-Es does not change.

In the case of Company D, the stock sold in an average P-E range of 16x to 25x while it was achieving an earnings growth record averaging 10 percent per year. If Company D is expected to continue to grow at 10 percent, the P-E range of 16x to 25x might be considered reasonable. *But if the growth rate is expected to increase or decrease for an extended period, the P-E range might also be expected to increase or decrease.*

Words such as *overpriced, fully valued, undervalued, cheap,* and the like are constantly used on Wall Street and are best thought of in terms of the price-earnings ratio. The distinction between undervalued and fairly valued, or between fairly valued and fully valued or overvalued, is fuzzy and subject to individual interpretation. Nevertheless, the following charts for Company D might help to put some perspective on these words.

Company D—Historical record and future estimates

	1977	1978	1979	1980	1981	Estimates 1982	1983
EPS..........	$ .91	$ .96	$1.11	$1.25	$1.33	$1.60	$1.75
High price.....	22¾	26⅞	27¾	33¾	34½		
Low price	12¾	15⅜	16⅝	20	21¼		
High P-E......	25x	28x	25x	27x	26x		
Low P-E	14	16	15	16	16		

P-E range	Evaluation
Over 26......	High, overpriced, overvalued.
26–23	Fully priced, fully valued.
23–19	Fairly priced, fairly valued.
19–16	Low, underpriced, undervalued.
16–14	Cheap!
Below 14.....	Very cheap!

Again, these ranges are subjective. Another writer might say the stock is overpriced, or overvalued only above 28x earnings, undervalued only below 17x, and so on.

A would-be investor once asked a Wall Street magnate how to make money in the stock market. The magnate replied, "Buy low and sell high." The would-be investor walked away muttering to himself, ". . . yes, but how do I know what is low and what is high until the end of the year, and then it is too late."

In light of this chapter it is evident that the would-be investor misinterpreted the answer. What the magnate meant was this: Buy a stock only if it is selling at the lower end of its price-earnings range relative to your best estimate of earnings for the present or the coming year, or both. Then the probability of price appreciation is greater than the probability of price decline as the future unfolds. If you already own a stock and it is selling at the high end of its historical P-E range relative to your best estimate of earnings for the present or the coming year, or both, perhaps you should sell the stock, not because it cannot go higher, but because the probability of its going much lower exceeds the probability of its going much higher.

To further emphasize the importance of the P-E and the unimportance of the absolute price level of the stock in determining investment attractiveness, consider the following. How often have you heard someone say, "I would not buy that stock, the price is so high that I could not buy enough shares to matter"? The following example illustrates the fallacy in that statement.

Suppose it is October 1982 and an investor calls his broker and says he has $1,200 to invest. The broker recommends buying ABC Industries, which is currently selling at $60 per share. The broker estimates earnings per share this year, 1982, to be $5.00, but expects earnings to leap ahead by 50 percent next year to $7.50. Therefore, the stock is currently selling at 12x this year's earnings. Further, the broker expects that the price-earnings ratio will remain at about 12x in the future. Thus, the broker is assuming the following:

	Estimated EPS	P-E ratio	Current price
Current: 1982	$5.00	× 12x =	$60
Expected one year out: 1983	$7.50	× 12x =	$90

The investor with $1,200 would then be able to buy "only" 20 shares and make a projected profit of $600, or 50 percent.

	Number of shares		Price per share		Total dollars	
Bought:	20	×	$60	=	$1,200	
Sold:	20	×	90	=	1,800	= Profit of $600 or 50%

But what if ABC had a 5-for-1 stock split in September 1982? In the event of a stock split, the stock price and earnings per share are divided by the amount of the split. So after the split the stock would look like this:

	Estimated EPS	P-E ratio	Current price
Current: 1982	$1.00	× 12x =	$12
Expected one year out: 1983	$1.50	× 12x =	$18

After the split the stock is still selling at 12x estimated earnings, but now the investor with $1,200 can buy 100 shares. ABC's earnings are still expected to grow at 50 percent in 1983; but as a result of the 5-for-1 stock split, the new EPS estimate for 1983 is $1.50 per share ($7.50 ÷ 5). The price-earnings ratio does not change because of the stock split. Therefore, the investor with $1,200 would now have the following projected investment results:

	Number of shares		Price per share		Total dollars
Bought:	100	×	$12	=	$1,200
Sold:	100	×	18	=	1,800 = Profit of $600 or 50%

Note that the projected profit is the same with or without the stock split (i.e. the profit is the same whether the investor bought 20 shares of the higher priced stock or 100 shares of the lower priced stock. What determines the gain (or loss) in a stock is not the initial absolute price level of the stock, but is either 1. or 2. (below), or both together:

1. *The growth in earnings.* Assuming the price-earnings ratio stays the same.

2. *A change in the price-earnings ratio.* Recall that changes in the P-E have nothing to do with whether the stock is selling at $60 or $12; they are related to (*a*) investors' perceptions of expected changes in the future growth rate of the company's earnings and dividends, and (*b*) changes in investors' confidence that their best estimate of earnings growth will prove to be correct.

Changes in forecasts of earnings growth rates as well as changes in confidence can result from almost anything that happens in the world. The following list includes commonly occurring factors but is far from comprehensive:

A. *Changes in the company:*
   1. New products.
   2. New management.
   3. Increasing or decreasing profit margins.

B. *Changes in the industry:*
   1. New product uses or product obsolescence.
   2. Competitors dropping out.
   3. Competitors introducing superior or lower-cost products.

C. *Changes in the economic environment:*
   1. Inflation or deflation in raw materials' cost.
   2. Easing or tightening of government regulatory, taxation, or export/import policies.
   3. Changes in interest rates.
   4. Threat of war, especially in a country producing a vital raw material, such as oil.

16

Wall Street

In the last chapter we looked at the price-earnings ratio as a way of measuring what someone will pay for a share of stock. We saw that P-Es and stock prices fluctuate substantially within or around some presumed true range of value. We also saw that this "true" value can vary depending on one's projection of future earnings and dividends. In this chapter we will look at some of the people and institutions who are directly involved in the investment process and make these projections and P-E judgments, and how this process can benefit you.

Sell-side institutions

On Wall Street we talk about the "buy side of the street" and the "sell side of the street." Sell-side institutions are firms that earn money by taking commissions when selling or buying stocks for customers. Stock brokerage firms are sell-side institutions. There are currently over 2,400 stock brokerage firms in the U.S., ranging from giant Merrill Lynch, Pierce, Fenner & Smith, the largest, to small regional firms whose names are not even familiar to many Wall Streeters. Buy-side institutions include mutual funds, trust companies, pension funds, endowment funds, and others. These are discussed later.

Brokerage firms, to repeat, make money on commissions when they buy and sell shares for customers. For example, if you bought 100 shares of a $30 stock from a large full-service brokerage firm today you would pay a commission of about $68. If you bought 1,000 shares of a $30 stock you would pay a commission of about $450. Your individual stockbroker gets part of that commission and the rest of it goes to his firm. A stockbroker who deals with individuals is called a retail stockbroker. The retail or individual business is distinguished from the institutional business, which refers to mutual funds, pension funds, and the like.

Why should an individual do business with one brokerage firm or another? One reason, of course, is convenience. The firm is near you, the broker is a relative or a close friend. Another, perhaps better, basis for choosing a stockbroker is that you have reason to trust his judgment. Perhaps his recommendations to other people have worked out well.

Judgment in stock picking is, of course, the ultimate test of a broker, but in the stockmarket, judgment can be no better than the information it is based on. Stockbrokers all have numerous sources of information. Sources include: published investment services, such as *Value Line, Standard & Poor's, Moody's Investor Services*; newspapers, such as *The Wall Street Transcript, Barron's*, and *The Wall Street Journal;* magazines, such as *Fortune, Forbes,* and *Dun's Review*. In addition, there are company reports, press releases, and prospectuses, as well as specialized industry publications, such as *Ward's Automotive Reports, Modern Tire Dealer, Electronic News,* and hundreds of others that you can subscribe to or find in libraries but do not appear on news stands. In fact, the amount of information available is far too much for any one person to digest. Consequently, many brokerage firms have staffs of people called security analysts who specialize in analyzing information to help their stockbrokers and clients make buy and sell decisions.

Most big firms have many analysts, each specializing in one or more industries. One analyst, for example, may specialize in analyzing stocks in the automotive and tire industries, another may specialize in insurance stocks, another in computer stocks. These analysts usually devote their full time to researching stocks. They analyze a company and its industry, make forecasts of earnings and dividends for individual companies, and based on that information make judgments about those stocks' outlooks. In most firms the analysts write reports, which are available to their stockbrokers and clients. The reports typically give both the most relevant information and the analyst's judgment about it. Thus the stockbroker, instead of trying to do all his research himself, can read his analysts' reports. He can then use this information in recommending stocks to his clients. Of course, he also uses his own judgment. Just because his firm's analysts are recommending certain stocks does not mean that he has to recommend them to his clients. He may disagree with the judgment of the analyst. Thus a broker's recommendations may come from his firm's research department (security analysts) or they may come from his own sources. The security analysts' salaries are paid by the firm out of the firm's portion of the sales commissions.

Some investors do not want or need advice from stockbrokers. They have their own sources of information and just use a broker to execute their orders. In this case they may prefer to use a *discount* broker. There are a number of brokerage firms, called discount brokers, who charge much lower commissions because they do not keep a staff of analysts and do not offer advice. These firms are also sell-side firms, in that they earn money on commissions when customers buy and sell stocks; but, because they do not provide as much service, they can afford to charge lower commissions. One large discount broker, for example, was charging about $35 for buying or selling 100 shares of a $30 stock and about $110 for a 1,000-share order of a $30 stock at the date of this writing. These commissions are much lower than the full-service firms' commissions. The discount broker, however, gives you less service. For example, a broker at a full-service firm can usually give you much more time to discuss your stock ideas and will often get you a lot of information about stocks that interest you. You can choose whichever broker seems appropriate for you. Obviously, if a broker is recommending stocks that go up and is consistently making money for you, you should stay with him regardless of the size of the commission.

Buy-side institutions

Suppose you want to have your money invested in the stock market but do not want to be actively involved in the decision of which stock or stocks to own. One way to avoid this is to give your broker discretion to buy and sell as she sees fit. Another possible solution would be to put your money into a mutual fund.

There are many kinds of mutual funds. Some funds invest primarily in stocks, others primarily in corporate bonds or municipal bonds, or U.S. Treasury Bills. We will only discuss common stock mutual funds here, but many of the concepts apply to other kinds of funds as well.

A common stock mutual fund is a large pool of assets (common stock or cash), which is owned by all of the individuals putting money into the fund. Each person's ownership is in proportion to the amount of money he or she put in. By having a large pool of money the fund can afford to either hire a staff of investment professionals to do the investing for it, or contract with a mutual fund management company to do its investing. A mutual fund management company is an organization that specializes in investing money and has its own full-time staff of securities analysts and other investment professionals. A mutual fund management company is a buy-side institution.

Buy-side institutions are firms that invest other people's money for them. These institutions make their money by taking a percentage of the assets (money) they manage. That percentage is small, typically ranging from ½ of 1 percent to 1 percent. Suppose, for example, a fund had $100,000,000 in it. If the fee was ½ of 1 percent per year it would be $500,000. With that money, the mutual fund management company pays for its staff of analysts, fund managers, investment library, and so on. Now, suppose the fund manager or managers chose stocks very well and a year later the fund had grown to $160,000,000. In that case the fee at ½ of 1 percent would be $800,000. While the management company could use the entire increased fee to hire more analysts, it is likely that they will keep some of it as increased profits. Thus, since the management fee goes up with the assets, and perhaps even has an incentive bonus for good performance, the management company has the same goal the investors do—to make the fund go up as much as possible.

While mutual fund management firms make the decisions to buy and sell stocks for the funds they manage, they still do their buying and selling through brokerage firms (sell-side institutions) and have to pay a commission. Buy-side institutions are particularly attractive customers for brokerage firms, because they typically have substantially larger sums of money than individuals and thus generate far more commission business over a period of time, even though their large size enables them to get lower commission rates for a given purchase or sale. How brokerage firms compete for this enormous commission business of mutual funds and other buy-side institutions is important and we will come back to it shortly, but first let's look at an example of a mutual fund that invests in common stock and see how it works.

How a mutual fund works

Let's say that Mr. Adams, Mr. Burt, and Mr. Chen formed a mutual fund company and called it ABC Management. ABC Management felt there were a large number of potential investors who would like to invest in high-technology stocks but did not know which companies to buy. So ABC Management decided to start a new common stock mutual fund that specialized in buying high-technology stocks. They called the new fund ABC Technology Fund. Before they could accept money for the fund from the public, it was first necessary to register with the SEC and state agencies and publish a prospectus. Assuming all the legalities have been taken care of, ABC would now advertise the fund and accept money for it by selling shares of ABC Technology Fund.

ABC Management initially sold shares of ABC Technology Fund at $10 per share on March 1, 1980. On that day five individuals bought some shares of the fund, as follows:

	Amount invested	Price per share March 1	Number of shares purchased March 1
Mr. Davis	$1,000	$10	100
Ms. Evans	500	10	50
Mr. Frank	1,500	10	150
Mrs. Gibbs	1,000	10	100
Mrs. Hunt	2,000	10	200
	$6,000 =	10 ×	600 Shares

Thus on March 1, 1980, there were 600 shares of ABC Technology Fund outstanding and there was $6,000 to invest. On the morning of March 2, the fund manager of ABC Technology Fund called a brokerage firm and bought the following five stocks for the fund.

Stock	Price paid	Number of shares purchased	Amount invested
SFC Corporation	$50	40	$2,000
Smith Electronics.	80	25	2,000
General Computer. . . .	10	100	1,000
Data Electrix.	50	10	500
National Robotics.	25	16	400
Remaining cash*			100
Total worth of fund . . .			$6,000

* The example ignores commissions.

Do not confuse shares of ABC Technology Fund with the shares of SFC, Smith Electronics, and so on, owned by this Fund. Smith Electronics, for example, has 150 million shares outstanding, 25 of which are owned by ABC Technology Fund. ABC Technology Fund has 600 shares outstanding, 100 of which are owned by Mr. Davis, 50 by Ms. Evans, and so on. Although Davis, Evans, and so on do not directly own shares of SFC, they do own shares of SFC indirectly through their ownership of ABC Technology Fund. When people talk about owning shares of a mutual fund, they are talking about owning shares like ABC Technology Fund. They are not talking about the shares of SFC and the others held by the fund. However, an individual can certainly call a broker and buy shares of SFC or Smith Electronics for himself, which he then owns directly. Thus it is possible that Davis can both own some shares of SFC directly and own some indirectly through his ownership of ABC Technology Fund.

Returning to ABC Technology Fund, by the end of the day three stocks had gone up, one had declined, and one was unchanged. The next table shows what the fund was worth at the end of the day. The amount of gain assumed in each stock is much larger than would normally occur in one day's trading, but the larger figures make the example easier to follow. Also, the cash would have been invested in something that earned interest, but the amount of interest earned in a day is small enough to be ignored in this example.

Stock	Price at end of day	Number of shares held	Amount invested
SFC Corporation	$ 65	40	$2,600
Smith Electronics......	100	25	2,500
General Computer.....	9	100	900
Data Electrix..........	70	10	700
National Robotics	25	16	400
Cash.................			100
Total worth of fund			$7,200

At the end of March 2, the total net worth of ABC Technology Fund was $7,200. Since there are 600 shares of ABC outstanding, we say the *net asset value* per share of ABC Technology Fund is now $12:

$$\frac{\text{Net asset value}}{\text{Shares outstanding}} = \frac{\$7,200}{600} = \$12/\text{Share}$$

Since ABC initially sold shares at $10 per share and they are now worth $12 per share, each share has appreciated by 20 percent—not surprising since the fund's net assets appreciated by 20 percent, from $6,000 to $7,200. Thus, each of the original five investors has seen each's investment go up by 20 percent. For example, look at Davis's account:

Original
 investment: 100 shares × $10/share = $1,000
Current worth: 100 shares × $12/share = $1,200 = 20 percent gain

With the net asset value per share of $12 at the end of the day, ABC Management would be willing to sell new shares of ABC Technology Fund the next day for $12 per share. Similarly, ABC Management would be willing to redeem shares of the fund for $12 per share from Davis, Evans, and the others. This is called an *open-ended fund.* An open-ended fund is one that is always willing to sell new fund shares or redeem outstanding fund shares at the current net asset value per share, usually the value at the close of that day. When more people are buying fund shares than redeeming them, there is obviously an increase in the amount of cash, which the fund manager can use to buy more shares of stock for the fund. If there has been a net redemption of fund shares (more shares redeemed than new fund shares sold), the fund manager will have to sell shares of stock from the fund to raise cash to meet the redemption if there is not enough cash available. In addition to buying new shares of stock when more money comes into the fund, and selling stock when shares of the fund are redeemed, the fund manager can also change stocks within the fund. For instance, he may think Data Electrix has gone as high as it is likely to go, so he would sell it and buy another stock he feels is more likely to go up. Or he may decide he was wrong in buying General Computer and want to sell it before it goes any lower and reinvest the proceeds in something more attractive.

A *closed-end fund*, unlike an open-end fund, does not usually issue new fund shares or redeem outstanding shares. In a closed-end fund, the number of fund shares outstanding is usually fixed forever. There are some exceptions. Some closed-end funds will redeem existing shares but not issue new shares. Some closed-end funds will issue new shares but only at specific times, which may be less than once a year. Thus, in most cases, if you want to buy some shares of a closed-end fund you have to find someone who already owns them and is willing to sell them to you. Similarly, if you want to sell your shares in the kind of closed-end fund where the management company does not redeem them, you must find someone to buy them. Thus, closed-end funds are usually traded over the counter, much like stocks, and the price of such a fund will vary depending on what people are willing to buy or sell it for. That price is usually close to the net asset value per share of the fund. Open-ended funds, of course, are not traded because the fund management company is always willing to buy or sell directly to you.

Load versus no-load funds

Mutual funds are either *load funds* or *no-load funds*. In a no-load fund, the management company takes its entire fee, called a management fee, as a percentage of the assets. For example, if a management fee were 1 percent per year, the management company might take 1/365 of 1 percent of the assets every day. In some funds the management fee may vary depending on the performance of the fund. For example, the management fee might be 0.5 percent of the assets per year, but go up to 0.6 percent if the fund's net asset value appreciates by a specified percent in any year.

In a *load fund*, the management company also takes an annual management fee; but in addition, when you first put your money in, the management company takes a one-time-only "load" or sales charge to cover the expenses and commissions of the people selling the fund to you. This load varies substantially by fund, but is typically about 4 to 8 percent of the amount of money you put in. For example, assume you had $10,000 you wanted to use to buy shares of a mutual fund, and you were deciding between a no-load fund, which had a net asset value per share of $10, and a load fund, which also coincidently had a net asset value per share of $10. If you bought shares of the no-load fund, you would be able to purchase 1,000 shares with your $10,000. If you bought the load fund, you would only get 920 shares for your $10,000 because 8 percent or $800 would be taken out as a sales charge. Some people think that the management fee of a load fund is smaller than for a no-load fund because of the load, but this is generally not so. The range of annual management fees for load funds tends to be about the same as for no-load funds.

There are no inherent advantages to load funds. The load is not buying you superior management. The purpose of load is primarily (if not entirely) to pay the sales charge. Load funds are often sold through stockbrokers or through other large sales staffs, and the load goes to pay the brokers or sales staff. Load funds are best suited for persons who do not know about mutual funds or how to contact no-load funds and what to ask them. The load fund salesman can bring his expertise to these people and help them decide what kind of fund would be most appropriate for them. No-load funds are typically sold by putting advertisements in newspapers and magazines and on TV, which invite you to call the management company directly and inquire about the fund and obtain a prospectus.

Choosing between a mutual fund and investing yourself

The decision of whether to choose stocks yourself with the help of your broker or whether to buy a mutual fund is a personal one and may be based on how much money you have to invest, how much time you want to devote to it, and your attitude toward risk. There are advantages to both methods of investing.

Advantages of mutual funds include:

1. *Diversification of risk.* Whereas an individual can only buy a limited number of stocks without running up big commissions, mutual funds can easily diversify substantially because of the large amount of money they manage. The advantage of diversification, of course, is that if you bought only one or two stocks and they both went down you could incur a substantial loss. Through diversification, one or two unexpected losses will not have a major impact, and, in fact, might not even be noticed if the rest of the stocks in the fund go up.
2. *Bookkeeping.* Most mutual funds keep track of your fund for you, and regular mailings tell you about your gain or loss, your tax consequences, and the like.

3. *Lower commission rates when buying stocks.* Because of their large size, mutual funds usually get lower commission rates from brokers.
4. *Access to expertise.* Mutual fund management company research departments devote their full efforts to working for their funds. Their research reports and stock recommendations are not available to stockbrokers or to the public, as are brokerage firms' research reports and recommendations. Further, buy-side institutions have access to most brokerage firm research departments and thus can choose the best of all research available.
5. *Family-of-funds concept.* Many mutual fund management companies offer a variety of no-load funds, including growth stock funds, income stock funds, corporate bond funds, municipal bond funds, money market funds, and so on. Such management companies usually allow you to switch your money back and forth between funds free or at minimal cost. Again, all the bookkeeping is done for you by the management company.

Advantages of individual investments:

1. *Concentration of investment.* If you have a strong conviction that a certain stock is going up, you can put all or as much of your money into it as you wish.
2. *Control of investment.* Buying stocks yourself gives you total control over the nature and diversification of your stocks at all times. For example, you could quickly move from energy stocks to computer stocks or to a diversified portfolio. In addition, you can buy or sell stocks any time the market is open. Open-end mutual funds are usually bought or sold (redeemed) only at the end-of-day price.
3. *Access to information.* Individual investors are free to call their broker for information or advice on their stocks anytime. Mutual fund management companies generally do not give investment advice beyond the information provided in the prospectus.

Other buy-side institutions

Pension funds.   Many corporations have set up pension funds for their employees. The pension arrangement usually specifies that when an employee retires, the company will pay him a certain monthly or yearly pension as long as he or his spouse lives. In order to have money available for those future payments, companies set aside a certain amount of money each year, based on the number of employees, their ages, and other factors. That money is put into the pension fund. While that money is in the fund it can be invested as the company sees fit, within the guidelines of federal laws governing pension funds. Most pension funds are invested in stocks and bonds. The reason companies like to have their pension money in the stock market is that the more profit they make in the market, the less they have to put into the fund from the company's cash. Pension funds are sometimes managed by the company sponsoring the fund, but more frequently the sponsor has the money managed by an investment management firm.

There are many investment management firms that specialize in pension funds. However, many mutual fund management companies also manage pension funds. The investment expertise needed to manage mutual funds can also be applied to pension funds. Pension funds also are run by trust companies and trust departments of large banks. Pension fund management companies, like mutual fund management companies, charge a management fee. Such fees are typically in the range of 3/10 of 1 percent to 5/10 of 1 percent per year, but some are higher or lower. Since pension funds, like mutual funds, often amount to hundreds of millions or billions of dollars, even this small fee can be enough to maintain a full-time staff of analysts and other investment personnel.

Trust companies.   A trust company is also an investment management company that makes its money by taking a small percentage of the assets of the money it invests. A trust company typically manages money for personal trusts and estates, charities, pension funds, and others. For example, a deceased person's will might specify that the money be invested by a trust company and only a small amount be paid monthly to the beneficiaries. While most estates are small compared to hundred million dollar pension funds and mutual funds, if you manage a lot of them you can earn enough money from small fees to pay for a professional staff of investment personnel. Thus trust companies, like pension fund management companies and mutual fund management companies, are buy-side institutions—that is, they make investment decisions on stocks and bonds for the benefit of their clients, and take a small percent of the assets under management as a fee.

Almost all buy-side institutions use brokerage firms to execute buy and sell orders. In recent years a few buy-side institutions have bought their own seat on the stock exchange so they can do their own trading, rather than give the commission to brokers, but these exceptions are few.

Other buy-siders.   University endowments, insurance companies, charity, and private foundations are some additional buy-side institutions. Many of their pools of money amount to hundreds of millions of dollars and thus are big enough to enable the institution to maintain a professional investment staff and operate independently. Smaller endowments or foundations that could not afford to maintain their own investment staff might pay an existing management company to do it for them.

The relationship of buy-side and sell-side institutions

Let us now return to the question of how the brokerage houses compete for the commission business of the large institutions. One important factor is their ability to continually execute orders at favorable prices. While any brokerage firm can take a small order to the specialist on the floor of the exchange and have it executed, a large block of stock, say 20,000 shares, might be difficult to buy or sell without forcing the price of the stock up or down substantially. Thus a brokerage firm that keeps its eyes and ears open may know where there are buyers or sellers for a big block of stock and be able to execute an order faster or at a better price than a less well-informed broker. Similarly, the broker may be willing to buy all or part of the block for itself if a buyer cannot be found when a client wants to sell a large block. This is called "positioning" the stock. A brokerage firm that is willing to position stocks is likely to get called first on big orders.

A second way brokerage firms compete for institutional business, and more important for our purposes, is by providing research services. Many brokerage firms maintain research staffs, which include: security analysts, who research individual stocks and industries; market analysts, who research ways to predict the moves in the stock market as a whole; and economic analysts, who research and make forecasts on the economy as a whole and on individual segments of the economy, and how they might influence the stock market. This research is then made available to the analysts at the buy-side institutions. The buy-side analysts look at all this research material and choose what is most helpful to them, and whichever brokerage firms have been most helpful are then paid for this research by getting the most commission business. Thus, each buy-side institution can use its commission business to buy research from whichever brokerage firms it wants in whatever proportion it wants.

The question arises: If buy-side institutions have their own research staffs, why do they need research from sell-side (brokerage firm) analysts? The answer is that there is so much information available to analyze on so many stocks that it is not practical for a buy-side research department to do it all by itself—it would need a gigantic staff. Thus buy-side analysts can cover more companies and more industries more thoroughly with the assistance of the sell-side analysts. This assistance is not absolutely necessary, but it is widely used because it is very helpful for the buy-side institution that wants to cover a very broad list of stocks and still cover them in depth. As a result of the extra commission business generated by buy-side institutions, brokerage firms are able to keep much larger staffs of analysts than they might otherwise keep just to assist their stockbrokers who deal with individuals (the retail business).

The influence of research on stock prices

The intensive stock research that results from both the institutional and retail needs can have a strong influence on stock prices. The most obvious way is when an analyst disseminates some significant information about a company that was not previously known or understood. Stocks can react quickly to important new information. More typically, though, stocks react more gradually. For example, assume a brokerage firm analyst has written a research recommendation which was then sent to buy-side institutions' analysts and portfolio managers. While the portfolio managers might buy the stock immediately on the recommendation of the brokerage firm analyst, more likely they will ask their own analysts to review the report or do their own research on the company. After that, the portfolio manager might still want to watch the stock for a while to get familiar with its trading pattern. Thus, the original analyst's buy recommendation may in fact have had an impact on the stock, but because it occurred over a period of months, it is hard to judge if that recommendation alone caused the stock to move or if other developments were involved.

Another important way research can influence stock prices is as follows. Because the best research analysts are able to generate substantial institutional brokerage commissions for the firms they work for, many brokerage firm analysts become particularly knowledgeable on certain stocks. While they may not be right every time on their earnings forecasts or buy or sell recommendations, such analysts often develop a strong following on Wall Street, and their changes in recommendations or earnings forecasts can impact stock prices immediately, just from their reputation.

When a lot of information about a company and the analyses of future earnings potential of that company are widely disseminated among investors, they should be better able to anticipate future company results and therefore have a better feel for what a stock is worth. On Wall Street, we often say a stock is trading "efficiently" if it is intensely followed (researched) by many analysts (i.e., if a lot of information is disseminated to many potential investors). On the other hand, it may be harder to make confident buy or sell judgments on such efficient stocks because the price at any time, in theory, has already moved up or down to reflect the well-informed judgments of a large number of investors. To what extent intensive research impacts stock prices is a subject of great debate on Wall Street.

How to take advantage of Wall Street research

Since the reader of this book presumably does not have time to do in-depth stock market research, how can you take advantage of all the research being done? One way is to put your money into a mutual fund that does maintain a full time professional staff. For those who prefer to make their own investment decisions, one thing to do is to choose a broker who works for a firm that has a large research department. This way you should have access to reports written by that firm's analysts. You could then call your broker and ask if there are any recent reports available on stocks of interest to you, and also ask him to send you any recent reports the firm has written recommending any other stocks, or about the outlook for the market in general.

Also, you might split your business between two or more brokers and thereby have access to two or more research departments. You will also find that you can walk into many brokerage firms and find research reports on individual stocks or on the market in general that are free for the taking. Research reports from many brokerage firms are also printed in a newspaper called *The Wall Street Transcript*. Other publications, such as *The Wall Street Journal* and *Barron's*, often make reference to brokerage firms' research conclusions. In addition to brokerage firms' research departments, there are also research services available from *Value Line*, Moody's Investor Service, and Standard & Poor, Inc. These are often available in public libraries or by subscription. Some of these are quite expensive, but there are also less expensive investment magazines and services, which you will find advertised in *Barron's* and other publications.

17

Making an earnings estimate

Since the price of a stock relates to a large extent to the future earnings potential of a company, forecasting future earnings is an important part of investment analysis. It is one of the primary tasks of security analysts, besides, of course, making buy and sell recommendations. How forecasts are made is a subject for a whole book and a lifetime of experience. We will look at it briefly here, first to increase the readers' appreciation of the discussion about Polaroid in the next chapter, and second, because these techniques are useful in one's own analysis.

The best place to start when making an earnings forecast for a company is by looking at what happened to that company or to similar companies in the past, and then try to determine what will change in the future to make the company grow faster or slower. The analyst looks first at sales growth and then at expenses or profit margins. The following illustration is a real-world example.

Let's assume it is March 1977 and we want to make an earnings estimate for the full year 1977 for Polaroid. We will look first at Polaroid's 1976 income statement and then we will forecast changes.

In the following presentations, each line is numbered for easy reference to the subsequent comments.

POLAROID

Line	(1)	1976 Income Statement (from Annual Report)		
	(2)	($Millions Except per Share)		
	(3)	Sales..........................	$950.0	
	(4)	Less: Cost of sales	511.8	
	(5)	Less: Selling, advertising, research, distribution and administrative expense.................	294.9	
	(6)	Equals: Profit from operations......	143.3	
	(7)	Operating profit margin............		15.1%
	(8)	Plus: Other income (mostly interest)	14.4	
	(9)	Less: Interest expense	3.3	
	(10)	Equals: Profit before tax...........	154.4	
	(11)	Less: Federal, state, and foreign income taxes	74.7	
	(12)	Tax rate		48.3%
	(13)	Net earnings	$ 79.7	
	(14)	Shares outstanding 32,855,000		
	(15)	Earnings per share	$ 2.43	

The following comments help clarify the terms above.

Line (1) The numbers are all taken from the annual report but the layout here is modified slightly.

(2) (**$ Millions Except per Share**):   This tells you that each of the dollar figures below (in the statement) is in millions except for the last line, which is expressed per share. For example, sales were $950 million or $950,000,000. Cost of sales were $511.8 or $511,800,000. But earnings per share were $2.43, not $2.43 million.

(4) **Cost of sales:**   This is what Polaroid calls cost of goods sold.

(5) **Selling, advertising, research, engineering, distribution, and administrative expense:**   This looks like what we normally call Selling, general, and administrative expense, but Polaroid tells us that research and engineering are also in here. Notice that depreciation expense is not included as a separate line. This probably means some of the depreciation is in each of the expense items (4) and (5), but we don't know how much is in each.

(6) **Profit from operations:**   We have not used this term before but it is obviously the profit calculated before considering interest expense and other income (i.e., the profit earned just from making and selling products).

(7) **Operating profit margin:**   This is profit from operations divided by sales. It is very similar to the pretax profit margin discussed in Chapter 4, but here it excludes interest income

and interest expense. Thus, it is an even better measure of the underlying profitability of Polaroid's manufacturing and selling of goods.

(8) **Other income (mostly interest):**   Primarily comes from the interest earned on the Marketable Securities found on the balance sheet (not shown here).

(9), (10), and (11):   Mean exactly the same as they did in Chapters 2 and 3.

(12) **Tax rate:**   The actual tax paid, line 11, divided by the profit before tax, line 10.

(13), (14), and (15):   Same meaning as throughout the book.

Now let's look at how the analyst projects 1977 earnings specifically, and future growth in general.

Line   (3)   **Sales:**   A look at the past 10 years' sales from old company annual reports or from investment service data, such as Standard & Poor's or the *Value Line* indicates that Polaroid's sales growth averaged 10.7 percent per year. The best year was the economic boom year 1973, when sales were up 22.2 percent. The worst year was the recession year 1970, when sales declined 3 percent. This is not surprising since one would expect consumers to be more cautious about spending in a recession, when unemployment is high and people are worried about layoffs. Interestingly, sales were up in the 1974–75 recession years, but it turns out all the growth was foreign, where Polaroid was expanding rapidly. Domestic (U.S.) sales were almost unchanged in 1974 and 1975.

Factors affecting the 1977 sales outlook include the following.

Favorable : (*a*) U.S. economy expected to be expanding as recovery from the 1974–75 recession continues; (*b*) the increase in cameras sold in 1976 (stated in annual report) suggests film sales will be up in 1977; (*c*) the expected introduction of a Polaroid movie system late in the year should add substantial sales.

Unfavorable: (*a*) Kodak introduced an instant camera in 1976. Thus, Polaroid should lose some camera sales it would otherwise have had; (*b*) Polaroid is unlikely to raise prices in the year it is meeting competition for the first time.

Conclusion: In an economic recovery year, sales should grow more than average, but sales lost to competition will hurt. On the other hand, if a movie camera is introduced it could add importantly to sales as dealers stock up.

Estimate: Sales up between 11 percent and 14 percent.

(4) **Cost of sales:** Too hard to project for this company. There is no way to know how much of which raw materials it buys and how much it pays.

(5) **Selling, advertising, etc:** Likely to be up more than sales. Competition from Kodak suggests selling and advertising expenses will be up more than normal. Expected introduction of movie camera suggests big increases in research and engineering expenses.

(6) **Profit from operations:** We cannot estimate this directly because we have no estimate of Cost of sales. But we can estimate it indirectly by estimating the profit margin first and multiplying sales by profit margin.

(7) **Operating profit margin:** *Favorable influences:* Big increase in SX-70 film sales should help margins as Polaroid becomes more efficient at making it, and because overhead (fixed costs) stay the same despite unit sales increases.

Unfavorable influences: (*a*) increased research and engineering on the movie camera whether or not it is introduced; (*b*) probable excess cost on early movie systems if it is introduced. This is normal at the introductory stage of a major new product for many companies; (*c*) likelihood of no price increases to offset cost increases. This is due to competitive threat from Kodak.

Conclusion: operating profit margin will probably decline or be flat at best compared to 1976.

Estimate: 13% to 15%.

(8) **Other income:** Most of this is interest income and is almost sure to be up. Polaroid began 1976 with $158 million in marketable securities, and is beginning 1977 with $205 million in marketable securities, almost 30 percent higher. Also, the interest rate received is likely to be higher since interest rates have tended to move up in economic recoveries in recent years. Of course, some of the money could be spent, but since earnings should be up this year much of the spending needs will come from current earnings.

Estimate: $18–$20 million.

(9) **Interest expense:** According to the footnotes in the annual report, all of Polaroid's borrowing and interest expense are foreign. Since foreign business is continuing to grow, let's assume another increase.

Guess: $4–$6 million.

(10) **Profit before tax:** Derived using above numbers.

(11) **Taxes:** Derived using estimated tax rate.

(12)   **Tax rate:**   Assume it remains the same because we have no basis for assuming a change.
   Estimate: 48.3%.
(13)   **Net earnings:**   Derived.
(14)   **Shares outstanding:**   No reason to expect change.
(15)   **Earnings per share:**   Derived.

Since we have used ranges for most of the estimates above, the "analyst's worksheet" below will project both an optimistic earnings estimate using the high ends of the ranges, and a pessimistic estimate using the low ends of the ranges. Note that in the estimates we are dropping the number to the right of the decimal since our estimates could not be that accurate anyway.

Analyst's Worksheet
1977 Estimated Earnings

			Pessimistic	Optimistic
		Sales change from 1976 level......	Up 11%	Up 14%
Line	(3)	Sales	$1,055	$1,083
	(4)	Cost of sales..........	No attempted estimate— for lines 4 and 5—go to operating profit margin, line 7.	
	(5)	Selling, adv. etc.		
	(7)	Operating profit margin	13%	15%
	(6)	Operating profit........ $	137	$ 162
	(8)	Other income	18	20
	(9)	Interest expense.......	4	6
	(10)	Profit before Tax (derived)........	151	176
	(11)	Tax rate..............	48.3%	48.3%
	(12)	Taxes (derived)	73	85
	(13)	Net earnings.......... $	78	$ 91
	(14)	Shares outstanding	32.855	32.855
	(15)	Earnings per share .... $	2.37	$ 2.77

We have now calculated an estimated earnings range of $2.37 to $2.77 per share, compared to the $2.43 earned in 1976. As we will see in Chapter 18, we could use both estimates and try to make a stock market judgment assuming either was equally probable. A second alternative would be to make our estimate in the middle of the range, which would be $2.57 per share. A third alternative is to use our judgment and ask what looks best. In this case, the low-end estimate is actually lower than the 1976 earnings and, although it was derived using seemingly realistic assumptions, it somehow just looks too low in what should be a good economic year. Thus, we could choose the high-end estimate of $2.77, or we could take a figure somewhere between the midpoint and the high end, say $2.65 or $2.70. Thus, we might present our conclusion as follows:

> We think Polaroid is going to earn about $2.65 per share in an expected range of $2.50 to $2.75. We do want to call attention, however, to the possibility that the impact of Kodak's competitive threat and costs associated with the expected movie camera introduction could cause earnings to be roughly flat or even decline slightly from the 1976 level.

The long-term growth forecast

The same type of reasoning process is used to make a long-term earnings growth forecast. The analyst looks at the past earnings growth and tries to forecast what will change, given the changing economic and competitive environment. As one projects further out beyond one year, however, the estimates become more subjective. For example, if an analyst was asked in March 1977 to make a five-year projection of Polaroid's earnings growth rate, he would not be likely to do a detailed income statement projection as we did above. Rather, he might reason as follows. Polaroid's growth rate in the past 10 years averaged 10.7 percent per year. What could change that? First, the introduction by Kodak of an instant camera should definitely hurt Polaroid, for two reasons. First, because some people will buy Kodak's camera and film instead of Polaroid's, and second, because the competition between them will probably prevent Polaroid from raising prices as freely as in the past for fear of losing more sales to Kodak. However, with lower prices, perhaps more people will buy cameras and hence more film will be consumed. Also, with both Polaroid and Kodak advertising instant cameras, an increased consumer awareness could lead to increased sales. Even with lower prices, increased sales could lead to greater profits. Thus, there is both an optimistic and a pessimistic way to look at the Kodak introduction.

What else will affect Polaroid's growth rate? The introduction of a home movie system could accelerate Polaroid's sales and earnings growth if it is successful—or hurt earnings growth if it fails. So, what is the likelihood that the instant movie system will be successful? Photography industry statistics show that home movie camera sales have had almost no growth for 10 years. But will the idea of "instant" developing increase its attractiveness? That's hard to judge. Conclusion: The Kodak competition and my uncertainty about the instant movie camera make me think Polaroid's growth rate is more likely to slow than to accelerate in the next five years. Thus I'll guess earnings growth will average between 6 percent and 10 percent, and I'll use 8 percent if you want a single best estimate. This does not mean exactly 8 percent growth each year. Growth will continue to be better in good years and worse in bad years. Of course, the analyst could have considered many other factors too, such as economic assumptions for consumer spending.

The current year's earnings estimate (and ultimately the actual earnings) are important, first because they give you a benchmark along the way to see if your long-term estimate is reasonable, and second because they give you numbers against which to apply a price-earnings ratio to determine whether you think the stock is currently overpriced, underpriced, or fairly valued. Recall that the P-E one should pay for a stock is related to the expected earnings growth rate.

Having made a full year's earnings estimate, the next thing the analyst does is look at each quarter's reported earnings as a benchmark to see if the full-year estimate is reasonable or has to be changed, and if so, reassess his or her opinion of the stock.

Quarterly earnings analysis

All publicly traded companies are required to report quarterly earnings, usually within 45 days of the end of the quarter, except at year-end when they are allowed 90 days. Most companies, in fact, report earnings well before the 45 or 90 day limit. A summary of the report, usually just sales, earnings, and earnings per share, is published in *The Wall Street Journal*, the *New York Times*, and other major newspapers. A more detailed report is mailed to stockholders, filed with the SEC, and is usually published in Moody's and in Standard & Poor's news services.

A company's year does not have to coincide with the calendar year. While a majority of companies use a calendar year, it is very common to find companies that end their year on January 31 or February 28, and so on. Retail stores, for example, frequently use a January 31 year because they want to have their after-Christmas returns in the same year as the Christmas sales. We refer to the company's year as its fiscal year. Sears, Roebuck's year, for example, ends on January 31. Thus the year that ended on January 31, 1980, could be called "fiscal 1980" even though 11 of the months fell into 1979. Other people would call that year "fiscal 1979" even though it ended in January 1980. When you are talking about a company whose fiscal year is not a calendar year, you have to be careful to specify exactly which 12 months you are referring to. Polaroid uses a calendar year, so its first quarter ends March 31, its second quarter June 30, and so on. Since the Sears year ends January 31, its first fiscal quarter, or just first quarter, ends April 30. In Wall Street reports, it is common to abbreviate first quarter as 1Q, second quarter as 2Q, etc. 2Q does not mean two quarters; it means just the second quarter. We will use that convention in the remainder of this book.

When a company reports its quarterly results, it usually compares them to the same quarter a year ago. For most companies that is a more valid indication of a company's progress than a comparison to the previous quarter. For example, a retail store would have its biggest earnings in the calendar fourth quarter (Oct-Nov-Dec) every year as a result of the Christmas season. Thus, the best indication of the store's growth would be to compare its fourth quarter to the previous year's fourth quarter. To compare the 4Q to the 3Q would be meaningless, because the 4Q is always seasonally higher. But it would be fair to compare the 3Q with other years' 3Qs. For companies whose business is not seasonal, it would be fair to compare sequential quarters.

Since quarters are relatively short periods of time, it is possible that special circumstances could affect the sales or earnings and make it unfair to compare the quarter to any other quarter. Nevertheless, it is all the investor has to go on so one should look at it as closely as possible to monitor the company's progress. We will do that frequently in Chapter 18 to watch Polaroid's progress relative to our expectations, so let's learn how to analyze a quarter now by looking at Polaroid's actual results in the first quarter of 1977, which we can abbreviate 1Q 1977. Since we made a forecast for the full year 1977 earlier in the chapter, we can use the 1Q 1977 to see if our forecast still looks reasonable.

POLAROID
Quarterly Results
(Millions except per Share and Percent)

Line (1)		1Q 1976	1Q 1977	% change
(3)	Sales......................	$182.1	$191.8	+ 5.4%
(4)	Cost of goods	103.4	99.5	− 3.8
(5)	Selling, adv., etc.	61.5	68.0	+ 10.6
(6)	Operating profit..............	17.1	24.4	+ 42.2
(7)	Operating profit margin........	9.4%	12.7%	Good gain
(8)	Other income			
	(mostly interest)	3.3	3.9	+ 18
(9)	Interest expense..............	.4	1.0	+150
(10)	Pretax profit..................	20.0	27.3	+ 36.8
(11)	Pretax margin	11.0%	14.2%	
(12)	Taxes	9.4	13.3	
(13)	Tax rate	47.0%	48.6%	
(14)	Net profit	$ 10.6	$ 14.0	+ 32.7
(15)	Shares outstanding	32.855	32.855	
(16)	Earnings per share ....$	.32	$ .43	+ 34.4

This is a complete display of Polaroid's 1Q earnings comparison. As we will see when we go through it line by line, it is not necessary to look at every item and as a result we will show a condensed version below that shows enough of the essentials to lead us to the same conclusion as if we looked at every figure. It is part of the analyst's job to eliminate the unessential and call attention to those numbers which are useful indicators.

Line   (1)   *(Millions except per Share and Percent):*   This means that all figures are in millions except the profit margins, the tax rates, the changes, and the earnings per share. Now that the reader knows that we talk in *millions* for Polaroid, we can drop that comment.

(2) *1Q 1976 . . .:*   Analysts commonly present quarterly earnings in this format, first showing last year's quarter, then this year's quarter, and then a column showing the change or comments. We will use this format in Chapter 18.

(3) *Sales:*   Up 5.4 percent in the 1Q. This is well below our forecast of 11–14 percent sales growth for the year, and thus may indicate that the Kodak competition is having a more serious impact than expected. Perhaps our full-year estimate will have to be revised downward. Even so, we were expecting the biggest sales gains later in the year, after the expected introduction of the movie camera, so let's not make any change yet.

(4) and (5):   As in the full-year forecast, these items are too difficult to forecast and it is easier to look at them together— by simply looking below at the *Operating profit margin.*

(6) and (7) *Operating profit:*   Up 42 percent even though sales were only up 5.4 percent. Thus the *Operating profit margin* was up from 9.4 percent to 12.7 percent. This is very encouraging. When sales are up a lot, one normally expects profits to be up more, because some expenses are fixed; but this was a very small sales gain, which produced a very strong earnings gain. However, the 1Q 1977 operating margin of 12.7 percent was still below our estimated range of 13–15 percent. But then, if you look back at Polaroid's history, you discover that the 1Q margin was usually the lowest of the year except in recession years. Thus, we can say the operating margin was in line with expectations.

(8) *Other income:*   Up, in line with expectations.

(9) *Interest expense:*   Up 150 percent, more than our full-year forecast; but in this case the actual dollars involved are small, compared to the *Operating profit* and so are not worth changing.

(10) *Pretax profit:*   Up slightly less than *Operating profit* because of the sharp increase in *Interest expense*, and the lesser increase in *Other income.*

(11) *Pretax margin:*   Notice that this was up 3.2 percentage points and the *operating margin* was up 3.3 percentage points. These margins tend to behave similarly because the *Other income* and the *Interest expense* are small dollar figures. Thus, to simplify the presentation, we could leave out lines 8 and 9. Since we are also dropping lines 4 and 5, we can now jump directly from *Sales* to *Pretax Income* and

Pretax margin without altering our conclusion about the quarter.

(12) and (13) *Taxes and tax rate:* Since one obviously determines the other, there is no need to present both. We will choose to show the tax rate because that is the most helpful way to see if our full-year projections are on target. It also shows us—quickly—if a major change in the tax rate has distorted the quarterly earnings.

(14) *Net profit:* Up 32.7 percent. This is slightly less than the 36.8 percent gain in *Pretax profit* and is due to the slightly higher tax rate.

(15) *Shares outstanding:* This has not changed at all in recent years at Polaroid, and thus can also be dropped from the presentation unless a change occurs.

(16) *Earnings per share:* Up 34.4 percent. If each quarter's earnings were up 34.4 percent, the full-year 1977 EPS would be $3.27/share, well above our forecasted range of $2.37 to $2.77. Perhaps we should revise our estimate upward, but two things must be kept in mind. First, 1Q earnings are seasonally unimportant (i.e., are usually the lowest of the year for Polaroid), and thus, a few cents per share difference can badly distort the comparison percentage. Second, the disappointing sales gain suggests that we should be cautious about changing our earnings estimate because it may be an indication that earnings will be disappointing (i.e., up less than expected) in later quarters. Note finally that EPS were up 34.4 percent but net earnings were up only 32.7 percent. Since the number of shares outstanding did not change, the entire difference must be due to rounding.

It now seems that we can come to the same conclusions about the quarter even though we use the short report form shown below.

POLAROID
First Quarter Results

	1Q 1976	1Q 1977	Percent change
Sales............	$182.1	$191.8	+ 5.4%
Pretax margin	11.0%	14.2%	
Pretax profit......	$ 20.0	$ 27.3	+36.8
Tax rate	47.0%	48.6%	
Net profit.........	$ 10.6	$ 14.0	+32.7
EPS............	$ .32	$ .43	

We will use this shortened quarterly report form in Chapter 18 unless circumstances suggest otherwise.

18

What makes stocks go up—An 18-year history of Polaroid's stock

The price of a stock, with perhaps some rare exceptions, is not determined by a small group of wealthy investors, nor is it set by a brokerage firm, a mutual fund, a big bank or a trust company. Nor is its value determined by some guru's computer-driven statistical "valuation" model. As much as some people look for simple explanations of things they don't understand, there is rarely a simple or hidden explanation of stock price behavior. Rather, the price of a stock reflects the "market's" opinion (i.e., the anonymous result of the opinion of everyone who is thinking about that stock).

Actually, in the very short run, the price of a stock can be set by one person. For example, if someone buys a stock heavily and pushes it way up, he has obviously determined the price. But as soon as he is finished buying, perhaps even before he is finished buying, stockholders who now see the stock as overpriced will begin to sell and cause the price to fall back down to its "true" range of value. Such occurrences however are short-lived.

It is the thesis of this book that the true value of a share of stock relates to the value of the current dividend plus all future dividends that an investor can expect to receive from that share. Many investors, of course, are not actually interested in receiving present or future dividends. They just want the stock to go up. But ultimately, what is going to make it go up is its value in terms of current and future potential dividends.

203

For experienced investors, what a stock is worth, or how high or low it may go, is to a large extent an intuitive judgment. Few investors actually sit down and calculate the future stream of dividends. And when they do, there is still the question of how much to pay for that stream of dividends given the fact that you don't get them for a number of years, and the risk that your estimate may be wrong. It should not be surprising that few investors actually calculate the value of the expected future dividends. By analogy, few people betting on a sports event actually try to "calculate" who will win. True, there are systems for weighing the strong and weak points of a team based on its past statistics; but ultimately the decision to bet on a given team depends on one's intuition of key factors that results from having watched the teams and read the available news about them. The same thing applies to valuing stocks. Most investors don't actually calculate the future dividends or earnings beyond a year or two, but they do closely watch their favorite companies, studying their past statistics and reading the current news about them. Then the decision to buy or sell is usually an intuitive one based on what they see as the key factors or changes that will improve or lessen the likelihood of future earnings and dividend gains. Those key factors might be within the company itself, the industry it serves, the economy, or the stock market as a whole. Examples where each of these appears to be the key factor will be seen in the history of Polaroid's stock price.

At first, it is fascinating to think that for every buyer who thinks a stock is undervalued, there is a seller who thinks the opposite. But that should not be so surprising for two reasons. First, when talking about stock prices we are dealing with expectations for the future, for which there is very little certainty. When you put your money in the bank, there is a very high degree of certainty about the amount of interest and the likelihood of receiving that interest. But when you buy a stock, you are really making assumptions about the future of the economy, the future of that company's products in the economy, the future of that company's competitive position against other companies making that product, the earnings that will derive from sales of the product, the amount of these earnings that will need to be put back into the business for plant modernization as well as expansion, and finally, of the profits left over—how much the board of directors will choose to pay out as a dividend. Thus, with a high degree of uncertainty about all these factors for the future, it is not surprising that investors have substantially different views of what the stock is worth.

There is another reason why it should not be surprising that each stock sale reflects opposite opinions about the stock's worth. Suppose there was no one who thought the stock was overvalued. Everyone who owned it, or was considering an investment in it, felt that it was undervalued (too low). In that case, they would obviously buy it. To do so, they would have to offer higher prices to induce someone to sell. In fact, they would keep buying until they had forced the price up to the point where the investors who thought it was undervalued approximately balanced the investors who thought it was overvalued. The reverse would happen if almost everyone thought the stock was overvalued (too high). It would fall until it reached the point where the investors who thought it was overvalued balanced those who thought it was undervalued. Thus, the price of a stock almost always reflects exactly that price where investors who think it is overvalued exactly balance those who think it is undervalued. Otherwise, the stock would necessarily move up or down until it reached exactly that point.

This chapter on why stocks go up or down, then, is not about how to calculate the future stream of dividends or earnings but is really about what factors cause investors to change their minds about that future stream of dividends and earnings and, hence, the value of the stock.

To put it another way, the price of a stock today *already* reflects the combined anonymous opinion of what investors expect for earnings and dividends in the future. If you foresee something occurring that you think other investors do not see, and you think this occurrence would cause them to raise their expectations of earnings and dividends, then you should buy the stock *now* because it should go up when other investors see what you see. How far the stock will go up should be related to the long-term effect the new information will have on the outlook for earnings and dividends.

Recall that we said the price of a stock reflects the opinions of all the investors who are thinking about that stock. This leaves out those investors who are *not* thinking about this particular stock. Thus, another key to projecting stock prices is being able to forecast what might change that will call attention to a stock which appears undervalued but has been overlooked by other potential investors.

In predicting stock prices, there is no substitute for experience. An investor should watch closely the price behavior of a stock he is interested in. He should watch how much it moves up or down daily and weekly as news emerges about the company, its products, its earnings, its dividends, and any news about the economy or the world in general that may affect his company. This will give an investor insights into the stock and a feeling of confidence in his ability to predict its price movements that cannot be had from a textbook.

The remainder of this chapter will attempt to create some of that experience by giving an 18-year running history of Polaroid. The discussion will proceed as if the future was unknown and periodically give the reader the opportunity to make a judgment about the stock before turning the page to see what actually happened.

This analysis of Polaroid cannot include all the factors that affected Polaroid's stock price behavior. That is not possible; first, because there are too many factors, and second, because analysts would have different opinions about what were the major influences on Polaroid's stock price movement in any given year. Thus, this chapter only discusses those factors that the author believes were the major influences on the stock price. Other investors or followers of Polaroid will have their own theories and may totally disagree with the information presented here. It is the author's belief, however, that the reader will come away with a substantial insight into Polaroid's stock price movement, and therefore into the stock price movement in general.

Charting

Throughout the chapter, the price behavior of Polaroid will be shown on charts similar to the following. Chart 1 shows for each month the price range and the closing price on the last day of the month. It also shows the volume or number of shares traded that month. Similar charts, but on a daily basis rather than monthly, will be used beginning with the year 1979.

Chart 1 shows that in January 1964 Polaroid sold as high as $23.00 per share, as low as about $19¼ per share, and closed on the last day of January at about $19⅝ per share. It also shows that about 2½ million

CHART 1

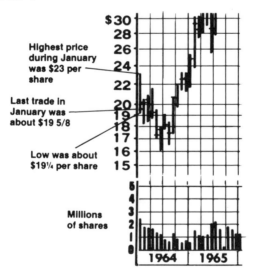

Highest price during January was $23 per share

Last trade in January was about $19 5/8

Low was about $19¼ per share

Millions of shares

Trading volume in January was about 2½ million shares. Volumes in February, March and April were slightly below 2 million shares per month shares of stock were bought and sold that month. On all the charts in this chapter both the volume and the price level have been adjusted for stock splits that took place in 1965 and 1968. Similarly, all the earnings per share figures have also been adjusted for the stock splits. Thus all the charts, prices, earnings, and price-earnings ratios are consistent throughout the chapter.

Technical analysis

Many investors believe that by watching the price changes in a stock and the related volume, they can see patterns in the stock's behavior that frequently indicates whether to buy or sell. This type of stock analysis is called technical analysis. There are many books that dwell on technical analysis and it will not be covered here. Rather, this book has concentrated on the other type of stock analysis, which is called fundamental analysis. Fundamental analysts attempt to project sales, expenses, profits and dividends, and future growth rates of profits and dividends and then determine a price-earnings ratio that reflects both the earnings and dividend growth and the confidence that those projections are accurate, in order to project future stock prices. Most technical analysts would agree that these fundamental factors are what determine the long-run price behavior of a stock, but they also believe that investors' best projections of all these fundamental factors, whether accurate or not, are all reflected in the price and volume behavior of the stock and thus correct reading of this price and volume behavior can often enable one to make the correct buy or sell decision without doing the fundamental research yourself.

We will not attempt technical analysis here, but the reader is welcome to test his or her technical skills as the chapter proceeds. Let us now turn to Polaroid.

POLAROID

The growth years

As Chart 2 shows, Polaroid's stock moved up substantially in the mid-1960s. The years 1964, 1965, and 1966 were years of rapid growth for Polaroid. Earnings per share (EPS) in those years were $.58, $.93, and $1.51. Thus the EPS growth rate was 60 percent in 1965 and 62 percent in 1966. This is a very impressive growth rate. A growth rate of 20 percent for a big company is considered a very good year, and 40 percent would be considered an outstanding year. Polaroid was experiencing outstanding growth years as a new line of cameras and film came out that made picture taking easier. Lower-price cameras were also

CHART 2

Price ($)

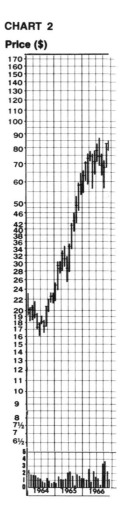

introduced, making instant[1] photography available to more people. With more people owning cameras, more film was being purchased. In addition, film users were shifting from black and white film to an increasing proportion of color film, and color film sales were more profitable to Polaroid.

---

[1] Instant photography in this chapter refers to the Polaroid process in which the photographer gets the finished picture in a matter of minutes at the most; as distinguished from conventional photography, in which the film has to be taken to a store to be developed.

Looking first at 1964, Polaroid earned $.58 per share. During the year the stock got as high as $23 per share at one point and as low as $16 per share at another point.[2] Thus we could say the price-earnings ratio (P-E) got as high as 40x[3] earnings at one point:

$$\frac{\text{Price}}{\text{Earnings}} = \frac{\$23.00}{\$.58} = 39.655x$$

Also, the P-E got as low as 28x (28 "times") earnings when the stock was at $16. Thus we can set up the following table:

	EPS	Price range High	Low	P-E range High	Low
1964 ..... $.58		$23 –	$16	40x –	28x

In 1965 the stock moved up almost steadily. Its low point early in the year was about $22 per share and its highest price was $65 late in the year. Since earnings came in at $.93, the P-E ratio during 1965 ranged from a high of 70x to a low of 24x.

	EPS	Price range High	Low	P-E range High	Low
1964 ..... $.58		$23 –	$16	40x –	28x
1965 ..... .93		65 –	22	70 –	24

The table of P-Es above can be misleading. While it is true that the stock sold as low as $22, and it is true that earnings were $.93, and therefore it is true that the low P-E was 22x, it is probable that no one actually thought he was selling the stock (or buying it) at 22x earnings. For example, the person who sold it at the beginning of 1965 at $22 may have been estimating 1965 earnings at $.70 per share, not the $.93 that earnings actually came in at. Thus, he thought he was selling the stock at 31x earnings where he may have felt the stock was overpriced.

$$\frac{\text{Price}}{\text{Estimated earnings}} \quad \frac{\$22.00}{\$.70} = 31.4x$$

---

[2] Throughout most of this chapter stock prices will be rounded off. In fact Polaroid sold as high as $23⅜ and as low as $16¼ in 1964. The rounding off is too small to matter.

[3] P/Es (like 39.655x in the ratio) will also be rounded off in most of this chapter.

Had he been more accurate in estimating earnings (i.e., had he been estimating earnings at $.93) he might have felt the stock was fairly priced or even undervalued at 22x estimated earnings and not sold the stock. Similarly, no one actually thought he was paying 70x earnings. By the end of 1965, when it became apparent that earnings were growing rapidly and seemed likely to continue to do so in 1966, investors were probably making their decisions based on projected 1966 earnings. Thus, in December 1965, someone who paid $65 per share may have been estimating 1966 earnings at $1.30 per share. Thus he thought he was paying 50x earnings, not 70x earnings. If he had projected 1966 earnings at exactly the $1.51 it came in at, he would have thought he was paying 43x earnings. Had he been overly optimistic about Polaroid's 1966 earnings prospects and been estimating earnings of $1.65, then he would have thought he was paying 39x earnings.

Price	Projected earnings	Projected P-E
$65	$1.30	50x
65	1.51	43
65	1.65	39

During 1966 earnings continued to grow steadily and rapidly each quarter and, for the full year, earnings came in at $1.51. During the year the stock got as high as $87 per share and as low as $54. But this year the stock's rise was not as steady as in 1965. In fact, as Chart 3 shows, the high point of the year of $87 was reached in August, following which the stock declined to $54 in October before rebounding to the $80s in December.

What caused that sharp late-summer move downward and then the equally sharp rebound? Was some new information revealed that suddenly changed the outlook for Polaroid for the worse, and was followed by some additional information that changed the outlook for the better? Possibly. More likely, Polaroid was just moving with the stock market in general. In 1966, the stock market averages had been declining more or less steadily since the beginning of the year, but took their worst plunges in August and again in October before making a gradual recovery from the October low until the end of the year. Thus Polaroid's sharp late summer decline and fall recovery coincided with the market in general, and therefore were probably caused more by the market than by anything at Polaroid. This is a key point to remember. No matter how attractive the outlook for a given company, regardless of how high or low the P-E is, it is possible that a sharp market decline or rally can carry the stock with it and make all your estimates of earnings and dividends seem

CHART 3

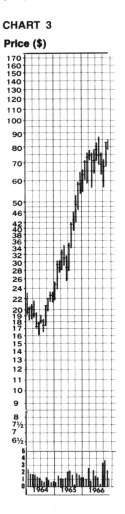

Price ($)

irrelevant over the short-run—perhaps one to three months, and sometimes longer. Over a longer period, however, stock performance does
seem to respond to earnings growth. For example, in 1966 the outlook
for Polaroid's future earnings growth did look better than the earnings
growth outlook for the market as a whole, and Polaroid's stock did do
better. In fact, Polaroid was rising for much of the time from January to
August 1966 while the market averages were falling. Polaroid also did
better than the market in the October to December recovery. As a
result, Polaroid ended the year at about $78, a good gain from the
January level in the $50s, while the market averages ended the year with
a loss despite the recovery late in the year.

Thus there were opportunities to make gains or losses in Polaroid in

1966. Those who bought the stock in August saw it fall to the $50s in two months. At this point, they might have either sold it at a loss or held it into 1967 when it went higher, and thus had a profit despite the poor timing of their purchase.

Had their timing been better, of course, they could have bought the stock in October at a much lower price, and hence bought more shares and made a greater profit. The conclusion here is that short-term stock price movements may sometimes appear volatile and irrational, but over longer periods a stock's movement is likely to reflect its true record and outlook.

We can now add 1966 to our table:

	EPS	Price range		P-E range	
		High	Low	High	Low
1964	$ .58	$23 –	$16	40x –	28x
1965	.93	65 –	22	70 –	24
1966	1.51	87 –	54	58 –	36

In 1967 Polaroid's earnings growth was slower. EPS was $1.81, only a 20 percent increase from the 1966 level. In 1968 EPS increased only 3 percent to $1.86. Nevertheless, the stock continued to trade at very high P-Es for a number of reasons. First, there was a mystique about Polaroid's research and innovativeness, which suggested that there was always a new product being developed with great potential. Investors felt that even if earnings growth was slow for a year or two, it was probably just a lull before a new generation of products, and surely the new products would send earnings and hence the stock rocketing again. In addition, an upgraded line of cameras introduced that year seemed likely to keep film sales and hence profits rising near term. Finally, Wall Street analysts' estimates for 1967 and 1968 had been slightly too optimistic and thus investors had thought they were going to see more rapid growth in those years than what actually occurred. As a result, the stock continued to move higher but at a slower rate than in 1965–66.

	EPS	Price range		P-E range	
		High	Low	High	Low
1964	$ .58	$ 23 –	$16	40x –	28x
1965	.93	65 –	22	70 –	24
1966	1.51	87 –	54	58 –	36
1967	1.81	127 –	77	70 –	43
1968	1.86	134 –	88	72 –	47

CHART 4

Price ($)

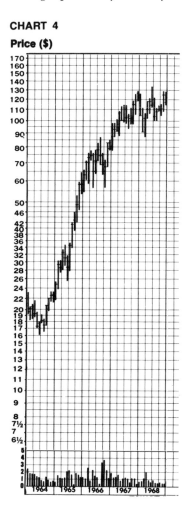

The transition years—No earnings growth, but great promise

In 1969 the stock market averages declined more or less steadily all year. Polaroid declined through May but then turned up sharply. There was much to be optimistic about for the near future. There was talk of many new products, including what Polaroid was then calling the "Ultimate" camera—a camera that would fold up and fit into your pocket, and which would use a new type of film that completely developed itself and had nothing to peel apart and throw away. In addition, an office copier was demonstrated at the company's annual meeting, and a transparency film was discussed, which could mean either slides or movies. But it was mostly the "Ultimate" camera that had some analysts saying that Polaroid might earn $4 per share in a few years when this new generation of cameras and film was in full production. In addition to the excitement surrounding these future products, investors were optimistic about a new line of cameras, which was introduced in February 1969, including the first inexpensive camera that could use both black-and-white film and color film. With all this potential for sharp earnings gains, the stock reached a high of $145 before retreating to close the year at $125. Earnings for the year, however, were $1.90—another year of minimal growth.

	EPS	Price range High	Low	P-E range High	Low
1964	$ .58	$ 23 –	$ 16	40x –	28x
1965	.93	65 –	22	70 –	24
1966	1.51	87 –	54	58 –	36
1967	1.81	127 –	77	70 –	43
1968	1.86	134 –	88	72 –	47
1969	1.90	145 –	102	76 –	54

Why did someone pay $145 per share? Obviously he thought it was going higher. Polaroid had traded as high as 70x earnings at some point in four of the past five years (see preceding table). Since earnings of $4 seemed likely in a few years the stock might be expected to reach 70x $4, or $280 per share. Even if it only went to 60x $4, or $240 per share it was still a good gain from the current level of $145. In other words, the historical P-E range, combined with the outlook for earnings, suggested there was still a lot of room for Polaroid to move up. That did not happen, however.

In 1970, the economy slid into a recession. The stock market went nowhere in the first quarter, but Polaroid declined to about $100. Was the stock a "buy" or a "sell"?

The buyers would say that it still looked like Polaroid could earn $4 per share in two or three years. Thus, with the stock now at $100, it was selling at 25x that estimate, which is as low (in terms of P-E) as it had sold in the past seven years. Thus when the $4 EPS figure was actually reached in a couple of years, the stock should at least double when the P-E returned to 50x earnings—a more typical P-E for Polaroid in recent years. Therefore, even though the stock could go lower near term, it was better to buy it now, rather than risk missing it if it began to move up immediately. Furthermore, there have been many times when Polaroid declined sharply for a couple of months before rebounding to a new high. Look, for example, at August to October 1966, or January to March 1968, or February to March 1969. Therefore, with Polaroid having declined to the $90s in the first quarter of 1970, it looked like another buying opportunity.

The sellers disagreed. They pointed out that Polaroid's earnings had now shown minimal growth in 1968 and 1969 and, because of the recession, were not likely to show much growth in 1970. With three years of minimal growth, it was hard to justify a P-E of 50x. Therefore, why take a chance? Furthermore, the market was declining and Polaroid could well be expected to decline with it, as it had done in 1966. So why worry about earnings, dividends, and P-E ratios—why not just sell before it goes any lower? Others may have sold simply because in a recession they needed money. All this selling, of course, triggers other holders who see their profits evaporating and don't want to lose more.

Was the stock a "buy" or a "sell"?

CHART 5

Price ($)

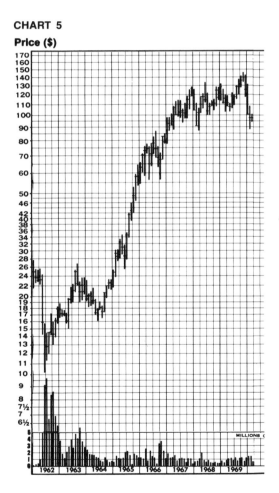

CHART 6
Price ($)

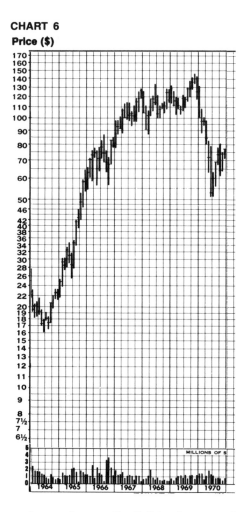

As it turned out the stock was a "sell." In the second quarter of 1970 the market declined sharply and Polaroid went down with it. Although the market stopped going down in May 1970 and began to recover, Polaroid continued to decline in June and reached $51 before it began to recover.

Two factors that may have accelerated a decline are *short selling* and *margin selling*. Both of these factors, discussed in Appendixes 1 and 2, typically occur in sharp market declines, such as happened to Polaroid's stock in early 1970. In fact, they may be partly responsible for the suddenness and depth of such declines.

Margin sales and short selling can occur anytime and may have nothing to do with the fundamental outlook for earnings and dividends. Thus we see again that, *in the short run*, human psychology can have more to do with determining stock prices than the fundamental outlook for a company.

By the end of 1970 the stock had recovered to about $77. Earnings for the year 1970 were $1.86, a small decline from the 1969 level.

	EPS	Price range		P-E range	
		High	Low	High	Low
1964	$ .58	$ 23 – $ 16		40x – 28x	
1965	.93	65 – 22		70 – 24	
1966	1.51	87 – 54		58 – 36	
1967	1.81	127 – 77		70 – 43	
1968	1.86	134 – 88		72 – 47	
1969	1.90	145 – 102		76 – 54	
1970	1.86	130 – 51		70 – 27	

In early 1971 the stock market recovered and Polaroid recovered with it despite the fact that earnings were not recovering very much. Investors, however, were still looking forward to the earnings of $4/share or even $5/share that seemed probable when the "Ultimate" camera and new film were in full production. In late 1971 the stock gave up part of its early year gain, perhaps declining with the market and perhaps reflecting the fact that earnings were disappointing. (See Chart 7.) In 1971 Polaroid again earned $1.86/share. Although sales were up, the company reported that earnings were held back by heavy research and development expenses related to the new line of cameras and film.

	EPS	Price range		P-E range	
		High	Low	High	Low
1964	$ .58	$ 23 – $ 16		40x – 28x	
1965	.93	65 – 22		70 – 24	
1966	1.51	87 – 54		58 – 36	
1967	1.81	127 – 77		70 – 43	
1968	1.86	134 – 88		72 – 47	
1969	1.90	145 – 102		76 – 54	
1970	1.86	130 – 51		70 – 27	
1971	1.86	117 – 76		63 – 41	

Entering 1972, the introduction of Polaroid's new camera and film were imminent and the stock moved up to a new high of $150 in May as investors became more confident of the company's ability to earn $4 per share or higher a year or two out. Earnings for 1972, however, came in at $1.30, and thus at the price of $150 it could be said that the stock was

CHART 7

Price ($)

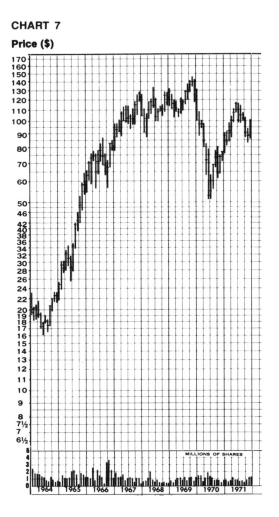

selling at 115x earnings. Again, nobody thought they were paying 115x earnings, first, because in the early part of the year most analysts expected 1972 EPS to be higher, perhaps around $2 per share, and second because they really did not care about 1972 earnings. In early 1972, optimistic investors still believed the new generation of cameras would propel earnings sharply higher in 1973 and beyond, just as a new generation of cameras had pushed earnings up sharply in 1964–66. Recall that in 1965 and 1966 EPS grew at 60 percent per year. If 1972 and 1973 EPS were each up 60 percent, beginning with the 1971 level, then 1973 EPS would be $4.76. In that case the stock was probably quite attractive since it was selling at only 32x EPS.

$$\frac{\text{Current price}}{\text{Projected earnings}} = \frac{\$150.00}{\$4.76} = 32x$$

Here is a case of where investors may have been using the past as a guide to the future.

In October 1972 the new camera, now called the SX-70, was first introduced to the public. The SX-70 differed from the older cameras in many ways, but one of the most important was that the SX-70 picture was automatically ejected from the camera and was entirely self-developing. Unlike the older cameras there was nothing to pull out, no need to wait 60 seconds and then peel the negative away from the final picture. While some people liked the SX-70, others were disappointed. First, it was not as compact as expected. You could not put it in your pocket comfortably, as Polaroid had initially indicated. In addition, some people were disappointed with the quality of the pictures it produced. Further, the camera was very expensive. This meant relatively few people could afford it, which in turn would keep film sales low, and therefore profits might never be as high as some hoped.

Immediately after the introduction the stock declined. While this may have been due to the disappointment with the camera and film, it also may have been simply that the excitement had passed and there was no more good news to happen that had not already been anticipated. *The stock market always anticipates.* With the stock selling between $110 and $150 for much of 1972, perhaps it was already anticipating the introduction of the SX-70 and the substantial earnings gains that it was expected to produce. According to this reasoning, perhaps Polaroid only deserved a P-E multiple of 25x to 35x, and thus the reason the stock moved up over $100 in 1971 and 1972 was in anticipation of selling at 25x to 35x an estimate of about $4. Thus at $150, the stock was overvalued at 37x earnings. Even at $120 the stock appeared fully priced at 30x earnings, and thus there was no reason why it should go higher for now (i.e., until something else came along, perhaps another new product, that had the potential to push earnings even higher than the $4 per share level that was anticipated from the SX-70 system). Therefore, with little reason to expect the stock to go higher, it might as well be sold because what if earnings never reached the $4 per share level? What if earnings only went to $2.50 or $3.00 per share? Would that deserve a P-E of 30x or 40x? For whatever reason, enough investors were worried that the stock got no higher than $130 in the four months after introduction, and in fact got as low as $104. (See Chart 8 on page 220.)

Earnings for 1972 came in at $1.30/share, well below early-year expectations; but again it was due to unusually high research and development costs associated with the SX-70 program, and it could be reasonably assumed that these costs would decline soon because the SX-70 camera and film were now on the market.

	EPS	Price range		P-E range	
		High	Low	High	Low
1964	$ .58	$ 23 –	$ 16	40x –	28x
1965	.93	65 –	22	70 –	24
1966	1.51	87 –	54	58 –	36
1967	1.81	127 –	77	70 –	43
1968	1.86	134 –	88	72 –	47
1969	1.90	145 –	102	76 –	54
1970	1.86	130 –	51	70 –	27
1971	1.86	117 –	76	63 –	41
1972	1.30	150 –	87	115 –	66

CHART 8

Price ($)

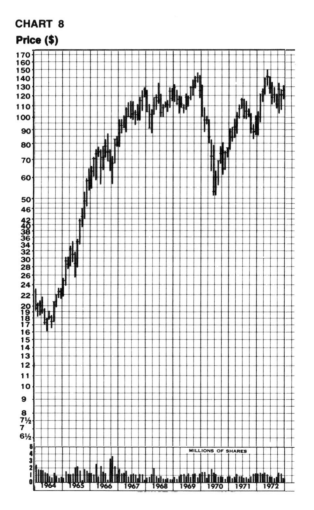

Many investors were not disappointed with the SX-70 introduction; rather, they were quite excited about its prospects. Although it was an expensive camera, Polaroid had always introduced an expensive camera first, and then followed with a family of less-expensive cameras so more people could afford them. Assuming this were to happen again, it was very easy for analysts to make reasonable assumptions about sales that would enable earnings to reach the $4 per share level or higher. Thus, in the first half of 1973, the stock moved up again, reaching the year's high of $143 in June, despite a steadily declining market. In the last half of 1973 Polaroid came down sharply, closing the year at $70 per share. Sales figures were showing nice gains as the year progressed, but the earnings reported each quarter were below what most Wall Street analysts had forecast.

Was it time to buy the stock or was it a sell? The big earnings gains anticipated continued to be held back by development costs (expenses) relating to the SX-70 system, but it was still easy to demonstrate that Polaroid could earn $4 per share when things improved. In addition, the stock market averages were also declining in the last half of 1973, so perhaps Polaroid was just declining with the market, as it had done in 1970, and would recover sharply when the market recovered. **Was it time to buy the stock or was it still a sell?** To test your judgment, look at the chart on page 222 before looking at the chart on page 224.

The recession years—and the market "correction"

In February 1974, Polaroid reported its 1973 earnings per share at $1.58, well below early 1973 expectations by most analysts. The elusive $4 EPS figure seemed further out of reach, and the stock continued to decline.

The historical summary table on page 222 now also includes the Pretax profit margin and the Return on equity ratios. Note that the Pretax margin declined steadily since peaking in 1968. This, in fact, was the reason that earnings declined more or less steadily despite sales growing nicely throughout this period. Further, the declining profits also caused a declining return on equity. Watching the trends in profit margin and return on equity provide a kind of bird's-eye view of what is happening at a company, and the historical summary tables from here on will show these figures.

At the beginning of 1974, some Wall Street analysts were estimating 1974 earnings to be as high as $2.60 to 2.80 per share, up from 1973's $1.58. But consumer spending slid into a recession, and sales and earn-

CHART 9

Price ($)

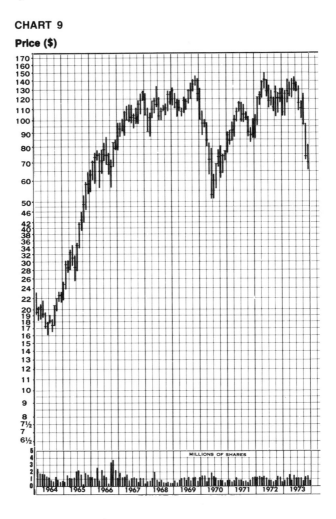

		Price Range		P-E range		Aftertax return on	Pretax profit
	EPS	High	Low	High	Low	equity	margin
1964	$ .58	$ 23 –	$ 16	40x –	28x	22.7%	25.8%
1965	.93	65 –	22	70 –	24	29.7	28.4
1966	1.51	87 –	54	58 –	36	38.1	30.0
1967	1.81	127 –	77	70 –	43	33.7	30.6
1968	1.86	134 –	88	72 –	47	26.6	32.1
1969	1.90	145 –	102	76 –	54	23.3	28.1
1970	1.86	130 –	51	70 –	27	14.4	25.6
1971	1.86	117 –	76	63 –	41	12.4	21.6
1972	1.30	150 –	87	115 –	66	7.8	13.0
1973	1.58	143 –	65	91 –	41	9.0	12.9

ings were disappointing all year. With each quarter's earnings disappointing, most Wall Street analysts were continually lowering their earnings estimate for the full year. Full-year 1974 earnings came in at a surprisingly low $.86/share, the lowest since 1964. The disappointingly low earnings were undoubtedly one of the reasons, but probably not the only reason, for the stock's decline. Nevertheless, it is instructive to look at the reasons for the earnings decline to see if they reveal any hints as to future earnings and stock price behavior. For instance, if the earnings decline was clearly due to either temporary problems that could be solved or was due to the economic recession, then one could assume that when the recession ended and consumer spending picked up again; or when the "temporary" problems were solved, that EPS would spring back upward and the stock would recover with it. But if the earnings disappointment was due to problems that seemed likely to be with the company for years, then one might conclude that earnings recovery was unlikely and thus the stock might be going down further, or at least not be likely to show much recovery.

All the reasons for the earnings decline cannot be known for sure, but the two reasons most apparent to Wall Street analysts included:

1. Demand for the new SX-70 camera and film was disappointing relative to expectations. Whether due to disappointment with the product, too high a price, or the consumer recession is not clear. Or perhaps it was simply that expectations by the company and the investment community were too high. In fact, over 1.2 million SX-70 cameras were shipped by Polaroid. But the company was geared for an even higher level of camera and film sales than actually occurred, and thus the shortfall definitely hurt profits.

2. Sales of the old peel-apart line of film and cameras declined as could be expected when the new line was introduced, but the peel-apart line was making very high profits and the new SX-70 line was making very little or losing money. Thus, as sales shifted from the old to the new, profits were certain to decline until profitability increased on the new line.[4]

In fact, both of these problems seemed likely to be temporary, and those who bought the stock in the $70s and $60s and $50s, all the way down, probably were thinking along these lines, and therefore the stock

---

[4] It is common in many companies that when a new product is first introduced it makes little or no profit, or even loses money. This typically occurs for two reasons. First, there are many fixed costs associated with manufacturing and selling the product, which have to be expensed whether or not the product has reached a high selling rate.

Second, the manufacturing process is often inefficient at the beginning and a lot of money is wasted due to excess labor time or products that come out defective and have to be thrown away. As the company gains more experience with making the product it modifies the process to eliminate the inefficiencies.

CHART 10

Price ($)

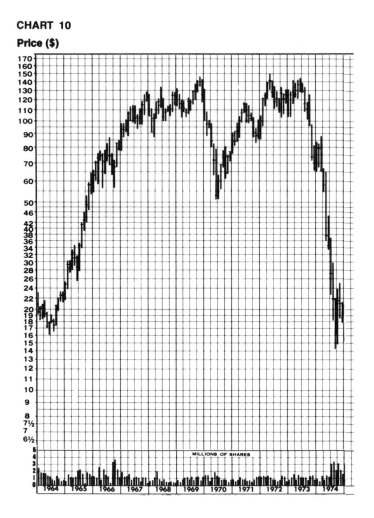

looked "cheap" relative to its earnings recovery potential when camera sales picked up and profitability on the new SX-70 line improved.

In addition to the disappointing earnings, two other factors may also have contributed to the stock's decline:

1. Eastman Kodak was now talking about making its own instant camera that would compete directly with Polaroid. Without the competitive threat from Kodak, investors knew that Polaroid had complete freedom to raise its camera and film prices whenever it wanted and thus had some control over its earnings. But once Kodak had a directly competitive product, price increases might be limited because, if Polaroid raised its prices and Kodak did not, potential camera buyers would be likely to choose a Kodak camera instead of

a Polaroid camera. While it was too early to assess exactly how serious this threat might be, particularly since no one knew what the Kodak camera would look like or what the quality of the picture would be, it was nevertheless reasonable to assume that things would not be as easy for Polaroid as they were in the past.

2. In the 1971–73 period a small group of stocks, which came to be known on Wall Street as the "Nifty Fifty," performed substantially better than the rest of the market. The price-earnings ratios of these stocks went much higher than the P-E of most other stocks in the market. That group of companies had certain things in common, including a good earnings growth record, a high pretax profit margin, and a high return on equity. Polaroid tended to behave like these stocks. From 1964 to 1969, Polaroid had a very high pretax margin, and a very high return on equity. The earnings growth rate, however, began to slow in the late 1960s. In the early 1970s, earnings actually declined, the pretax margin came down to half its mid-60's level, and return on equity also fell sharply. However, the stock market was evidently not disturbed by the deterioration of these ratios in 1971–73 as Polaroid moved up steadily with this group of stocks (probably, as we have seen, in anticipation of renewed earnings growth as the new SX-70 products reached high volume). In 1974, most of these Nifty Fifty stocks came tumbling down as their price-earnings ratios came back to more normal levels. Polaroid came down with them.

Looking back at the P-Es and charts of these stocks, it now seems they were substantially overpriced before they tumbled. Yet this stock market "fashion" or fad for companies with high pretax margin and return on equity persisted for perhaps two years before ending. Here is another example of how short-run (although in this case two or more years) stock behavior can seem irrational and independent of any "true" value based on dividend and earnings outlook.

For whichever of these or other reasons, Polaroid reached a low of $14⅛ in late 1974, a level that was almost unthinkable a few years earlier. It represented a 90 percent decline from the $143½ price just 16 months previously.

Was Polaroid really worth 90 percent less than it had been 16 months ago? Had the outlook for future earnings and dividends deteriorated by 90 percent in 16 months? Probably not. Then why the 90 percent decline? The answer lies partly in that the outlook for future earnings and dividends seems to have deteriorated, although not by 90 percent, and partly in that the stock market, especially in the short run, is not perfectly rational in pricing stocks. Even ignoring the uncertainties in projecting future earnings and dividends, it is debatable exactly how much one should pay today for a given stream of expected future earnings and dividends. Therefore, stocks reasonably should fluctuate in a fairly wide range of "true" value. But more important, the stock market frequently exaggerates moves in either direction. The market, in this sense, has an "emotional" aspect to its behavior (or perhaps reflects the emotional characteristics of humans who make the buy and sell decisions) in that it can get wildly enthusiastic about a stock and seem to overlook the risks, pushing the stock up to levels that seem much too high relative to potential earnings and dividends, or the market can become overly worried about a stock and push the price down to a level that suggests things were never going to get better. It is usually these extremes of emotional behavior in the market, or more correctly of people who buy and sell stocks in the market, that cause extreme highs and extreme lows.

Perhaps, then, Polaroid was trading substantially above its range of true value when it was over $120, and perhaps it was trading well below its range of true value below $20. This in fact seems likely since the stock sprang back sharply in early 1975.

The lesson here is that there may be great risk in paying a record high P-E for a stock. Not because the stock may not go higher, but because there is a possibility that the new high P-E reflects not only an improving outlook for the company but may reflect an unsustainable enthusiasm, and thus the stock may come down even if the company's earnings and dividends do improve as was anticipated. Similarly, the optimal time to buy a stock may be when everyone hates it and the outlook is the bleakest. Of course one must also do some analysis to be sure that there is some reason to believe the company is going to recover and not go out of business.

Let us turn to the question of why the stock's decline stopped at $14 rather than $10, or $20, or some other price. Of course, there cannot be a precise answer. Possible partial answers include:

1. The market in general stopped going down in September 1974. Perhaps there was nothing magic about $14 per share except that happened to be Polaroid's price when stocks in general stopped going down.
2. Some people who had been "short" stock (see Appendix 1) decided to cover their short (i.e., replace the stock they borrowed). In order to do this they had to go into the market to buy stock. This buying pressure caused the stock to go up, or at least prevented it from going down further.
3. Margin selling (see Appendix 2) may have stopped. That is, people who had bought on margin and were forced to sell when the stock went below a certain level relative to their "margin," or money borrowed, may have all been forced out of the stock. Or others who were afraid of getting margin calls if the stock went any lower may have

already sold their stock. Margin selling, in particular, is one of the causes of a stock appearing to go below its "true" worth in a sharp decline.

4. Book value per share at June 30, 1974, was $19 per share. Some investors look at book value per share as a psychological point below which stocks are cheap. Thus, when Polaroid went below $19, it began to attract buyers. When it reached $14, it was at 74 percent of book value, which appeared extraordinarily cheap by most historical standards for a company that still had reasonable growth prospects and whose survival was unquestioned. This made Polaroid interesting to a whole new group of investors. We might call them "value" or "asset value" investors. These people would not have considered buying Polaroid in 1970 at $51/share. At that time the book value was about $15 per share, so even at $51 at the bottom of the 1970 decline the stock was selling at more than three times or 300 percent of book value. It was also selling at a P-E of 27x that year's earnings. At the 1974 bottom of $14, it was selling at a P-E of 16x that year's eventual earnings, and an even lower P-E based on the higher earnings estimates that most of Wall Street was actually using late in 1974. Furthermore, 1974 earnings seemed unusually depressed for reasons mentioned above.

These so-called asset value investors, on the one hand, would not have bought Polaroid at the 1970 bottom and missed a subsequent tripling of the stock over the next two years. On the other hand, they would also not have bought Polaroid in 1973 just before its 90 percent decline. Some people feel they are more adept at picking "value" in stocks. Others feel they are more adept at trading the high flyers, such as Polaroid in the 1960s or early 70s. Either way is good if it works for you.

Polaroid's earnings for 1974 came in at a very disappointing $0.86 per share.

	EPS	Price range		P-E range		Aftertax return on equity	Pretax profit margin
		High	Low	High	Low		
1964	$ .58	$ 23 –	$ 16	40x –	28x	22.7%	25.8%
1965	.93	65 –	22	70 –	24	29.7	28.4
1966	1.51	87 –	54	58 –	36	38.1	30.0
1967	1.81	127 –	77	70 –	43	33.7	30.6
1968	1.86	134 –	88	72 –	47	26.6	32.1
1969	1.90	145 –	102	76 –	54	23.3	28.1
1970	1.86	130 –	51	70 –	27	14.4	25.6
1971	1.86	117 –	76	63 –	41	12.4	21.6
1972	1.30	150 –	87	115 –	66	7.8	13.0
1973	1.58	143 –	65	91 –	41	9.0	12.9
1974	.86	88 –	14	103 –	16	4.6	5.9

The table above shows that Polaroid's P-E got as high as 103x in 1974. Again, it should be pointed out that no one thought he was paying 103x earnings. The person who bought the stock at the beginning of the year in the $70s or $80s probably felt earnings had bottomed in 1972 and was estimating 1974 earnings at well over $2.00—possibly as high as the $2.60 estimate published by one respected brokerage firm. At the other extreme, the stock sold as low as 16x earnings, well below even the 1970 bottom level. This new low P-E as well as the lows in the other ratios in the table suggest that things had changed for Polaroid and the high-flyer days might be over.

The competitive years begin

Throughout 1975 and 1976 the stock recovered, reaching a high point of $46 in late 1976.

CHART 11

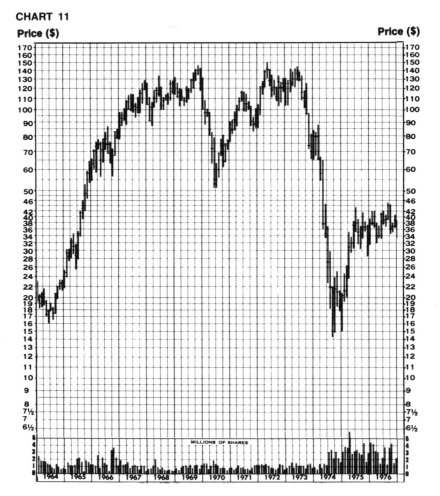

	EPS	Price range		P-E range		Aftertax return on equity	Pretax profit margin
		High	Low	High	Low		
1964	$ .58	$ 23 –	$ 16	40x –	28x	22.7%	25.8%
1965	.93	65 –	22	70 –	24	29.7	28.4
1966	1.51	87 –	54	58 –	36	38.1	30.0
1967	1.81	127 –	77	70 –	43	33.7	30.6
1968	1.86	134 –	88	72 –	47	26.6	32.1
1969	1.90	145 –	102	76 –	54	23.3	28.1
1970	1.86	130 –	51	70 –	27	14.4	25.6
1971	1.86	117 –	76	63 –	41	12.4	21.6
1972	1.30	150 –	87	115 –	66	7.8	13.0
1973	1.58	143 –	65	91 –	41	9.0	12.9
1974	.86	88 –	14	103 –	16	4.6	5.9
1975	1.91	44 –	15	23 –	8	9.8	14.9
1976	2.43	45 –	31	19 –	13	11.6	16.0

The initial recovery in early 1975 was rapid. From January to April 1975 the stock recovered from a low of $14 to a high of $34, more than a double. Did the outlook for future earnings and dividends suddenly look twice as good during that period? Not likely. More likely, the sharpness of the rebound simply supports the idea that the market over-exaggerates moves in either direction, and that the late 1974 decline to the mid-teens went well below the company's true "worth." Again, we cannot state precisely what that "worth" is, but in retrospect it seems clear that the stock was very undervalued in late 1974.

Earnings recovered in 1975 and 1976. EPS in 1975 bounced back to the previous high area of $1.91 and set a new record in 1976 of $2.43. But the stock did not go back to its old high level or to its old P-E multiple range. The reasons for the new lower valuation of Polaroid shares are probably related to the outlook for earnings. Although EPS did recover sharply from the 1974 low, profit margin and return on equity never recovered to their late 1960's level.

The main reason that earnings were higher was simply that sales were much higher, but to generate big gains in earnings to the $4 or $5 per share level would also require a recovery in the profit margin. The new lower level of margins may have reflected the introduction of a competitive product by Kodak. This resulted in both lower selling prices and higher marketing expenses as both Polaroid and Kodak stepped up their advertising and selling programs in order to get the consumer to buy their cameras. Lower selling prices and higher marketing expenses both mean lower earnings. Also, research and development costs (all of which

Polaroid expenses) moved up as Polaroid accelerated development of a movie camera and other products. This also hurt the pretax profit margin. As a result of all these pressures on pretax margins, Polaroid's earnings, while up, were never quite as high as expected and, *these near-term disappointments made investors more cautious about the long-term ability of Polaroid to generate substantial earnings gains.*

In July 1976, Polaroid announced that the quarterly dividend was being raised from $.08 per share to $.12½ per share. While we have repeatedly said that dividends are the ultimate reason for holding a stock, Polaroid's stock did not seem to respond to the over-50 percent increase in the dividend. Why not? Because the price of the stock at any time reflects not just the current dividend, but the outlook for all future dividends as well. Thus, the market had long been expecting Polaroid's dividend to begin to move up as earnings moved up. While no one may have specifically guessed the amount and date of the increase, both amount and date were well within the range one might have expected. Thus, there was no surprise to immediately react to.

Another reason for Polaroid's lower P-E valuation by the market could be the psychological effect on investors of knowing that Kodak was there as a competitor. While many potential investors did not attempt to analyze the specific impact of the Kodak product, it seemed safe to say that the Kodak product would at least take some sales away from Polaroid, and that there was a good possibility that price wars might occur, which would hurt earnings. Although big earnings and dividend gains were still possible, they were far less likely, and therefore Polaroid was fairly priced at a much lower P-E level than it was in prior years when there was no risk from competition.

A third reason for Polaroid selling at a much lower P-E than in the late 1960s was that the market in general was selling at a much lower P-E. That is, investors in general seemed less optimistic about the long-term prospects for all companies' earnings and dividends. Some commonly heard reasons for the generally lower P-Es in the market included:

1. The oil embargo in late 1973, which made it clear that the U.S. economy was no longer as independent as it once was; therefore, long-term forecasts of earnings or dividends carried lower confidence.
2. The Nixon era caused less trust and confidence in the government, also implying less certainty of long-term earnings forecasts.
3. Ten years of increasing taxes and other legislation were discouraging capital investment for profits. With the government increasingly controlling profits or restricting companies' ability to increase profits and hence dividends, it decreased the return individual investors could expect from investing capital, or at least increased the risk.

4. A higher level of interest rates in the bond market than in the 1960s gave investors an attractive alternative investment to stocks. Thus, many investors sold stocks, pushing their prices down, in order to buy bonds or other high interest-yielding financial instruments. Further, given the high yields available on bonds, investors who stayed in the stock market would only be willing to do so with less risk, and that meant not paying high P-Es. In fact, as a general rule, whenever interest rates have been high, P-Es have tended to be low, and vice versa.

This list could be extended indefinitely, but these should be enough to demonstrate that international and domestic economics and politics can have a major effect on stock price performance.

For whichever of these reasons, and others as well, Polaroid and most other stocks were selling in P-E multiple ranges well below their 1960's levels.

Entering 1977, Polaroid was selling in the mid-$30s. Many published Wall Street estimates of 1977 EPS were around $3 per share. With the stock selling at 12x estimated EPS, its P-E was well above the P-E of most stocks in the market but well below Polaroid's historical levels. Throughout 1977 the stock worked its way lower (Chart 12). The sales gains as each quarter was reported were disappointing. Each quarter's sales were only about 7 percent above the sales level of the same quarter a year ago, much lower than one would expect from Polaroid in a year when consumer spending was picking up. This indicated that the competition from Eastman Kodak was taking its toll on sales. Earnings suffered accordingly. In fact, on October 19, the day that Polaroid reported its third quarter sales and earnings, the stock fell two points from $27⅞ to $25⅞.

Not only were sales and earnings disappointing all year, but there appeared to be no other reason to get excited about the stock. Earnings estimates of $4 per share or big growth rates were not being heard anymore. In addition to the Kodak competition, there were rumors that Fuji and other foreign companies might enter that instant photography market. Also, Polaroid introduced its long-anticipated home movie camera, but it was expensive and the picture was not as good as many Wall Street analysts hoped, and analysts' expectations for sales and earnings from it were lowered. In fact, instead of adding to earnings, many analysts thought it was quite possible that the movie system could be a money loser for a long time, particularly in the first year or two because sales volume was low and overhead costs and start-up costs were high. In addition to these costs (expenses), Polaroid was rapidly increasing its marketing expenses in its battle with Kodak and was selling its cameras at what most analysts believed to be lower profit margins than in the past

CHART 12

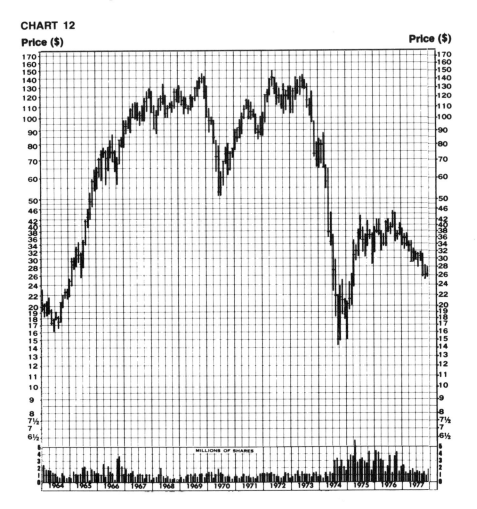

for fear of losing even more sales to Kodak. On top of all that, while sales of the SX-70 family of cameras and film were increasing, sales of the old peel-apart film continued declining. Since it was generally assumed that the peel-apart line still had much higher profit margins than the SX-70 system, analysts feared that even if sales were up, profits could be down. They were afraid to recommend buying the stock. Further, investors did not know what the difference was in profit margins between the old and the new lines, or how much more decline was possible in the highly profitable peel-apart business.

Note that the analysts could have been entirely wrong about the difference in profitability between the SX-70 family and peel-apart family. Perhaps the difference was minor. Perhaps most of the decline in peel-apart was behind and SX-70 was now reaching a sufficiently high volume level that its profitability was equal to or greater than peel-apart. But analysts did not know, and generally speaking, when there is uncertainty about something that might produce substantially lower than expected earnings, investors tend to either avoid the stock or are only willing to buy it at a much lower P-E than previously.

In fact, as each of the first three quarters' earnings were reported—and were disappointing—investors saw it as confirming all their worst fears about long-term earnings problems. It is also interesting to note that during 1977 three of the major stock averages, the Dow Jones Industrials, the S & P 500, and the NYSE Common Stock Index, all declined. Each of these averages is heavily weighted to big companies.

The only averages that were up in 1977 were the American Stock Exchange Index and other indexes that have a lot of small stocks in them, such as over-the-counter stocks. Thus, with nothing to get especially excited about at Polaroid, and with the market "action" moving away from big stocks, it is no surprise that Polaroid's stock had a bad year.

		Price range		P-E range		Aftertax return on equity	Pretax profit margin
	EPS	High	Low	High	Low		
1964	$ .58	$ 23 –	$ 16	40x –	28x	22.7%	25.8%
1965	.93	65 –	22	70 –	24	29.7	28.4
1966	1.51	87 –	54	58 –	36	38.1	30.0
1967	1.81	127 –	77	70 –	43	33.7	30.6
1968	1.86	134 –	88	72 –	47	26.6	32.1
1969	1.90	145 –	102	76 –	54	23.3	28.1
1970	1.86	130 –	51	70 –	27	14.4	25.6
1971	1.86	117 –	76	63 –	41	12.4	21.6
1972	1.30	150 –	87	115 –	66	7.8	13.0
1973	1.58	143 –	65	91 –	41	9.0	12.9
1974	.86	88 –	14	103 –	16	4.6	5.9
1975	1.91	44 –	15	23 –	8	9.8	14.9
1976	2.43	45 –	31	19 –	13	11.6	16.0
1977	2.81	39 –	25	14 –	9	12.2	14.9

1978—Beginning of a new era?

In the first three months of 1978, Polaroid traded in a narrow range between $23⅜ and $26¼. On January 31, the company held a conference for the press and investment analysts. At the conference, management first discussed the major new products for the year: the Polavision movie system and a new faster developing SX-70 film. Second they said that in the fourth quarter of 1977 sales were up about 20 percent from the fourth quarter of 1976. This was a pleasant surprise following the first three quarters of 1977, when sales were up only 7 percent. Nothing, however, was said about earnings. Third, they said camera sales were up 68 percent in the U.S. led by the One-Step, Polaroid's lowest-priced SX-70 film-using camera, which had been introduced in August 1977. In fact, sales of that camera were so strong that Polaroid was still backlogged to meet demand. Finally, Polaroid stated that SX-70 film manufacturing margins had improved substantially in 1977. Was the stock a buy or a sell?

The sellers would point out that things were really no better than last year. First, the Polavision movie system still looked like a possible failure and could cause losses for a long time to come. Second, Kodak had proved itself to be a real force in the market. This was reflected by Polaroid's disappointing sales in the first nine months of 1977, and by the price wars which waged all through the Christmas season in 1977. While Polaroid's fourth quarter sales were up sharply, earnings were not expected to do as well for a number of reasons.

1. The introduction of the Polavision home movie system was probably very expensive due to both marketing costs and manufacturing start-up costs. The volume of sales at this time was likely to be sufficiently low so as to result in a loss.

2. Sales were heavily weighted to the One-Step cameras where the competitive price-cutting was occurring, so profit margins were not likely to be very high.

3. Heavy advertising and other promotion expenses were incurred in the marketing battle against Kodak.

4. The older peel-apart film sales were still believed to be declining and were still probably the most profitable product in the company. Furthermore, the sellers argued that SX-70 film could never be as profitable as peel-apart because the SX-70 film pack came with the battery in it, which was an extra cost that the peel-apart film did not have.

The sellers' arguments seemed particularly valid when Polaroid's 4Q 1977 earnings were reported on February 22, 1978. While sales were up 21 percent as expected based on the January 31 company announcement, earnings per share were only up 17 percent. Normally when sales are up, particularly by such a large amount as 21 percent, earnings can be expected to be up even more because overhead costs remain relatively fixed. However, far more worrisome was the fact that earnings before tax *actually declined* by 2 percent despite the 21 percent gain in sales. The only reason net earnings after tax were up was because the effective tax rate was much lower than normal, and that could not be depended on to last for very long.

POLAROID
4Q Earnings Comparison
(Millions except per Share)

	Fourth quarter 1976	Fourth quarter 1977	Percent change up or down
Sales......................	$303.0	$366.6	+21%
Pretax profit margin..........	20.5%	16.6%	
Pretax profit.................	62.1	60.7	− 2
Taxes......................	30.2	23.0	
Effective tax rate	48.6%	37.9%	
Net profit	$ 31.9	$ 37.7	+18
Shares outstanding (million)...	32.86	32.86	
Earnings per share	$ .98	$ 1.15	+17

Thus, for whichever of the above reasons, or perhaps for others, if Polaroid's pretax profit fell in a quarter when sales were up sharply, there was real cause to worry about earnings in 1978 and beyond. Additionally, sellers pointed out that following the big burst of heavily promoted lower-priced camera sales in 1977 it was hard to see how camera sales could do as well in 1978. Finally there were the perennial arguments that Japanese companies would get into the instant photo field, further increasing competition, and that Polaroid was primarily interested in advancing the art of instant photography and was not really concerned with earnings growth.

With all of those near-term and long-term pressures on earnings, it was hard to foresee substantial growth in earnings, if any, so why should the stock sell at a P-E multiple any greater than most other stocks? Since Polaroid was selling at about $25 during most of the first quarter of 1978 and was expected by most analysts to earn between $2.50 and $3.00 per share in 1978, its P-E ratio was therefore between 10.0x and 8.3x, which was still slightly greater than the stock market average, so what was there to get excited about? Of course, the stock would fluctuate and could bounce up to perhaps $30 in the event of a strong market or of some better-than-expected news, but that was hardly worth the risk of what might happen if the economy slid into a recession and earnings declined again as in 1974 and 1975.

The buyers, of course, knew all these arguments but interpreted some differently and felt that some other factors were even more important.

First, at the January 31 meeting, Polaroid announced that manufacturing profits on SX-70 film had improved. This was no surprise, as unit sales volume was growing and the company was becoming more experienced at making it. So it could be projected that manufacturing profits would improve again in 1978, particularly as film sales should be higher. In fact, film sales should be substantially higher because camera sales were so strong in the fourth quarter. All those additional camera owners were bound to buy film for their new cameras in 1978. Thus, it became very easy to forecast both a good sales gain and an increase in profit margins in 1978. Net earnings could be up substantially.

Second, the buyers recognized that Polaroid probably lost money on Polavision in 1977, but that was not necessarily bad because, like all other Polaroid products, when volume increased and manufacturing efficiency improved with experience, that too might become profitable and thus add to company earnings. Therefore, with the new Polavision profits on top of profit growth in the rest of the company, earnings could be up substantially. And even if Polavision turned out to be a failure, as some predicted, if the company simply stopped making it and spending money advertising it, they would stop losing money on it, and thus total company earnings would be higher just from the absence of Polavision losses.

Third, buyers pointed out that the competition from Kodak, while important, was now a known factor, and, in fact, Polaroid still held the larger market share and was believed to be way ahead technologically. The uncertainty associated with the Kodak threat was now behind. In addition, Polaroid was suing Kodak for patent violation; while the case was likely to be in the courts for years, it could only help Polaroid if it won, and couldn't hurt if Polaroid lost because Kodak was already behaving as if it had won (i.e., was selling products using what Polaroid claimed were its patents).

Fourth, buyers believed that while peel-apart sales were likely to decline further, it was possible that the worst of the decline was behind already and, in fact, the substantial decline in the highly profitable peel-apart products may have been one of the reasons that earnings did so poorly in 1977.

Therefore, with the possibility of good sales and earnings gains in 1978, additional gains in 1979 could easily enable earnings to reach $4 per share. With the stock now at $25, it was selling at about 6x that earnings level. While right now most investors were probably skeptical of Polaroid's ability to ever earn that elusive $4 figure, it would look quite real for 1979 by late 1978 if, in fact, 1978 earnings were up over the $3 level. Also, if earnings growth was resuming, it might get enough investors excited to cause the P-E to expand again. Actually, looking at the historical table, Polaroid has reached at least 14x earnings every year, so if Polaroid went to 14x an earnings estimate of $4 for 1979, it would be a $56 stock, a substantial gain from the current level of $25. And if the stock was on its way to the $50s in 1979, it would surely anticipate a lot of that in 1978 (i.e., move up to the $30s or $40s or perhaps even into the $50s). Meanwhile, how much lower could the stock go? Book value was up to $25 per share, which meant that if the stock price went much lower it would be likely to attract the value buyers again. Therefore, the upside potential looked quite good if things went well (and there were a lot of reasons to believe they would) and downside risk seemed somewhat limited. Furthermore, the stock was totally out of favor in 1977 and had declined more or less steadily. Maybe investors would be ready to come back to Polaroid.

Notice that there were persuasive arguments on both the buy side and the sell side. The decision to buy or sell is rarely clear-cut. It always comes down to an individual investor's judgment about the relative likelihood of the bullish (buy) arguments and bearish (sell) arguments. **Would you buy the stock here, or sell it?**

CHART 13

Price ($)   **Price ($)**

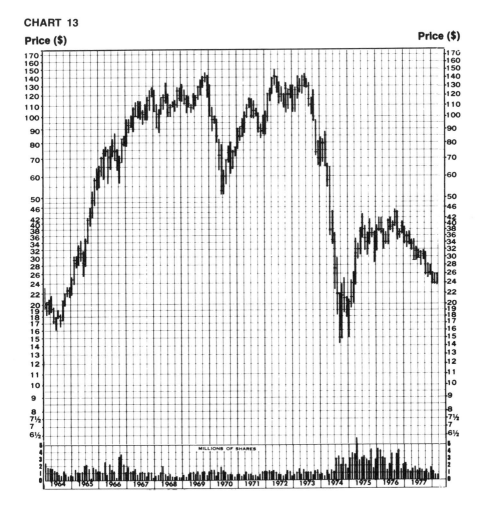

CHART 14

As it turns out, the stock market began to move up in April 1978 and Polaroid moved up sharply with it, touching a high of $60 in September. Were the buyers of Polaroid right, or were they just lucky and made money because the market went up and carried Polaroid with it? There are a few ways to answer that question. First, although the market did move up sharply in the April to September period, Polaroid moved up much further. The Dow Jones Industrial Average was up 20 percent but Polaroid was up 140 percent. That suggests Polaroid was really moving "on its own." However, when the market backed off sharply in September and October, Polaroid backed off sharply with it. Similarly, when the market turned back up in November, Polaroid turned back up with it. This suggests that Polaroid simply moves in the same direction as the market but is more volatile (i.e., Polaroid will usually have a bigger percentage gain or loss than the market averages over a period of a steadily rising or falling market). If this is true, an investor does *not have to know anything at all about Polaroid*. When the market seems likely to go up, simply buy Polaroid and you should do better than the market averages. When the market is going down, sell your stock and hold cash. One flaw in this theory is that many investors find it harder to predict the market as a whole than an individual stock. The other flaw is that Polaroid has not always moved in the same direction as the market, although it has done so most of the time over the period we have examined. Even when Polaroid does move directionally with the market, the actual time of a Polaroid bottom or top has not always coincided perfectly with the market. Furthermore, the fact that Polaroid has historically tended to move in the same direction as the market does not guarantee that it always will, and thus one is well advised to keep an eye on the fundamental outlook for the company (i.e., its near- and long-term earnings forecast).

Investors who use this technique of first making a judgment on the market as a whole, and then buying volatile stocks such as Polaroid when they think the market is going up, usually buy more than one such stock. The reason for buying more than one is the risk that this time the stock may not move with the market. By buying a group of stocks that are expected to behave that way, even if one fails to go up there is still a good chance that you can make money on the group. The major risk of this investment technique is that you may be wrong about the direction of the market.

Let us now return to the question of whether the investor was right when he bought Polaroid at $25 in early 1978. Of course, since the stock went up—and that is the goal of the investment—we could simply say, "Of course, he was right." But our purpose here is to improve our skills in stock valuation, so the real question is, Were the buyers right for the right reason? Since their decision to buy was based on a judgment of the improving outlook for earnings, let's look at what happened to earnings to see if they were right.

First quarter earnings were reported in April 1978. Sales were up 25 percent, but earnings before tax were down. Once again, only a lower effective tax rate enabled net earnings to rise slightly. However a blizzard in eastern Massachusetts in February closed Polaroid's plants for a week, which hurt earnings both because Polaroid elected to pay its employees during the shutdown and because of the big expenses associated with getting the film manufacturing equipment back to peak efficiency. In fact, Polaroid said that were it not for the storm, earnings would have been up in line with sales. Thus, both the bulls and the bears could be encouraged. The buyers noted that sales were up a substantial 25 percent, which confirmed their belief that SX-70 film sales were taking off as a result of the surge in camera sales in late 1977. Further, a 25 percent earnings gain rate (were it not for the storm) implied earnings for the full year of $3.50. That, in turn, made at least $4 easily predictable for 1979. The bears, though, noted that, even if there were no storm and the earnings gain matched the sales gain, it would have been a disappointment. With a 25 percent sales gain, earnings should certainly have been up more because many of the costs are fixed. Thus, there was still a profit margin problem somewhere in the company. In that regard, management announced that the sales mix in the quarter was worse than in the first quarter of 1977 (i.e., the products the company was selling in the 1Q 1978 had, on average, a lower profit margin than the products that were being sold in the 1Q 1977). This could have been due to: (a) the big increase in One-Step camera sales, (b) the continued decline in highly profitable peel-apart film sales and the increase in lower profit SX-70 film sales, and (c) the increase in Polavision sales, which were probably losing money. For whichever reasons, the problem might continue for an unknown period.

The stock continued to move up through the summer of 1978. Despite the ambiguity of the first quarter earnings report, most Wall Street analysts interpreted it positively and raised their full-year 1978 earnings estimates over the next couple of months. In addition, Polaroid announced and showed a self-focusing camera at the annual meeting in April and later said it would be introduced in the fall. The self-focusing feature was interpreted favorably by Wall Street because it could provide a boost to sales and hence earnings. First, it might cause some people to select a Polaroid camera rather than a Kodak instant camera which lacked the self-focusing feature, and second, it might convince some people to buy a Polaroid camera who previously had trouble with focusing and thus did not want to use a camera. Any new camera owners would also help increase Polaroid's film sales, and increasing film sales were likely to be highly profitable now that Polaroid had become more efficient at SX-70 film manufacturing.

On July 19, Polaroid reported second quarter earnings as follows:

	Second quarter 1977	Second quarter 1978	Percent change
Sales	$249.3	$319.7	+28%
Pretax margin	15.5%	14.2%	
Pretax profit	38.5	45.5	+18
Taxes.	18.1	19.3	
Tax rate.	46.9%	42.4%	
Net income.	$ 20.5	$ 26.2	
EPS	$ .62	$ .80	+29

Sales were up a very encouraging 28 percent from the second quarter of 1977, and EPS was up 29 percent. However, the pretax earnings gain was only 18 percent because the pretax profit margin declined. It took a lower tax rate to enable EPS to climb 29 percent. Again, it was disappointing that earnings were not up more than sales. Nevertheless, the second quarter EPS of $.80 per share made it seem likely Polaroid was indeed going to earn well over $3.00 per share in 1978 and thus $4.00 per share was well within reach in 1979. In fact, at least two respected Wall Street analysts were projecting that earnings in 1979 could exceed $5 per share. Therefore, if the stock sold at a P-E of 14 times, a P-E level that had been reached or exceeded every year in the past 14 years, it would reach $70 per share. Thus, despite the deterioration in the profit margin, the stock's move upward seemed justified by the increasing earnings.

The stock, however, peaked at $60 in early September and then bounced down and up sharply until year-end. Interestingly, each of the peaks and troughs in the bounces coincided with peaks and troughs in the market averages. Once again we see Polaroid moving in the same direction as the market but with greater magnitude. In fact, that pattern persisted all through 1978 as both the market averages and Polaroid declined in January and February, made a slight recovery in March, moved up sharply from April to September, and then backed off. Again one might ask whether the fundamental outlook for earnings and dividends really matters or whether the stock simply follows the market.

Third quarter sales and earnings, reported in October, were up very strongly, and this time profit before tax was up more than sales as the pretax margin expanded from 13.7 percent to 15.4 percent.

	3Q 1977	3Q 1978	Percent change
Sales	$254	$342	+34%
Pretax margin	13.7%	15.4%	
Pretax profit	34.9	52.5	+50
Tax rate	42.6%	34.5%	
Net profit	$ 20.0	$ 34.4	
EPS	$ .61	$ 1.04	+71

A continued decline in the tax rate added even more to net profit and EPS. Further, in a letter to dealers dated December 4, Polaroid said that despite dramatically increased production, it would be unable to meet demand for One-Step cameras in 1978. This not only implied that camera sales would remain strong at least into early 1979, but that film sales were likely to remain strong throughout 1979 as all the new camera owners bought film. Thus the fundamentals (earnings and dividend outlook) continued to improve and analysts continued to raise their full-year 1978 and 1979 earnings estimates. Despite this improving outlook, the stock continued to decline in early November along with the market, and moved up in late November and December, but only when the rest of

the market was moving up. Should we then abandon attempts to predict
Polaroid's earnings in 1979? The answer will turn out to be "No." In 1979
Polaroid breaks with the pattern of doing what the market does.

	EPS	Price range		P-E range		Aftertax return on equity	Pretax profit margin
		High	Low	High	Low		
1964	$ .58	$ 23 –	$ 16	40x –	28x	22.7%	25.8%
1965	.93	65 –	22	70 –	24	29.7	28.4
1966	1.51	87 –	54	58 –	36	38.1	30.0
1967	1.81	127 –	77	70 –	43	33.7	30.6
1968	1.86	134 –	88	72 –	47	26.6	32.1
1969	1.90	145 –	102	76 –	54	23.3	28.1
1970	1.86	130 –	51	70 –	27	14.4	25.6
1971	1.86	117 –	76	63 –	41	12.4	21.6
1972	1.30	150 –	87	115 –	66	7.8	13.0
1973	1.58	143 –	65	91 –	41	9.0	12.9
1974	.86	88 –	14	103 –	16	4.6	5.9
1975	1.91	44 –	15	23 –	8	9.8	14.9
1976	2.43	45 –	31	19 –	13	11.6	16.0
1977	2.81	39 –	25	14 –	9	12.2	14.9
1978	3.60	60 –	23	17 –	6	14.3	13.9

As 1979 began, Polaroid's outlook continued to look good. Indications
were that fourth quarter sales stayed strong right through year-end, and
even sales of Polavision, the instant movie system, apparently picked up,
although with the help of expensive promotion. In January and early
February many Wall Street earnings estimates for 1978, the year just
ended, were in the range of $3.70 to $3.90/share, and estimates for 1979
in the range of $4.50–$5.50 were common. When the fourth quarter and
full-year 1978 earnings were reported on February 23, 1979, they were
disappointing. Full-year earnings were $3.60 per share. Although this
was a strong 28 percent gain from the 1977 EPS level of $2.81, and was
much higher than most people had been estimating earlier in 1978, it was
below the most recent expectation of $3.70–$3.90. Before the earnings
were reported the stock was selling at about $50, but the disappointment
produced an immediate influx of sell orders for which there were no
matching buy orders. As a result, the specialist on the floor of the New
York Stock Exchange who was in charge of trading Polaroid had to
temporarily stop trading the stock. In Wall Street jargon, "Trading was
halted due to an imbalance of orders." Before the stock could be re-
opened (i.e., trading resumed), the specialist had to wait until enough
new buy and sell orders came in at matching prices. The new price
turned out to be $44 per share. At that price some people were now
willing to buy, and probably some people who wanted to sell at $50

changed their minds and cancelled their sell orders because they thought the stock had fallen far enough to reflect the disappointment, which, after all, seemed minor compared to expectations. The stock kept falling, however, and two days later reached $39 before stablilizing for most of March in the $40–$41 area (see chart 15 below).

Why did Polaroid fall so sharply given the excellent year the company actually had? The answer is simply that investors were anticipating a better year. In fact, due to the improving outlook during 1978 the stock closed that year much higher than it started the year; but had the "market" been projecting earnings of $3.60 rather than $3.70–$3.90, the stock would probably not have gotten as high as it did in August. The lesson here, repeated many times. is that *the stock market anticipates.*

CHART 15
Price ($)   **Price ($)**

MILLIONS OF SHARES

When anticipations are raised, or earnings come in better than anticipations, stocks usually rise. When expectations are lowered, or earnings come in below expectations, stocks generally fall. A notable exception to that rule occurred in late 1978. Recall that when Polaroid reported third quarter earnings in October, they were better than expected and caused analysts to raise their full-year 1978 and 1979 forecasts. Nevertheless, the stock declined more or less steadily through mid-November along with the rest of the market. This inconsistency, *that a stock sometimes behaves on its own and sometimes reacts with the market as if it had no behavior of its own, is a fact of life in the stock market.* This is one reason why stock moves, in the short run, are so hard to predict. Nevertheless, by continuously watching a stock's behavior in the market, how it reacts to company announcements of earnings, new products, and so on, and how it reacts with the market in general, you will develop an increased ability to spot these apparently irrational moves in a stock, and therefore develop an increased confidence in your ability to predict the stock's long-term behavior.

It is instructive to ask why the stock fell as many points as it did on February 23. Earnings of $3.60 were only 8 percent below the most optimistic estimates of $3.90, and only 3 percent below more "conservative" estimates of $3.70, but the stock declined $6, or 12 percent, immediately and was off 20 percent when it sold at $40 two days later. The answer then, at least partly, may be that when some investors saw they were wrong about earnings, regardless of by how much, they lost confidence in their earnings estimates for 1979 or, in general, lost confidence in their ability to understand the stock. As we have stated before, the price-earnings ratio is usually related to both the expected growth rate of earnings and *the degree of confidence investors have in their estimates.* In this case the impact on investors' confidence was probably more important than the actual earnings disappointment.

Here is the P-E based on expected 1978 earnings before results were announced:

$$\frac{\text{Price}}{\text{Estimated earnings}} = \frac{\$50.00}{\$3.80} = 13.2\text{x}$$

Now the P-E based on actual 1978 results after the announcement:

$$\frac{\text{Price}}{\text{Actual earnings}} = \frac{\$43.00}{\$3.60} = 11.9\text{x}$$

Other possible factors causing people to sell after the disappointing earnings included: (1) the expectation that earnings estimates would be lowered for 1979 and, (2) since experience suggests that there will be selling pressure on the stock following the disappointing earnings, some stockholders sold immediately just to get out ahead of others. Others may have shorted[5] the stock in anticipation of a further decline, thus putting even more selling pressure on the stock.

While some holders sold immediately due to the disappointment, others waited to see all the fourth quarter and full year-end figures in order to make a more informed decision on the 1979 prospects, and on whether to sell the stock, hold it, or buy more, given the lower price.

POLAROID
Fourth Quarter 1978 Results
($ Millions except per Share)

	4Q 1977	4Q 1978	Percent change
Sales............	$366.6	$474.5	+29%
Pretax margin	16.6%	15.2%	
Pretax income	$ 60.7	72.1	+19
Tax rate	37.9%	39.8%	
Net income.......	$ 37.7	$ 43.4	
EPS............	$ 1.15	$ 1.32	+15

Full-Year Results—1978 versus 1977

	1977	1978	Percent change
Sales............	$1,061.9	$1,376.6	+30%
Pretax margin	15.2%	14.1%	
Pretax income.....	$ 161.5	194.5	+20
Tax rate	42.8%	39.1%	
Net income	$ 92.3	$ 110.4	
EPS............	$ 2.81	$ 3.60	+28

The major disappointment in the 4Q was apparently that the pretax profit margin had declined again despite another big increase in sales. Thus pretax profit was up less than sales. This had occurred in the first and second quarters. But recall that in the third quarter, the pretax profit margin expanded, as would be expected given a large increase in sales, and this gave rise to expectations that it would expand again in the fourth quarter. Since it did not, it could again be assumed that the company was having cost pressures or product pricing problems which might persist in 1979. If these pressures were lowering the pretax margin when sales were up substantially, what would happen to the pretax margin, and hence profits, if sales were not up substantially? In addition, those who were bearish pointed out that 1979 might be a recession year, so sales probably would not be up much.

The bulls, however, pointed out that new camera sales were so strong in 1978 that film sales were almost certain to be strong in 1979. Further-

---

[5] See *Short Selling* in Appendix One.

more, film was generally assumed by Wall Street to have much higher profit margins than cameras, so 1979 should be a good year anyway, even if a recession did impact new camera sales. Then by 1980, the economy would be coming out of the recession and camera sales could be expected to pick up again.

The bulls were also encouraged because the Polavision movie system lost money in 1978. This was encouraging because if it should become profitable, that would add to earnings, but if it continued to sell poorly, the product would eventually be discontinued, and that would be good because the losses would stop. Polaroid did not reveal how much it was losing on Polavision, but the analyst from Merrill Lynch who followed Polaroid estimated that the loss on Polavision in 1978 was about $25–$30 million, equivalent to about $.40 to $.45 per share. Thus an investor could have reasoned as follows (see table below). Even if nothing else changed at Polaroid, just the swing from a loss on Polavision of $.40 per share to breakeven or a gain would add substantially to the company's net earnings.

Earnings per share	1978	1979 (Assuming no other changes, but Pola-vision earns a profit of $6 million or $.16 per share)	1979 (Assuming nothing else changes, but Polaroid gives up on Pola-vision and so the losses stop)
Estimated profit on all products except Polavision	$4.00	$4.00	$4.00
Estimated (loss) profit on Polavision	(.40)	.16	.00
Reported earnings	3.60	4.16	4.00

Thus a money-losing product is not necessarily bad from a stock-holder's point of view, because if it either swings to profitability or is discontinued, it can result in an increase in company earnings.

Despite the bullish arguments, the stock remained in the $38 to $42 range in March, below the level of the price break on February 23, when the disappointing earnings were reported. The price break can be seen dramatically on the daily chart (Chart 16). (We will continue to use daily charts from this point on.)

Polaroid had declined to $39 at the end of March 1979, a 25 percent decline from the $52 level reached at the end of 1978. The Dow Jones Industrial Average and the Standard & Poor's 500, however, were up about 7 percent and 6 percent, respectively. Here, then, is the first case in years where Polaroid stock moved meaningfully in the opposite direction from the market as a whole.

CHART 16

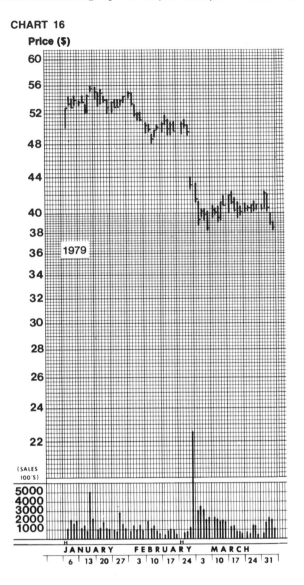

	EPS	Price range High	Price range Low	P-E range High	P-E range Low	Aftertax return on equity	Pretax profit margin
1964	$ .58	$ 23 –	$ 16	40x –	28x	22.7%	25.8%
1965	.93	65 –	22	70 –	24	29.7	28.4
1966	1.51	87 –	54	58 –	36	38.1	30.0
1967	1.81	127 –	77	70 –	43	33.7	30.6
1968	1.86	134 –	88	72 –	47	26.6	32.1
1969	1.90	145 –	102	76 –	54	23.3	28.1
1970	1.86	130 –	51	70 –	27	14.4	25.6
1971	1.86	117 –	76	63 –	41	12.4	21.6
1972	1.30	150 –	87	115 –	66	7.8	13.0
1973	1.58	143 –	65	91 –	41	9.0	12.9
1974	.86	88 –	14	103 –	16	4.6	5.9
1975	1.91	44 –	15	23 –	8	9.8	14.9
1976	2.43	45 –	31	19 –	13	11.6	16.0
1977	2.81	39 –	25	14 –	9	12.2	14.9
1978	3.60	60 –	23	17 –	6	14.3	13.9

Another recession?

Late in the first quarter of 1979, the Merrill Lynch analyst reported that she had taken a survey of photographic dealers and discovered that retail sales of Polaroid products had slowed. In addition, Polaroid revealed that it had ended 1978 with between 20,000 and 21,000 employees, versus 16,394 at the end of 1977. With the possibility that there would only be a minimal gain in sales, if any, and with labor expense obviously much higher due to the increased employment, it appeared that first quarter earnings might be lower than previously anticipated. As a result, she lowered her first quarter and full-year earnings estimates. Most other analysts were also lowering their estimates as a result of both the year-end 1978 disappointment and the indications that the first quarter was not going to be up as sharply as one might have expected, given the strong camera sales in 1978.

The first quarter of 1979 was reported in late April. Sales were up 10 percent, a substantial slowing from the sales gains of 1978. Earnings were up 18 percent from $.44/share to $.54/share. While the relative improvement in earnings versus sales could be interpreted favorably, it must be recalled that in the first quarter of the previous year, profits were held back by a big snowstorm that closed many Polaroid plants in February. The company had indicated then that the shutdown cost Polaroid roughly $.10 per share. Thus, after adjusting for the storm, earnings were essentially unchanged from the year-ago first quarter on a 10 percent sales gain, and were therefore disappointing. This illustrates an important point: One cannot simply look at an earnings gain or decline and say it is good or bad. Both the current and the earlier figure must be adjusted to remove nonrecurring factors, such as the snowstorm. Frequently, of course, such nonrecurring factors are unknown to investors, and even if known, the company may not say how big they were in terms of sales or earnings. In that case, the analyst has to make a guess, or alternatively, avoid the stock until the uncertainty is cleared up.

The balance sheet at the end of the first quarter also showed some disturbing results:

POLAROID
Part of Balance Sheet
($ Millions)

	12/31/78	3/31/79	Percent change
Cash and Marketable securities......	$179	$129	−28%
Total inventory:	407	512	+26
Finished goods	133	223	+68
Work in progress...............	149	150	+ 1
Raw materials	125	139	+11

In prior years, *Cash and Marketable securities* usually increased during the first quarter as dealers paid their bills after Christmas; this year, it decreased. Also, in each of the past four years, total inventory at the end of the 1Q was up between 7 percent and 13 percent from the year-end level as Polaroid began to rebuild following the heavy Christmas sales. This year, however, *Total inventory* was up 26 percent, and the *Finished goods* portion of the inventory was up an extraordinary 68 percent. This indicated that products were not selling as well as had been indicated by the dealer survey. While the weak sales and earnings performance (the income statement) indicated that a problem occurred in the first quarter, the cash and inventory problem (the balance sheet) indicated that the problem was continuing at the end of the quarter and therefore might be a continuing problem into the second quarter at least. The analyst can get a better idea of a company's near-term outlook by keeping an eye on the quarterly balance sheet as well as on the income statement.

The inventory problem was confirmed by Polaroid's management. It was not only surprised by the low level of sales, but it also said there were some product returns from dealers who were overstocked and that some dealers were cancelling orders. It was now clear that Polaroid's orders from dealers would be weak until the dealers' excess inventories were sold off.

At the company's annual meeting in late April, management said that it was "somewhat cautious about the outlook for the year." Reflecting this change in outlook, the stock declined to about $35 by the end of April. With the new outlook, but at the lower stock price, one could, as usual, be either bullish or bearish on the stock. With most Wall Street earnings estimates for 1979 now in the $3.10 to $4.00 range, the stock was selling in a P-E range of 11x to 9x estimated earnings, a low level by Polaroid's standards. **Was the stock a buy or a sell?**

CHART 17

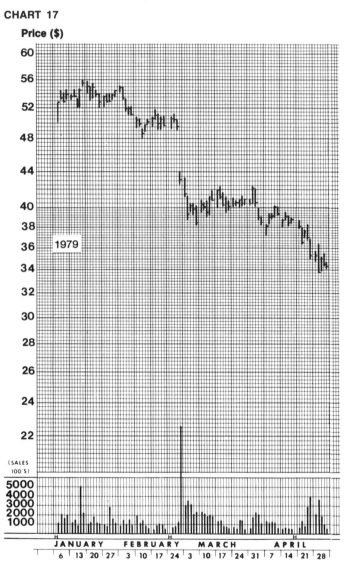

Evidently the disappointment in the first quarter news was not yet fully "absorbed" by the market at the end of April, as the stock continued to decline in May (Chart 18).

Sales and earnings prospects for the year continued to worsen through the spring and summer. In May, the company announced layoffs. In early July, Polaroid said it expected second quarter sales would be up 6 percent and earnings would be off substantially (actual results would be announced in late July.) Earnings estimates by Wall Street analysts continued to decline. When the second quarter was reported on July 26 it turned out that sales were up only 1 percent and earnings were off 50 percent. Inventory continued to grow and cash continued to decline with the result that the company had to increase its bank borrowings substantially. This also hurt earnings, as Polaroid had higher interest *expense* on the borrowings, and had lower interest *income* since it had lower marketable securities invested to earn interest.

At the end of July, Wall Street earnings estimates ranged from about $2.50 to $3.50 for 1979, and analysts were using wide ranges for 1980

CHART 18

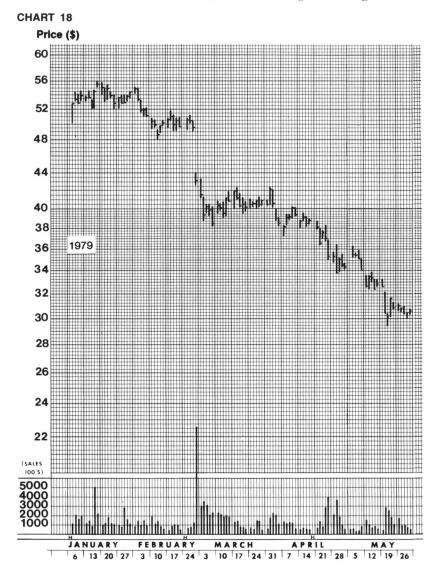

Price ($)

because it was unclear how long the lull in sales was going to last. Published Wall Street estimates for 1980 ranged from $3.20 to $4.75. The stock was selling for about $30 per share, which was slightly above the book value of $28 at the end of the second quarter. With the stock having come down to $30, reflecting the lowering of the current year's earnings outlook, but with most of Wall Street anticipating an earnings gain in 1980, was this the time to buy? Did the stock make a bottom in mid-July?

Recall that in 1974 the stock made a bottom well before the worst earnings figures were reported. In 1974, the stock bottomed at $14⅛ in September, bounced a bit, and then dropped back to $15 in January 1975 before moving up sharply. Earnings didn't reach a bottom until the quarter ended March 31, 1975, which was not reported until April 1975. *Again, stock prices always anticipate.* So if earnings were expected to begin to recover in 1980, it was reasonable, based on history, that the stock could bottom out in mid-1979. Look at chart 19 on page 253 and make your judgment before reading on. **Would you buy the stock here or sell it?**

The Polavision write-down

From mid-July to early September the stock bounced around in the $26–$31 range. On September 12, Polaroid made a major announcement. The company said it was taking a $68 million write-down in the third quarter to reduce the value of Polavision inventories to "nominal value" (near zero). What does this mean? Is it favorable or unfavorable for the stock? In the two weeks following the announcement the stock moved up from $27 to $29—too small a move to say the announcement had a significant impact on the stock. Although the announcement was of major importance to the company, why did it not have a major impact on the stock? Because it was anticipated. Not that anyone knew (at least no one publicly predicted it just before it happened), but it seemed apparent to analysts that Polavision was not going to be a successful product, and thus a write-off was inevitable eventually. Thus the write-down or write-off was generally anticipated.

CHART 19

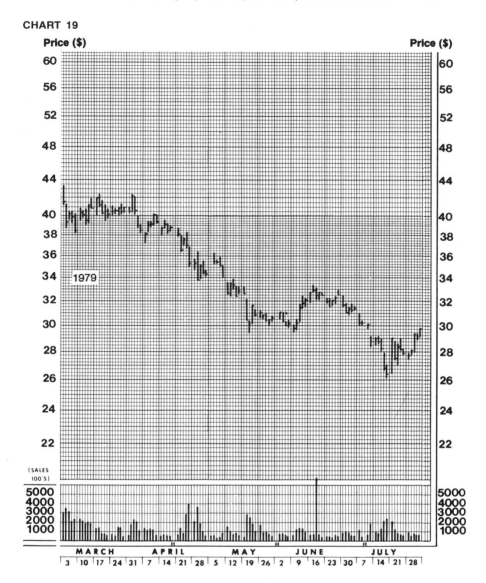

Management's decision to write down the Polavision inventory probably indicates that it had conceded the product was not going to be
successful and it would have to sell the remaining movie cameras and
film at a loss or scrap them. While some companies would give a lot of
details about such a write-down, Polaroid tends not to give out a lot of

CHART 20

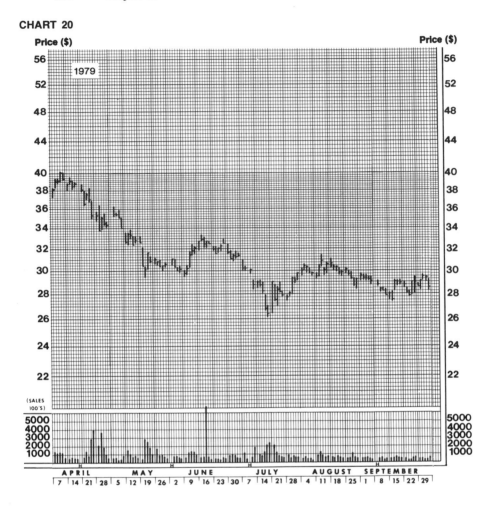

information, so investors are forced to make assumptions or guesses, or simply to ignore the stock. However, when Polaroid stock does move up, we have seen that it often moves up sharply and a lot of money can be made, so the stock has always been followed as closely as possible by investors to try to catch those big up moves.

The write-down was announced to be $68 million before considering tax savings. It included both some hardware (the camera, the screen, and some lighting equipment that could be bought with the system) and some film cassettes. Polaroid did say that it was staying in the business of selling the Polavision system and its film. Had Polaroid totally gotten out of the business, it would probably have had to write off the remaining book value of the plant and equipment, also.

Before we can attempt to anticipate the effect of the write-down on the stock, it is necessary to understand clearly what an inventory write-down is. Such write-downs often indicate major turning points in company earnings, and possibly in the stocks also. Thus, even though a major write-down is clearly a nonrecurring event—in fact, probably a rare event for most companies—it is worthwhile to get a clear understanding of the process. In the following explanation, the dollar figures used are entirely my own guesses, as Polaroid did not give out specific information; but even if the figures are way off, they are adequate to illustrate the write-down. Further, it shows the nature of estimates that investment analysts are forced to make and the reasoning process that enters investment judgments.

Before the write-down, let us assume that Polaroid sold a Polavision camera system (camera plus screen and lights, but excluding film) to a dealer for $400.[6] Polaroid did not manufacture the camera system, but had it made by another company under a contract. Let us assume Polaroid paid that company $350 per system. Thus every time Polaroid sold a system, it reported a gross profit of $50 (we are assuming).

```
Sales ...................... $ 400
     Less: Cost of goods sold ....   (350)
Equals: Gross profit. ..........  $  50
```

This however does not include marketing expenses, such as advertising to the public, advertising in trade magazines to dealers, displays for dealers to use in their stores, salesmen's salaries, special dealer bonuses, and other items. Let's assume that all the marketing expenses amount to about $250 per system, based on the number of systems actually sold. Thus, the real contribution to Polaroid's income statement would look more like this (for each system).

```
Sales ........................ $ 400
     Less: Cost of goods sold......   (350)
     Less: Marketing expenses.....   (250)
Equals: Loss ................. $(200)
```

A similar set of assumptions could be made to show the loss on each film cassette, but since the same idea would apply to film as to the camera system, we will not do it for both. (An interesting but probably irrelevant

---

[6] The dealer of course marked it up to a higher price when he sold it at retail in order to make his profit, but that is irrelevant here.

question is, How much of the marketing expense should be attributed to the camera system and how much to the film?)

Since the camera systems were not selling well, but had already been manufactured and sold to Polaroid, Polaroid carried them in its inventory, probably at about its cost of $350 per system. This was part of the reason Polaroid's inventory was so large all year. To write the inventory down to "nominal value," let's say $10 per system, probably means Polaroid realized it could only sell them at much less than its cost ($350) and therefore would incur a big loss. So, if the inventory value of each system is reduced from $350 to $10, it means a write-down of $340 per system. If we assume there were 100,000 systems in inventory, the write-down from the camera systems in total would be: 100,000 systems × $340/system = $34 million. This $34 million could either be added directly to *Cost of goods sold* or, perhaps, become a special line on the income statement called "Write-down Expense," or "Inventory Write-down Expense," or some similar title.[7]

Recall that the total write-off was $68 million, and our estimates have only accounted for $34 million. The rest might be assumed to be the film write-down. Film, of course, deteriorates over time, and if it is not used by a certain date after manufacture it is no good. Since Polaroid had anticipated selling many more camera systems, it probably manufactured a lot of film. Since this film was not expected to be sold now, it would shortly become worthless. Thus, this film also had to be written down or, in this case, completely written off (i.e., written down to zero because it was worthless).

The $68 million write-off expense, whether added to Cost of Goods Sold or put into the income statement as a special-line item would obviously reduce Polaroid's earnings for the year substantially. Thus, analysts had to reduce their 1979 earnings estimates again. The write-down also has an important effect on 1980 earnings. Let's assume that, in 1980, the camera system will be sold to a dealer for a much-reduced price of $200. Let's also assume that marketing expenses are reduced. Thus, the effect of selling a system in 1980 might look like this.

Sales........................	$ 200
Less: Cost of goods sold......	(10)
Less: Marketing expenses.....	(120)
Equals: Profit contribution.......	$ 70

---

[7] Polaroid announced later that $19 million of the inventory write-down (revaluation) was attributable to camera systems that were not yet in Polaroid inventory, but that Polaroid was required to buy from the supplier under contract. Accounting principles require that even though Polaroid did not have some of the products yet, since the loss on them was reasonably assured, it should report that loss now.

Or we could make different assumptions and the effect of selling a system might look like this:

```
Sales........................ $ 150
   Less: Cost of goods sold...... ( 10)
   Less: Marketing expenses..... (160)
Equals: Loss .................. $( 20)
```

Unfortunately, as analysts we don't known which of the above 1980 assumptions is more accurate, or even if either is close. About all we can say with sureness is that, as a result of the write-down, either the loss per unit sold in 1980 will be substantially reduced, compared to the 1979 experience, or perhaps the product will break even or show a profit. Therefore, the write-down has two effects. First, it lowers 1979 earnings, and second, it raises 1980 earnings—possibly just by reducing the loss that would otherwise have occurred in 1980, or possibly by also adding profit.

Let's now look at the process an analyst goes through in adjusting his earnings estimates for the write-down. First, we must convert the $68 million pretax write-down to an aftertax basis. This is done as follows:

```
Pretax write-off................ $68 million
   Less: Tax savings
      (assuming 47% tax rate).... (32)
Equals: Write-off after tax ...... $36
   Divided by
      shares outstanding......... 32.885
Equals: Write-off per share ..... $ 1.10 million
```

Now we can set up a worksheet for earnings projections:

Projection	1978	1979	1980
Estimated EPS excluding Polavision	$4.00	$2.70	$2.70
Est. Polavision operating (loss) or profit/share	(.40)	(.10)	?
Est. Polavision write-down per share		(1.10)	
Est. reported EPS (1978 actual)	$3.60	$1.50	$2.70

Analysts usually recognize they cannot be that precise in estimating the future, so their worksheets would more typically use ranges and look as follows:

Analyst's Worksheet

Projection	1978	1979 Range	1980 Range
Estimated EPS excluding Polavision	$4.00	$2.50 to 2.90	$2.50 to 3.50
Est. Polavision operating (loss) or profit/share	(.40)	(.10) to .00	(.10) to .12
Est. Polavision write-down per share	—	(1.10) to (1.10)	
Est. reported EPS (1978 actual)	$3.60	$1.30 to 1.80	$2.40 to 3.62

COMMENTS

1. *Estimated earnings excluding Polavision in 1979* is well down from the 1978 estimate. This is because the second quarter earnings were bad and most indications were that business was continuing weak.
2. *Estimated earnings excluding Polavision in 1980* is assumed by us to be between $2.50 and $3.50. Another analyst might use a lower range, such as $2.00 to $2.50 if he were worried about the consumer economy and Kodak competition. Yet another analyst might use a higher range such as $3.00– $3.80 if she thought the economy was going to recover and, perhaps, that Polaroid was going to introduce some successful new products.
3. *Estimated operating (loss) or profit from Polavision* refers to the loss or profit Polaroid earns from sales of Polavision products independent of the write-down. As shown above, because of the write-down we don't know if Polaroid will show a smaller loss or a profit in 1980. Thus, each analyst must use a range reflecting his own assumptions. We will guess that Polaroid could lose as much as $.10 per share in our pessimistic assumption. Other analysts might have higher or lower assumptions for 1980, and they might have a wider or narrower range of assumptions.

Having set up our earnings forecast worksheet, we can now turn to what this all means for the stock. As usual, a good place to start is to look at the price-earnings ratios. Since it is now September 1979, investors will no longer care about 1978 and will be focusing on 1979 and 1980. For both years one might look at both the low end and the high end of the estimated earnings range, or one might just choose a "best estimate" near the midpoint of each range. Our best estimate of 1979 earnings is $1.55, and our best estimate of 1980 earnings is $3.00.

Current price		Estimated 1979 EPS	P-E based on 1979 EPS estimates		Estimated 1980 EPS	P-E based on 1980 EPS estimates
$28	Low	$1.30	21.5x	Low	$2.40	11.7x
	Best	1.55	18.1	Best	3.00	9.3
	High	1.80	15.6	High	3.62	7.7

Notice that the P-E ratios for 1979 are high because the earnings estimates were all depressed by the $68 million or $1.10 per share write-down. Therefore, one could look at the P-Es for 1979, which are at the high end of the range for the past three years and say that the stock is overpriced and should be sold, or should not be purchased if not owned. However, the 1979 write-down of $1.10 per share will presumably not happen again and, therefore, such a "nonrecurring event" can usually be ignored by investors if it does not represent any serious threat to the company's long-term dividend outlook. In this case, Polaroid is expected to earn between $1.30–$1.80/share in 1979 and the dividend is $1.00 per share. While this represents a high payout ratio, there are clearly enough earnings to cover the dividend. Furthermore, with earnings expected to spring back to around $3 per share in 1980, the dividend would be very well covered. Thus, the dividend does not appear likely to be reduced either currently or over the long term as a result of the write-down. In fact, the result of this nonrecurring event is to stop or substantially reduce the losses on Polavision. This, in turn, will add to earnings in future years and possibly enable larger or earlier dividend increases. So the write-down can be interpreted favorably and the artificially high P-Es of 1979 can be ignored. As stock market investors, we are interested primarily in the ability of a company to generate an ongoing stream of earnings and dividends for the present and future, and we are not especially concerned with nonrecurring events if they do not affect our projections of future earnings and dividends. However, this nonrecurring write-down was the result of a poor management decision to pursue this product. If management of any company repeatedly makes poor decisions that result in major unsuccessful products and write-downs or write-offs, then the company will soon be in serious trouble.

Since the Polavision write-down was presumably nonrecurring, perhaps it would be more appropriate to look at the P-E based on a 1979 earnings estimate which excludes the write-off (i.e., an earnings estimate of $2.50–2.90). But why bother? By this time of year investors are beginning to focus on 1980 earnings, anyway.

Current price	Estimated 1980 EPS		P-E based on 1980 EPS estimates
$28	Low	$2.40	11.7x
	Best	3.00	9.3
	High	3.62	7.7

Is the stock expensive or cheap? What P-E could Polaroid be expected to sell at in 1980? To answer that question, let us begin by looking at the past and see if it might be a guide to the future.

	EPS	Price range High	Price range Low	P-E range High	P-E range Low	Aftertax return on equity	Pretax profit margin
1964	$ .58	$ 23 –	$ 16	40x –	28x	22.7%	25.8%
1965	.93	65 –	22	70 –	24	29.7	28.4
1966	1.51	87 –	54	58 –	36	38.1	30.0
1967	1.81	127 –	77	70 –	43	33.7	30.6
1968	1.86	134 –	88	72 –	47	26.6	32.1
1969	1.90	145 –	102	76 –	54	23.3	28.1
1970	1.86	130 –	51	70 –	27	14.4	25.6
1971	1.86	117 –	76	63 –	41	12.4	21.6
1972	1.30	150 –	87	115 –	66	7.8	13.0
1973	1.58	143 –	65	91 –	41	9.0	12.9
1974	.86	88 –	14	103 –	16	4.6	5.9
1975	1.91	44 –	15	23 –	8	9.8	14.9
1976	2.43	45 –	31	19 –	13	11.6	16.0
1977	2.81	39 –	25	14 –	9	12.2	14.9
1978	3.60	60 –	23	17 –	6	14.3	13.9

A review of the historical P-E ratios quickly suggests that all the pre-1975 data is irrelevant as being much too high. If we focus just on the past three years, 1976, 1977, and 1978, it appears reasonable to assume that the P-E will reach 14x at least once during the year. How low might it get? In 1978 it got as low as 6x, but that was when the stock was selling at $23 at the beginning of the year, when no one foresaw earnings as high as $3.60. Thus, a P-E of 6x probably did not reflect the market's true evaluation then and is not a good assumption to make now. Thus, we might reasonably assume the next lowest P-E, which was the 8x reached in 1975.

For the high-end P-E it is probably safest to stay with the 14x. If, in fact, the stock goes up to 17x or 19x or even higher, so much the better, but it appears safest not to assume that in making an investment decision at this point. Assuming very high P-Es might be classified more as hope than good investment judgment. Now let's look at the forecast for Polaroid stock, given the assumed P-E range and earnings estimates:

1980 estimate	Assumed P/E	Assumed price
Low estimate......$2.40	8x	$19
	14	34
Best estimate 3.00	8x	$24
	14	42
High estimate 3.62	8x	$29
	14	51

Is the stock attractive at $28? If the "best" estimate of $3 comes to pass, then it appears that the stock has $4 or 14 percent downside risk

($28 to $24) and has good upside potential of 50 percent ($28 to $42) if the P-E stays in our forecast range. That appears to be an attractive risk/ reward ratio. But what if the low end estimate comes to pass? Then the stock has downside risk of $9 ($28 to $19) and upside potential of only $6 ($28 to $34). That risk/reward ratio is quite unattractive. But what if the optimistic estimate is reached? Then it seems highly probable that the stock will move up substantially. Now we have to look at the subjective factors. For example, if your best estimate is wrong, is it more likely to be too high or too low? Experience has shown that even the best analysts' estimates are more often too high when earnings are falling and too low when they are rising. In other words, people underestimate how bad things can get in a recession, and then forget how quickly things recover in a boom. Therefore, since earnings had been disappointing early in the year, and the economy seemed about to slide into another recession, perhaps it would be safest to assume the worst for 1980 and make our investment judgment based on the low-end estimate. In that case, the stock is not especially attractive. However, everyone is probably thinking that way and, in so thinking, all the "weak" holders may have already sold their stock. As discussed earlier, the market behaves very emotionally, exaggerating the good news in good times, and exaggerating the bad news in bad times. With all the bad news currently known; earnings now having been disappointing for two quarters and almost everybody expecting a poor third quarter, a recession generally expected to begin shortly, and the write-off to distort near-term earnings downward, maybe this is one of those times when the stock is behaving as if things are never going to get better. Thus, it may be time to buy now regardless of the price-earnings ratio, because first, all the bad news is anticipated, and second, history shows that stocks almost always recover well before the company's earnings recover. **Is the stock a buy or sell?**

Look at the chart on page 263.

CHART 21

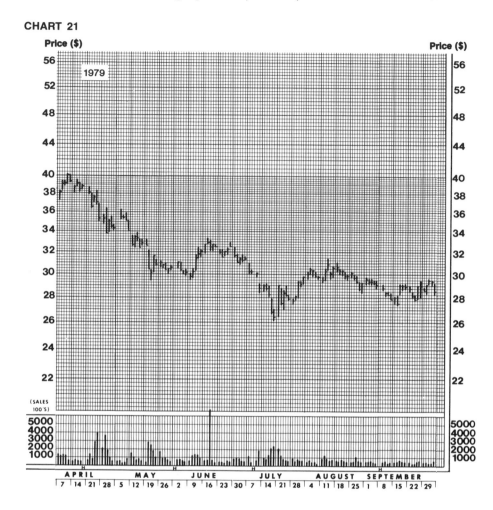

CHART 22

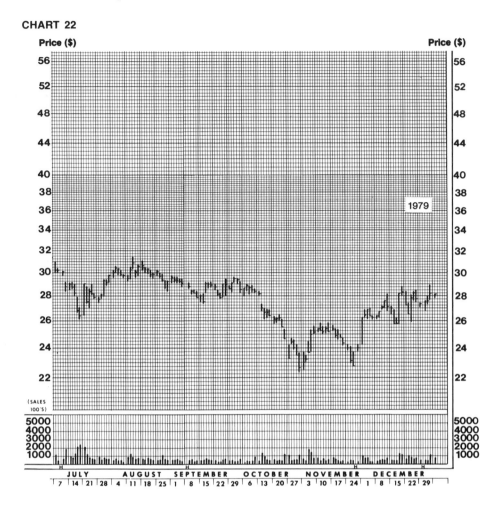

Following the brief rise after the September 12 announcement, the stock declined sharply in October along with the market and got as low as $22½ at just about the time third quarter earnings were reported.

POLAROID
Third Quarter 1979 Results

	1978	1979	Percent Change
Sales	$342	$348	+1.9%
Reported earnings (loss) per share	$1.04	$(.70)	
EPS, if no Polavision revaluation	$1.04	$ .48	Off 54%

On October 24, Polaroid reported the third quarter results. Sales for the quarter were up 2 percent. Earnings per share were a loss of $0.70 per share, but Polaroid announced that the Polavision write-down, which they called a "revaluation," came to $68.5 million and was equivalent to $1.18 per share. The $1.18/share included an adjustment for taxes and another minor item. Thus, third quarter earnings without the "revaluation" would have been $.48 per share, well below the $1.04 per share earned in the third quarter of 1978.

We had assumed the write-down or revaluation adjustment was going to be $1.10 per share. Our assumption was off by $.08 per share. The $.08 is small enough to ignore, considering the write-down is nonrecurring anyway, and investors should be more interested in the $.48 earnings figure—what Polaroid would have earned without the write-down. Even this figure was not especially meaningful, both because the write-down produces other accounting distortions, and because it was not known whether sales of Polavision systems in the quarter were now showing a profit, due to the write-down, or if they were still showing a loss. Thus, earnings estimates for 1979 were particularly unreliable. Also, for 1980, we were estimating earnings in a wide range from $2.40–$3.62. Thus, to change our best estimate by $.08 per share would not make a big difference.

After the earnings report, the stock recovered modestly until the end of the year, as did the stock market in general. The third quarter results, therefore, were pretty much as the market expected following the September 12 write-down announcement. Of course, had Polaroid not pre-announced the write-down, and just put the $68 million in the third quarter Cost of goods sold, without saying what it was for, then the quarter would have been an unexpected disappointment and the stock would probably have fallen sharply from whatever level it would have been at.

Early 1980 crosscurrents: An inflation problem, a new film, and finalizing the Polavision write-down

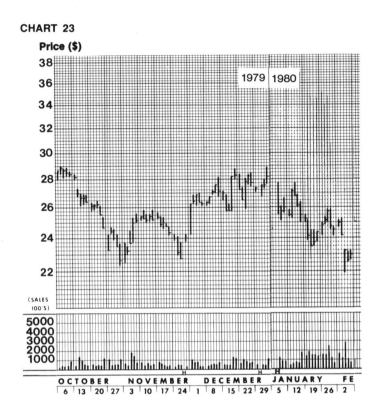

CHART 23

Price ($)

In January 1980, the stock worked its way lower. One reason was that inflation was increasing. The prices of raw materials, particularly silver, were rising sharply, and investors began to worry that Polaroid would be forced to raise its selling prices sharply. This could cause sales to fall and hurt earnings. In addition, Polaroid uses the FIFO method of inventory accounting, which requires using, in the Cost of goods sold, the cost of the oldest raw material in inventory when products are sold. Thus, in the fourth quarter of 1979, as Polaroid made sales, it had to put into Cost of goods sold the cost of the raw materials purchased early in the year when prices were lower. Therefore, the current level of reported profit was artificially high because it reflected the lower-priced raw materials costs that were no longer accurate. Thus, when Polaroid ran out of low-cost raw material and started selling goods using more recently priced higher-cost raw materials, earnings should then fall from current levels. Of course, Polaroid was raising prices to offset these cost increases, but there was no way for investors to know with certainty if the price increases fully offset the cost increases, and, of course, whether the higher prices would hurt sales.

Also, it was possible that Polaroid would change its accounting from the FIFO method to the LIFO method. LIFO accounting puts into Cost of goods sold the *most recent* raw materials cost in the inventory when products are sold. Therefore, if Polaroid made this accounting change, it would have the effect of immediately lowering pretax earnings and therefore also lowering income taxes. While a shift from FIFO to LIFO is actually good for a company because it saves taxes, the stock price might react negatively because the shift would lower reported earnings. However, it is possible that the market is already "anticipating" a shift to LIFO just as it "anticipated" the Polavision write-off. Thus, the stock may have already declined, or not gone up when it otherwise would have. There is no way to know. But since the inflation problem, especially the soaring price of silver, was well known to investors, it does seem probable that a shift to LIFO is already at least partly anticipated by the market. In other words, it is possible that if Polaroid shifts to LIFO, causing a sudden earnings decline, the stock price would stay at the same level, anyway. This means the market would be suddenly giving Polaroid a higher P-E, presumably because the risk of disappointing earnings due to FIFO accounting is now gone. Should that occur, Wall Streeters would say the shift to LIFO inventory accounting "was already in the price of the stock."

Current stock price	÷	1980 EPS estimate using FIFO	=	Price-earnings ratio
$26		$2.80		9.3x

Stock price assuming no change	÷	Possible 1980 EPS if Polaroid converts to LIFO	=	Price-earnings ratio if stock price does not change
$26		$2.20		11.8x

While, on the one hand, investors were worried about the rising raw materials cost problem, on the other hand there was optimism about a new faster developing film called Time-Zero, which Polaroid was introducing to replace the current SX-70 film. The new Time-Zero film not only developed itself in about 1½ minutes, much faster than the old

SX-70 film, but was reported to have much improved color rendition and clarity. Some Wall Street analysts believed that this new film would not only stimulate demand (with the help of advertising) but also had lower manufacturing costs and thus would increase profits. It also demonstrated that Polaroid continued to have a technological lead over Kodak in the instant photo field, a factor which increased analysts' confidence that Polaroid could continue to grow in the future. How much impact the new film would have, remained to be seen.

Fourth quarter profits were generally expected to be down but no one knew how much, of course. Recall that in the second and third quarters of 1979, sales had been up about 2 percent and earnings had been off about 50 percent, excluding the Polavision write-off. Thus, many analysts' full-year 1979 EPS estimates of $.80–$1.20 reflected that the 4Q profit might also be off by 50 percent (to get to $.80 for the full year) or perhaps would be off slightly less than 50 percent since the loss on Polavision should be much less than in the 4Q 1978 due to the write-down in September. Recall that quarterly results are always important to investors because they show the progress being made toward the long-term forecast for earnings and dividends. Since quarterly results are usually measured by comparing them to the same quarter a year ago, it is important to know what nonrecurring or unusual factors may have influenced the year-ago quarter in order to make as accurate a comparison as possible. Analysts should have recalled that the 4Q 1978 was very strong as dealers were stocking their shelves in anticipation of a very strong 1978 Christmas season. Of course, we later found out that they had been overly optimistic and thus their inventories were too high at year-end and reordering in January fell sharply. Nevertheless, recalling that the 4Q 1978 was particularly strong, perhaps excessively strong, investors should have anticipated that the 4Q 1979 might look weak in comparison, even under ideal circumstances. But with consumer spending having been weak all year, particularly for Polaroid's products, the comparison of 1979's fourth quarter to 1978's fourth quarter should have been expected to be particularly weak.

Nevertheless, analysts were apparently surprised when, on January 28, 1980, Polaroid announced that 4Q 1979 sales were off 10 percent from the 4Q 1978 level. No comment was made about earnings, but with a 10 percent decline in sales, it was a safe guess that earnings were off sharply. Earnings and final sales figures would not be reported until later in February. The announcement was made after the stock market was closed that day, so one could not immediately see if there was a market reaction. But the next morning there was such an influx of sell orders that the stock did not begin to trade until well after the usual 10 A.M. opening. When the stock finally opened (began trading), it was at $22, two points lower than it closed the previous day. Apparently, the market was not expecting such a sharp decline in sales. After the announcement, many Wall Street analysts lowered their 1979 EPS estimates again. Some analysts also lowered their sales and earnings estimates for 1980, perhaps because the surprisingly weak 4Q 1979 sales indicated that underlying demand for Polaroid products was weaker than they thought, and perhaps because their confidence in their ability to forecast Polaroid results had again been shaken. Most analysts, however, made no changes in their 1980 estimates, preferring to wait until final earnings were reported in a few weeks, with whatever explanations management might make in the press release.

On February 21, Polaroid announced the full-year 1979 and 4Q 1979 results.

POLAROID
4Q Results

	4Q 1978	4Q 1979	Comment
Sales............	$474.5	$426.6	Off 10 percent as preannounced
Pretax Margin	15.2%	5.9%	Way down
Pretax Profit......	72.1	25.3	Off 65 percent
Tax rate	39.8%		
Taxes	28.7	(3.6)	Tax credit
Net Profit	$ 43.4	$ 28.9	Off 33 percent
EPS............	$ 1.32	$ .88	Off 33 percent

The 4Q pretax profit was off 65 percent, worse than generally expected, but the net profit and EPS were only off 33 percent. The difference was that in the 4Q, instead of paying a tax, the company received a tax credit. This, of course, related in some way to the low level of earnings resulting from the Polavision write-down combined with normal tax credits. The 4Q tax credit also resulted in there being a small tax credit for the full year.

POLAROID
Full-Year Results

	Year 1978	Year 1979	Comment
Sales......................	$1,376.6	$1,361.5	Off 1 percent
Pretax margin	14.1%	2.6%	Includes effect of
Pretax profit................	194.5	35.8	Polavision write-down
Tax rate	39.1%	—	
Tax	76.1	(0.3)	
Net profit	$ 118.4	$ 36.1	
EPS......................	$ 3.60	$ 1.10	
Final adjusted effect of Polavision write-down ...		$ 1.00	
Earnings per share if no Polavision write-down ..		$ 2.10	

Polaroid stated that after making year-end accounting adjustments related to the write-down, the final cost of the write-down was now calculated to be $1.00 per share, rather than the $1.18 per share reported in the 3Q. Thus the actual earnings for the year were $1.10 per share, and the $2.10 EPS figure would be called "normalized" earnings (i.e., the best available figure for what the company would have earned under "normal" circumstances—without the extraordinary write-down).

By this time, however, no one really cared about the write-down. Earnings for 1979 were only of interest if you could remove Polavision effects and could see how the company was doing without it, and thus have a base from which to project 1980 earnings and beyond. Even the $2.10 per share normalized earnings was not an accurate base figure because it included both some accounting distortions caused by the write-down and the operating loss from Polavision sales early in the year, which would not happen in 1980. Thus, any detailed analysis of the 1979 figures was not worth the analyst's time, because none of the figures would be an accurate base from which to forecast 1980 earnings. Even the sales figure was distorted because it included some Polavision sales that were likely to decline substantially in 1980.

The historical summary table below shows the return-on-equity and pretax profit margin ratios both "as reported" and "normalized." In either case, even allowing for probable distortions associated with the write-down, it was not a good year for Polaroid. With the ratios approaching the levels of the 1974 recession, one could now say with a high degree of confidence that Polaroid had clearly become a cyclical company (i.e., its earnings were likely to decline in consumer-spending recessions).

	EPS	Price range High	Price range Low	P-E range High	P-E range Low	Aftertax return on equity	Pretax profit margin
1964	$ .58	$ 23 –	$ 16	40x –	28x	22.7%	25.8%
1965	.93	65 –	22	70 –	24	29.7	28.4
1966	1.51	87 –	54	58 –	36	38.1	30.0
1967	1.81	127 –	77	70 –	43	33.7	30.6
1968	1.86	134 –	88	72 –	47	26.6	32.1
1969	1.90	145 –	102	76 –	54	23.3	28.1
1970	1.86	130 –	51	70 –	27	14.4	25.6
1971	1.86	117 –	76	63 –	41	12.4	21.6
1972	1.30	150 –	87	115 –	66	7.8	13.0
1973	1.58	143 –	65	91 –	41	9.0	12.9
1974	.86	88 –	14	103 –	16	4.6	5.9
1975	1.91	44 –	15	23 –	8	9.8	14.9
1976	2.43	45 –	31	19 –	13	11.6	16.0
1977	2.81	39 –	25	14 –	9	12.2	14.9
1978	3.60	60 –	23	17 –	6	14.3	13.9
1979	2.10*	56 –	22	27 –	10	7.5	8.4 Estimated
	1.10**	56 –	22	51 –	20	3.9	2.6

  * normalized, i.e., excluding writedown.
** as reported, including writedown.

The high-end P-E figures of 27x and 51x were essentially meaningless. When the stock was selling at $56 at the beginning of the year, most analysts were forecasting EPS for 1979 of over $4. As those estimates declined all year, so did the stock price. The low-end P-E of 20x, based on the $1.10 EPS figure, is probably also meaningless since the write-down was a nonrecurring event and investors are generally concerned only with the company's ongoing ability to generate earnings.

By now the reader should have learned to be very wary of historical P-E ratios, because we have seen repeatedly that the high or low P-E figure in a given year often reflects a stock price based on an earnings outlook that turned out to be way off. This, in turn, demonstrates the importance of making as accurate as possible earnings estimates, and perhaps avoiding a stock where you do not have a lot of confidence in your earnings estimate. Or perhaps the more important point here may be that you should only buy a stock if it is selling at a "reasonable" P-E based on the lowest possible earnings you can foresee.

1980—Beginning of a new era?

Polaroid stock had declined substantially over the past 14 months— reflecting continuously disappointing news. At the end of February 1980, a week after 1979 earnings were reported, the stock was about $21, its lowest level since early 1975. But Polavision was now a thing of the past, and the long-term underlying trend of earnings was still up. While earnings had declined in 1979, the EPS—either including the Polavision write-down ($1.10) or excluding the Polavision write-down ($2.10)—were, in fact, higher than in the previous cyclical decline in 1974, when earnings declined to $.86 per share. Similarly, the peak earnings of $3.60 per share in 1978 were well above the peak earnings in the prior cycle. Thus, Polaroid might now be viewed as a cyclical growth company, meaning that, although earnings would move up and down with the economic cycle, the underlying trend over a long period would be upward. Now, with the cyclical decline in earnings having pushed the stock down, and the absence of Polavision likely to enable earnings to bounce up in 1980 regardless of the economy, perhaps the stock was down to a level where it was attractive relative to the company's prospects. Was it time to buy the stock or was it still a sell?

The buy arguments were as follows:

1. Earnings should be sharply higher than the $1.10 per share reported in 1979 due to the absence of the Polavision write-down. They should even be higher than the $2.10 per share figure, excluding the write-off, because there would be either no operating loss or a substantially reduced operating loss, compared to 1979 due to the ab-

CHART 24

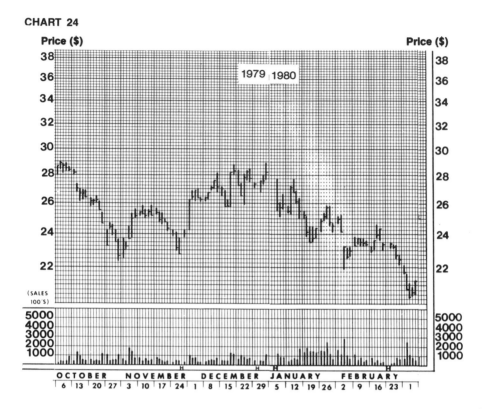

sence of Polavision sales. Some Wall Street analysts were estimating 1980 EPS at $2.50–$2.85. One analyst was using $3.65.

2. Earnings should benefit from the switch to Time-Zero film. Although no one knew what the cost savings might be, many analysts felt that the thinner Time-Zero film used less raw material and, therefore, necessarily had a lower cost.

3. Earnings should also benefit from a reduction of personnel costs. Polaroid said it was starting 1980 with 2,300 less people than at the beginning of 1979, and further reductions in personnel were expected to take place in 1980. Assuming the average employee costs the company $20,000 per year, including all benefits, the reduction of 2,300 people would save $46 million in costs over a year, which is equivalent, after adjusting for tax, to a savings of $.75–$.85 per share. Of course, some of that benefit was realized in 1979 because the personnel reductions actually began early in the year. Nevertheless, a lot of it should be felt in 1980.

4. The buyers recalled that in 1975 quarterly profit margins and earnings recovered much higher than analysts expected, beginning two to three quarters after a similar sharp reduction in personnel. A

similar pattern could occur in 1980, as most investors would again underestimate the significance of such labor cost reduction.

5. The new Time-Zero film promotion program should help Polaroid win sales from Kodak, as well as induce existing Polaroid camera owners to take more pictures than they might have otherwise. It is important to remember that Polaroid's sales have always responded to new products with enhanced features. In that regard, many Wall Streeters also expected Polaroid to introduce some new camera products in 1980, although there were no indications what the product might be.

6. At $21, the stock was selling at 8.4x the $2.50 EPS estimate and 7.4x the $2.85 EPS estimate. Further, even if earnings were only $2.30, by the end of the year investors would be focusing on 1981—and earnings for that year looked like $2.80 in a worst case. With the stock selling at 7.5x that estimate, very near the historical low P-E of 6x in 1979, it seemed there was very little downside risk. But if EPS appeared likely to reach $2.50 in 1980 and $3.00 in 1981, and if the stock reached 14x earnings, which it had every year on the table, it would be a $42 stock within two years, a double from the current level, and therefore certainly worth buying now. Even without making an actual earnings estimate, it was likely that when one or two earnings quarters came in much higher than expected, people would be raising their near-term and long-term EPS estimates again, and the stock would likely go up with it.

7. The stock at $21 was selling at 75 percent of the year-end book value of $28 per share. In the past, people who bought Polaroid well below book value were well rewarded.

The bears, or sellers, were more persuaded by different arguments:

1. Polaroid reported that its camera sales worldwide were 7.2 million units in 1979, down from 9.4 million in 1978. Since Polaroid camera owners use far more film in the first year after purchase than in subsequent years, the lower camera sales in 1979 than 1978 suggested lower film sales in 1980 than 1979.

2. Many analysts felt that Polaroid would probably not introduce any new products in 1980. Thus, camera sales could be down again in 1980 in the absence of any exciting new products, and film sales might then decline two years in a row.

3. Polaroid had raised film prices an equivalent of 13 percent over the previous year. This higher price for a luxury product could hurt sales in a year when the consumers' discretionary income was already being hurt by inflationary increases in such necessities as food and fuel.

4. Some Wall Street analyst surveys of photographic dealers revealed

sales at Christmas were below expectations. This indicated, first, that demand for Polaroid products continued very weak, and second, that the company's first quarter sales and earnings could be weak because dealers would work off their inventories before reordering from Polaroid, as occurred in early 1979.

5. The domestic consumer recession appeared likely to continue well into 1980, and Polaroid sales never did well in a recession.

6. Polaroid said that its international sales declined in the 4Q 1979. This was the first such decline in many years. Previously, Polaroid's products had been continuously introduced into new international markets, so that overall international sales had expanded even when some countries were in recessionary periods. Now, international sales had reached a high level where they, too, could not help but be impacted by a recession. Many economic forecasters were expecting a recession in Europe in 1980, and thus, an overall international sales decline might occur at the same time as a domestic sales decline. The impact on earnings could be substantial.

7. For all these reasons, earnings in 1980 could be well below the "normalized" $2.10 per share earned in 1979. In fact, some Wall Street EPS estimates for 1980 were as low as $1.50 to $1.75, with one analyst using $1.25.

8. If Polaroid earned $1.75 and sold at 14x earnings, it would be a $24½ stock, a 17% gain from $21. If it sold at 8x a $1.50 estimate, it would sell at $12, a 57% decline. Thus, the risk/reward ratio was quite unattractive at the current level.

9. Even if Polaroid earned $2.50 in 1980, which seemed doubtful, at what P-E should the stock sell? Long-term earnings growth was questionable. The record year 1978 was immediately followed by a collapse in earnings. The pretax profit margin had declined for three straight years despite increases in sales. Foreign growth could no longer be depended upon to carry the load when the domestic economy was in a recession. Finally, the company had given no indication it had any important new products to introduce that could bolster growth meaningfully. In fact, the company's last major product, Polavision, was a dismal failure. There were no consumer products being discussed. The company was now talking more about generating new sales from diversifying further into chemicals, and selling its flat battery to others. But there was little evidence of a substantial sales effort.

10. Polaroid was an exciting company with great technology, but to some people it seemed that the company was more interested in technological achievement than in earnings growth. Thus, in the absence of a clear case for continued earnings growth, why should it not sell at its historical low P-E, or even lower?

Forecast EPS		Forecast P-E		Forecast price
$2.00	×	6x	=	$12
2.50		8		20

With the stock currently at $21, it hardly looked attractive from this point of view.

11. We argued that a stock's worth is related to its current and future dividends. If Polaroid's earnings growth was going to be minimal, perhaps the stock should sell strictly on the basis of its dividend. The current dividend of $1 per share provides a yield of 4.8 percent based on the $21 stock price, hardly an attractive yield since you can get 5¼ percent in any bank. On the other hand, the $1.00 dividend may be an unrealistic assumption because, if Polaroid's earnings just recovered to the previous high of $3.60, the company should be able to pay a dividend of at least half that if they saw no growth prospects to use the profits for. But, if the company raised its dividend to $1.80, its yield would still be only 8.6 percent, not especially high by the stock market standards of today.

Once again we see that there are persuasive arguments both to buy the stock and to sell it. And once again, each investor must call upon his or her own judgment to weigh the bullish and bearish arguments and come to his or her own decision. **Would you buy the stock or sell it at the end of February 1980?**

CHART 25

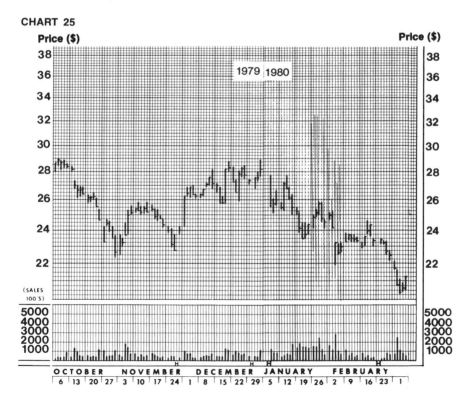

CHART 26

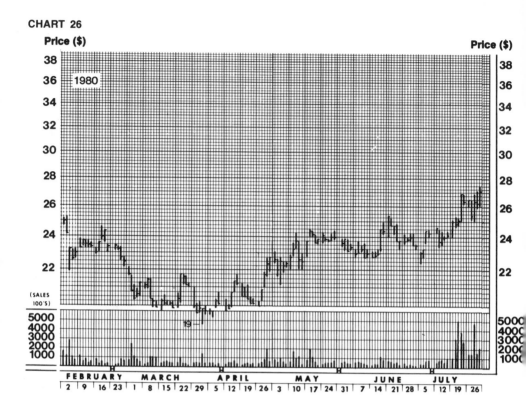

In the month of March, the stock declined to a low of $19 as the stock market declined sharply. From there it began to recover more or less steadily, as did the market throughout the summer. Was the stock just recovering with the market or was there a fundamental improvement in the company's outlook to support the recovery? Let's look at the news about Polaroid and see if there was any improvement in the outlook.

On April 17, the company reported the first quarter results. Sales and earnings were both better than most Wall Street analysts expected, but the stock hardly moved at all in the couple of days following the announcement. In fact, the results below could support the arguments of both the bulls and the bears.

POLAROID
1Q Results

	1Q 1979	1Q 1980	Comment
Sales............	$264.9	$308.3	Up 16.4 percent
Pretax margin	11.0%	9.3%	Down!
Pretax profit......	$ 29.1	$ 28.6	Down 1.7 percent
Tax rate	41.2%	39.0%	Lower rate enabled increase in net profit
Net profit	$ 17.1	$ 17.4	
EPS............	$ .52	$ .53	

The bulls were encouraged by the 16.4 percent increase in sales even though it did not result in an earnings gain. In the 1975 recovery, there was also a couple of quarters delay before the sales recovery translated into earnings gains. More important, with first quarter earnings up a penny, it looked as if the company could earn in 1980 at least as much as the $2.10 earned in 1979, excluding the Polavision write-off, perhaps more if there was a recovery in consumer spending late in the year. Also, the cost benefits of last year's personnel reductions were just beginning to be felt, according to President W. J. McCune Jr. at the company's annual meeting on April 22. McCune also said that although the company was being cautious due to uncertain economic conditions, he was looking for a "solid improvement in our operating results in 1980."

The bears looked at the first quarter results differently. First, a 16 percent increase in sales should have resulted in an increase in pretax profit, not a decline. The company said the decline was due to "increased manufacturing costs, as well as start-up costs associated with several new products, including Time-Zero film." This did not provide much encouragement, however. While start-up costs might decline as the company became more experienced at manufacturing Time-Zero film, it was likely that manufacturing costs would continue to rise. Certainly materials should keep rising, particularly silver and oil-based products, due to the sharp increases in those prices, and wage rates usually tend to rise also.

Second, the bears pointed out that Polavision losses were supposedly reduced substantially compared to the 1Q 1979, and that alone should have helped profits. Thus the 1.7 percent decline in pretax profit was even worse than it looked. Finally, the bears pointed out that the first quarter sales were probably artificially inflated by a film price increase announced for March 1. It seemed likely that dealers stocked up in the first quarter in anticipation of their second quarter needs in order to beat the price hike. Thus, it is possible that 2Q sales could be down and, therefore, earnings disappointing.

In sum, while the first quarter earnings report was slightly better than expected, it hardly seemed encouraging enough to change investors' perceptions of Polaroid's fundamental outlook for earnings and dividends. Nevertheless, the stock crept up in May and June and early July to the $23–$25 area. The percentage gain from the $20 level, then, was 25 percent to $25. Interestingly, both the Dow Jones Industrial Average and the Standard & Poor's 500 index were also up almost exactly the same percentage. This would seem to suggest that Polaroid was just moving with the market.

In late July the stock moved up to $27. The second quarter results were reported on July 22. Sales declined slightly but profits were up modestly.

POLAROID
2Q Results

	2Q 1979	2Q 1980	Comment
Sales	$321.8	$317.2	Down 1.4 percent
Pretax margin....	6.4%	7.8%	Up
Pretax profit	$ 20.7	24.8	Up 19.8 percent
Tax rate	35.9%	39.1%	
Net profit	$ 13.3	15.1	Up 13.5 percent
EPS	$ .40	.46	Up 15 percent

Once again the quarter could be interpreted positively or negatively. On the negative side, the sales decline of 1.4 percent was worse than it looked because prices were up about 12 percent, compared to the 2Q 1979. Therefore, unit sales of cameras and film were actually down, perhaps 10 percent. Also, Polaroid said that profits from operations increased, mainly due to lower Polavision expenses, compared to the year-ago 2Q, and that start-up costs on Time-Zero film continued to be substantial.

Thus from the bearish point of view, there still was no real improvement in Polaroid's profitability despite the substantial cutback in personnel over the past year. Furthermore, the start-up costs on Time-Zero film seemed to be continuing longer than expected, suggesting some difficulties with the film.

Again, the bulls looked at the earnings report differently. Their interpretation was that the company had now earned $.99 in the first half, despite the continuing start-up costs on Time-Zero film. Thus, since company sales and earnings are always stronger in the second half because of Christmas, and start-up costs on Time-Zero should decline over time, earnings for the second half of 1980 and the full year should be well above the second half and full-year 1979 even excluding the Polavision write-off. Thus, full-year 1980 earnings could easily be as high as $2.30–$2.70, depending on the strength of the Christmas season. And these earnings were being accomplished with a minimal sales increase. In this case, when the economy recovered and sales gains picked up, earnings might well exceed $3 per share. In fact, many analysts were already estimating over $3 per share for 1981. The earnings outlook looked, in some ways, like it did in the recovery from the 1975 recession; that is, the stage was set for a sharp increase in earnings when consumer spending picked up again. And, just as occurred in 1978, the sharp gain in earnings should be accompanied by a sharp gain in the stock price. In 1978, the stock almost tripled from its low of $23 to its high of $60, in about six months.

The circumstances were right for a repeat of the 1978 earnings and stock price recovery. It was just a question of timing, and in July 1980, with the stock selling at about $27, just about book value, and less than 9x the 1981 earnings forecast of over $3 per share, it was "cheap" enough to buy now and not risk missing the big move if the next quarter should produce a big gain in earnings.

The bears did not agree with that interpretation. While such an earnings surge was possible, it was far less likely than it was in 1978 because some circumstances were very different. First, by 1978 the economy was three years out of the depth of the 1975 recession. In 1981 or 1982 it would be, at most, one or two years out of the 1979–80 recession. Second, in 1978 Polaroid benefited from the 1977 introduction of the One-Step camera, the first really inexpensive camera which used the SX-70 film. In 1978, the company sold a record number of cameras and film packs. For 1981, there were no indications that the company would have any exciting new products to help sales. Most of the cameras, then, were likely to be just updated versions of the existing lines, and the Time-Zero film was really only a modest evolutionary improvement from the current SX-70 film. So the Polaroid product offerings for 1980, and perhaps 1981 and 1982, seemed likely to lack the excitement and newness that seemed so important for Polaroid to generate substantial sales increases.

Thus, the bears felt, that even if Polaroid did earn $3 per share in 1981, it certainly was not likely to merit a P-E of over 10x and, therefore, a price of $30 seemed "fully valued." With the stock currently just a few points below that, it was hardly attractive. **Would you buy the stock or sell it now?**

CHART 27

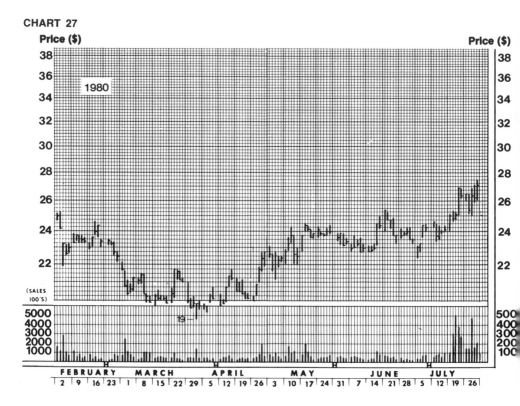

CHART 28

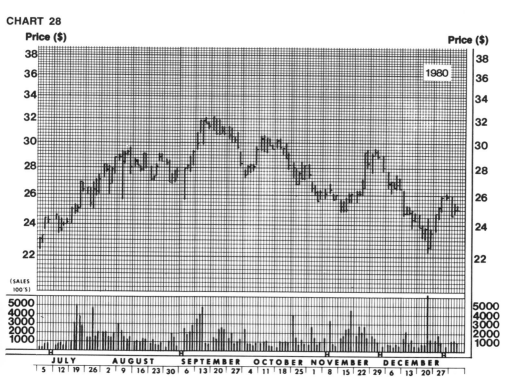

From the end of July until the end of December, the stock behaved erratically. In early September, it spurted to $32½ before working its way lower and closing the year at $25. Both the Dow Jones Industrial Average and the Standard & Poor's 500 Stock Average worked their way higher and closed the year above their respective July levels. Therefore, a nimble trader could have bought the stock in late July and made a quick profit by September, but longer-term investors would have been better off selling at the end of July.

A bond offering—But no impact on the stock

On August 4, Polaroid announced it would sell $125 million of bonds, the first public bond offering in the company's history. Should this have an impact on the stock, or was it just another event that is significant to the company, but either does not impact the stock, or was already anticipated by the market, and therefore should have little or no impact? Until now, the company had always had no long-term debt, and thus to some observers this debt offering was just another sign that Polaroid was no longer the glamour company and stock it was in the 1960s. Other signs, of course, were the lower pretax margin and return on equity ratios of the 1970s, compared to the 1960s. However, by August 1980, Polaroid had for a long time been carrying a lot of short-term debt, and about two thirds of the money raised from the bond offering was really just replacing short-term debt with long-term debt. The prospectus for the bond offering said the remainder of the money raised was just for "general corporate purposes." In the period from the time the bond offering was announced, August 4, until the offering was completed, August 13, and for a couple of weeks thereafter, the stock moved in a fairly narrow range, and thus we can deduce that the bond offering was essentially not a surprise (in the sense that the Polavision write-off was not a surprise) and so did not have a meaningful impact on the stock price.

Last half of 1980—A volatile stock

During the August to December period, news about the company was generally favorable. Many published Wall Street earnings estimates were raised, particularly after the third quarter earnings were reported—again better than expectations. Other positive news included a trade journal article in August, which said Polaroid was experiencing a 25 percent increase in camera sales in the geographic regions where it had introduced Time-Zero film. Whether this was true or not, perhaps it was a major cause of the early September stock spurt to $32. If such a 25 percent increase in camera sales where Time-Zero film was introduced were to occur all across the country when Time-Zero was introduced nationwide, it had enormous implications for 1981 earnings. To experienced followers of Polaroid, however, the likelihood of an evolutionary product improvement, such as Time-Zero, producing such a dramatic earnings increase, seemed very unlikely. Only a revolutionary new system with much improved convenience or features or lower price could be expected to produce a sustained 25 percent increase in sales.

The early September stock spurt to $32 is another demonstration of the short-term unpredictability of the market. If it was due to the magazine article, it shows that in the short run alert investors can make good profits by seeing an unexpected piece of news before the market in general. However, the stock's subsequent decline suggests that either (1) people who did not see it decided the stock was overpriced at $32 and sold, or (2) the market in general did see or eventually hear about the article, but decided it was not significant enough to make the stock worth $32. Thus they, too, were sellers until the stock declined back to a level where they thought it was fairly valued. If the spurt to $32 was not due to the article, then what caused it? Perhaps it was just a random fluctuation as some bullish investors accumulated the stock. At over $30, however, the anonymous majority still thought the stock was overpriced, and it quickly fell back.

On September 4, Polaroid held a major exposition of its professional, commercial, and industrial products (as opposed to its amateur products) for the press and the financial community. This show, however, produced nothing dramatic either positively or negatively that seemed likely to have a direct impact on the stock.

The third quarter was reported on October 22.

POLAROID
3Q Results

	3Q 1979	3Q 1980	Comment
Sales..............	$348.2	$364.7	Up 4.8 percent
Pretax margin	—	9.3%	
Pretax profit (loss)	$(39.2)	34.0	
Tax paid (credit)	$(16.1)	13.4	
Tax rate	—	39.3%	
Net profit (loss)	$(23.1)	20.6	
EPS (loss)	$ (.70)	.63	

The comparison is meaningless because of the Polavision write-off in the 3Q 1979. One could try to compare the 3Q 1980 to the 3Q 1978 to see what could be learned, but recall that the 3Q 1978 was part of a year of record earnings, Time-Zero film was not incurring large start-up costs, the Polavision system was still being sold, and the inflationary burst of 1979 and 1980 had not begun. Thus, the 3Q 1978 was too different to be a meaningful comparison. One could also compare 3Q 1980 to the 2Q 1980, but the seasonal difference would probably distort the comparison, unless we went back and looked at the 3Q compared to the 2Q for each of the past few years and developed a better understanding of the seasonal changes. We will not do this. Rather, we will simply look as closely as we can at the 3Q 1980 and make whatever judgment we can.

Sales were up 4.8 percent. But we know from published price increases that average prices were up perhaps 8 percent compared to the year ago 3Q. Thus, we can conclude that unit sales actually were down maybe 3 percent. This is no surprise compared to the trend in the first half of the year, but perhaps it disappointed some stockholders who were expecting an upturn. On the other hand, photography dealers knew that Time-Zero film would be available late in the year, and perhaps they stopped ordering the current SX-70 film to reduce their inventory to make room for the new film. If this were true, it would probably explain the disappointing 3Q sales volume and suggest that fourth quarter sales could therefore be up substantially as dealers restocked their shelves with Time-Zero film.

The company also indicated that start-up costs on Time-Zero remained very high, and again, this could be interpreted either negatively, that the product was difficult to manufacture and therefore might never earn very high profit margins, or positively, that when these start-up costs did come down, earnings would move up.

On balance, the quarter produced no big surprises. While most analysts raised their estimates shortly after it was reported, the stock declined from $27 just before the quarter was reported to a low of $24 two and a half weeks later, suggesting that some holders were disappointed in the quarter. However, the stock then jumped to $29 a week later. What conclusion can we draw? None are obvious to this writer. However, when one looks at the chart from August to November, one sees a lot of up and down activity, but no net movement. Perhaps the conclusion is that we are looking too closely at short-term moves. In essence, the stock has done nothing all year, while the stock market averages were moving up sharply. Of course, if one had been clever enough to buy Polaroid at the $20 level in March or April, and sell it over $30 in September, she or he had over a 50 percent gain. But all that is irrelevant now. The only relevant question, as always, is do we buy the stock now or sell it?

Contrary opinion—Perhaps the time to buy is when nobody likes the stock

The stock declined from September until the end of December, when it was hovering around the $25 area. Earnings estimates for 1980 were now generally in the $2.35 to $2.75 range. Estimates for 1981 generally ranged from $2.85 to $3.50. The bullish and bearish arguments were both similar to those of mid-year.

The bearish arguments were:

1. The consumer spending outlook still looked poor, due to high inflation and the continuing recession expectations.
2. Polaroid's sales volume was not making much progress and might not be expected to until some exciting new products were introduced, and none were expected.
3. With little likelihood for sustainable growth, Polaroid hardly deserved a high P-E.

The bullish arguments were:

1. Sales would recover eventually when the recession ended and, even if the sales recovery was small, reduced costs from the personnel cutbacks and probable declines in Time-Zero start-up costs would bring earnings much higher than expected.
2. With the stock selling at less than 8x 1981 earnings, near the low end of its historical P-E range, and selling below book value, it was better to buy now and be willing to wait, because, when higher earnings were achieved, the stock would likely move up quickly.

Stock price	Estimated EPS	P-E based on EPS estimate
$25	1980: $2.40	10.4x
	1981: 3.20	7.8

Perhaps now is the time to buy Polaroid. The stock has declined from over $30 to below $25 without any substantial change in the outlook. The stock is clearly "out of favor," and it is interesting to note that the best time to have bought Polaroid in 1980 was in March when earnings estimates had been coming down, not going up (i.e., when the stock was also clearly "out of favor").

The biggest gains are often made buying stocks when they are out of favor. If you bought Polaroid at the end of March at $20 or below, you could have made a 55 percent gain by selling at $31 in September. If you waited until after the 1Q was reported and earnings estimates for 1980 began to rise, you would have paid $22–$24 for the stock, and made only a 30–40 percent gain on the move to $31. Again, the biggest percentage gains are usually made by those who have the courage to buy "early" (i.e., when a stock has declined and nobody believes the bullish story). Of course, when a stock is out of favor may be exactly when the bullish story seems most improbable, and the probability of things going poorly for the company seems most likely. Inevitably, the biggest gains are made when the biggest risks are taken. So, of course, are the biggest losses.

What to do with Polaroid? The stock is clearly out of favor, but if it does go up from here, the percentage gain is likely to be much higher if you buy it now rather than if you wait for good news to emerge. By that time it will probably already be higher and the person who buys then will have a smaller percentage gain. **Is the stock a buy or a sell?**

CHART 29

CHART 30

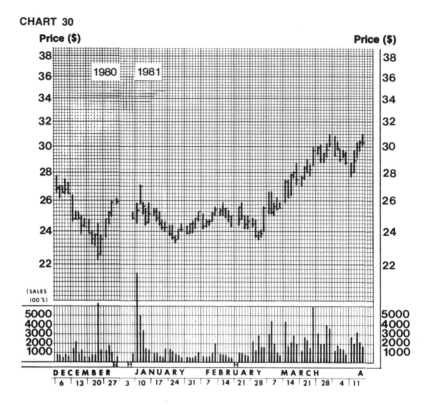

Anticipating a new product

The stock made no progress in January and February 1981. On February 19, Polaroid reported results for the 4Q and full-year 1980. The good news was that the earnings were $.20 to $.30 higher than most analysts were expecting. But there was also bad news. The press release said the company was "very cautious about the business and economic climate for 1981," and that "it is unlikely that the sales and earnings results for the 1981 first quarter will match the results of the same period a year ago, in part because retailers purchased heavily in the 1980 first quarter in anticipation of price increases. . . ." The announcement apparently caught many analysts by surprise and caused them to lower their 1Q and full-year 1981 estimates. Following the announcement, however, the stock declined only about one point over the next week before moving up to over $30 late in March. One reason for this strength in the stock may be that there were rumors on Wall Street that there would be a major new product introduced in 1981. Important new products have always stimulated Polaroid's sales and earnings growth. Also, if there were to be a major new product in 1981, it was most likely to be announced at the annual meeting in April, as has normally been Polaroid's practice in the past.

Upon hearing such rumors in February, risk-taking investors would have bought the stock in anticipation of the excitement that would surround such an announcement. With the stock having hovered around the $25 level for three months (through February), they reasoned, the stock had clearly not yet moved up in anticipation of such a new product announcement. Therefore, if there was no announcement there was little to lose. But more important, the stock might well move up as the annual meeting date approached and more people got excited about a possible introduction. Then, if there was a significant new product and the stock moved substantially higher, those who bought now would already have their position at a low price. But if the new product was not significant and not likely to stimulate accelerated earnings growth, then those who bought in February might still be able to sell at a small profit to the less-sophisticated investors who were either bidding up the price of the stock just before the annual meeting, or who bought afterwards, because they misjudged the importance of the new product.

Before we look forward, however, we should first examine the 4Q results and see what we can learn.

POLAROID
4Q Results

	4Q 1979	4Q 1980	Comment
Sales	$426.6	$460.5	Up 8.0 percent
Pretax margin	5.9%	12.4%	Way up
Pretax income	$ 25.3	$ 56.9	Up 124.9 percent
Tax paid (credit)	(3.6)	24.6	
Tax rate	—	43.3%	
Net income	$ 28.9	$ 32.3	+11.8 percent
EPS	$ .88	$ .98	

While sales were up 8 percent in the 4Q, pretax profit jumped an extraordinary 124.9 percent. Net earnings, however, were only up 11.8 percent because of the tax distortion in the 4Q 1979 results. The jump in pretax profit and margin is so unusual, compared to the prior history, that it should be examined to see what is distorting the figures, and, of course, we recall that the 4Q 1979 was badly distorted by year-end adjustments in the aftermath of the Polavision write-down. The full-year comparison between 1980 and 1979 is also not meaningful for the same reason. By early April the stock was up to the $28–$31 level. Was the stock a buy or a sell? The "buy" arguments were as follows:

1. The 4Q 1980 earnings were somewhat better than expected on a minimal sales gain, suggesting that Polaroid's cost-cutting measures and personnel reduction had been effective in lowering costs. Thus, when sales volume picked up, earnings should pick up sharply—as they did in 1978. In fact, even including the earnings decline now anticipated for the first quarter, Wall Street earnings estimates for 1981 were in a range of $2.75 to $3.45, and preliminary estimates for 1982 were in a range of $3.50–$4.50. With the stock at $30, its P-E based on those estimates was closer to the low end of the historical range. Despite this there was some downside risk if the low-end $2.75 estimate for 1981 became more probable.

Price	Earnings estimate range		P-E
$30	1981: Low	$2.75	10.9x
	High	3.45	8.7
	1982: Low	$3.50	8.6x
	High	4.50	6.7

2. While the 1Q was going to be down from the 1980 1Q, that was known because the company had announced it in the middle of February. Thus, there was unlikely to be any disappointment.

3. If the rumored new product was significant, it was likely that earnings forecasts would be revised higher either for 1982 or both 1981 and 1982, depending on the timing of the introduction.

The bears argued differently:

1. The stock had moved up from the $24–$25 level to $28–$30, pre-
    sumably (at least partly) in anticipation of new products. Now, if the
    product looked like it was going to be another disappointment, there
    might be a substantial decline in the stock. Thus, the "easy money"
    had been made in anticipation of the announcement. Why hold the
    stock and take the risk that it would be a flop?

2. While Polaroid had indicated the 1Q should be down, what if it were
    down more than expected? In fact, Polaroid probably would not have
    preannounced the down 1Q unless they expected it to be down a lot.
    And if the cost reductions in the 4Q were really that significant,
    should it not have cushioned the 1Q earnings decline? Perhaps Wall
    Street's 1981 earnings estimates were too high. After all, earnings
    had more than once come in well below early-year estimates. Why
    take the chance?

3. Foreign earnings, a new factor, now had to be considered. As could
    be seen in the footnotes in the annual report, foreign earnings were
    becoming a significant portion of total earnings, and Europe ac-
    counted for almost two thirds of the foreign earnings (in 1980). With
    many economic forecasters projecting a recession in most European
    countries, it was quite likely that Polaroid's sales there would be
    hurt. In addition, the American dollar had been rising against for-
    eign currencies in recent months, and, if that continued, it would
    make Polaroid products very expensive overseas as most of the com-
    ponents for Polaroid's overseas products had to be purchased from
    the U.S. Thus, the price of Polaroid products in France, for instance,
    would have to go up in French francs to enable Polaroid's French
    subsidiary to buy its product components from the U.S. Such price
    increases could hurt sales. Finally, there was the complex issue of
    foreign currency translation. The increasing value of the dollar had
    been causing Polaroid to incur losses associated with foreign cur-
    rency translation when the financial statements of its foreign sub-
    sidiaries were translated into U.S. dollars for the consolidated fi-
    nancial statements. These losses, of course, reduced the reported
    earnings of the company, and Wall Street analysts were saying that

as long as the dollar remained strong, Polaroid's earnings were likely to continue to be hurt.[8]

4. While the bears recognized the substantial upside potential of the stock if the new product announcement was meaningful and likely to produce good earnings gains, there seemed to be too many things that could go wrong, including the fact that there might not be an important new product.

In sum, if there was an impressive new product, one could easily see the stock at some point in 1982 selling at at least a P-E of 13x the 1982 estimate of $4.50, or $59 per share, a double from the current price. And in that case it would certainly be worth taking some downside risk now, because, if the stock were going to $59 in 1982, a lot of that move would be anticipated this year. Conversely, if there was nothing to get excited about and the stock went to 7x an earnings estimate of $2.75, it would be at $19, about a 33 percent decline. **Would you take the risk here or wait until the first quarter was reported and the annual meeting held?**

CHART 31

---

[8] The foreign currency translation accounting rules were subsequently changed in December 1981 to eliminate this problem, but in spring of 1981 the translation problem was both hurting earnings and increasing the uncertainty about the level of future earnings. As we have seen, the stock market does not like uncertainty and usually reacts negatively to it.

CHART 32

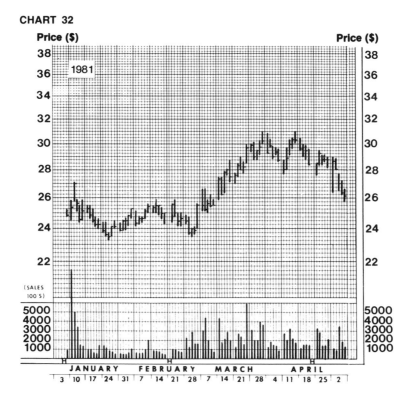

The first quarter was reported on April 16. Earnings per share were $.29 for the 1Q 1981 versus $.53 for the 1Q 1980, a 45 percent decline. This was worse than most analysts expected, even given the company's early warning that the 1Q would be down, and many analysts lowered their full-year estimates by $.15– $.30 per share. At the annual meeting on April 21, the company announced that there would be a new amateur photography system with "some entirely new features," but it did not show the product or give any details, saying only that the system would be introduced at the end of May.

By the end of April the stock had retreated to $26. There was still the uncertainty associated with the new product but, management was talking about it in superlatives, something they had not been known to do in recent years, especially if the new product was just a minor change from the old ones. Since the stock had retreated practically to its early-year level before the new system had been even rumored, perhaps the stock should now be purchased in anticipation of the late-May introduction. Before making an investment decision, however, it would be wise to look first at the first quarter results to see what they might indicate for the rest of the year.

POLAROID
1Q Results

	1Q 1980	1Q 1981	Comment
U.S. sales	$138.4	$127.8	Off 7.7 percent
Foreign sales	169.9	148.4	Off 12.7 percent
Total sales	$308.3	276.2	Off 10.4 percent
Pretax margin	9.3%	6.5%	
Pretax profit	$ 28.6	17.9	Off 37.2 percent
Tax rate	39.0%	46.8%	Big increase
Net profit	$ 17.4	$ 9.5	Off 45.3 percent
EPS	$ .53	$ .29	

In announcing these results, Polaroid said that foreign sales would not have been off as much were it not for the currency translation problem, but they still would have been down, not up. With sales also down in the U.S., it is not surprising that the pretax profit and margin declined. Also, the translation problem distorted the pretax profit down even further.

This pretax profit reduction caused by foreign currency translation also resulted in the 1Q 1981 tax rate being higher than it would otherwise have been. The result was that earnings per share were off 45 percent, although some analysts thought that EPS might have been off much less were it not for the currency translation problem. Even this, however, would not have been an encouraging quarter.

At the end of April the stock was back to $25 per share, somewhat below its book value of $29.25 at the end of the first quarter. Was it a buy or a sell? Published earnings estimates for 1981 had been generally lowered to a range of $2.60 to $3.50. Those who published estimates for 1982, however, still carried forecasts of up to well over $3 per share and in some cases approaching $4 per share. The new product announcement was set for late May and, although no one knew for sure, it was rumored to be the most significant development since the introduction of the SX-70 in 1972. In addition, recalling that the 1Q 1980 was artificially strong as dealers stocked up to beat the price increases, it follows that the second quarter of 1980 should have been artificially weakened as the dealers worked off their then-accumulated inventories. Thus, the 2Q 1981 should be an easy comparison (i.e., it should be easy for Polaroid to show a gain in sales and earnings), to the 2Q 1980, other things being equal. But, of course, other things were not equal. The U.S. dollar was continuing to strengthen, which could be expected to hurt earnings again, as it did in the 1Q. In addition, foreign and domestic business remained weak in line with poor consumer spending in recessionary environments in many countries. Also, U.S. business now might remain soft, because dealers would be reluctant to stock up on old SX-70 cameras and Time-Zero film while they awaited the new system. Also on the negative side, if the new system was as different as some expected, it might result in excessive start-up costs, such as those incurred in 1972 and 1974 with the introduction of the SX-70, or as occurred in 1980 with Time-Zero film. Recall that start-up costs in those years held earnings well below investors' expectations. Thus 1981 and 1982 earnings might also be disappointing due to start-up costs. However, Polaroid did say the new system was "in the SX-70 format," so perhaps start-up costs would not be significant this time.

All these potential negatives, however, were well known and maybe they were already in the price of the stock, and maybe now was a great buying opportunity. **Would you buy the stock now or sell it, or wait until after the late-May product introduction?**

CHART 33

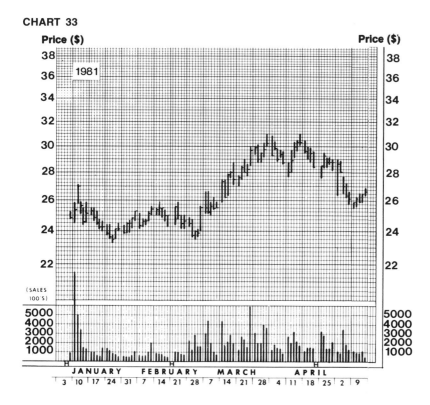

CHART 34

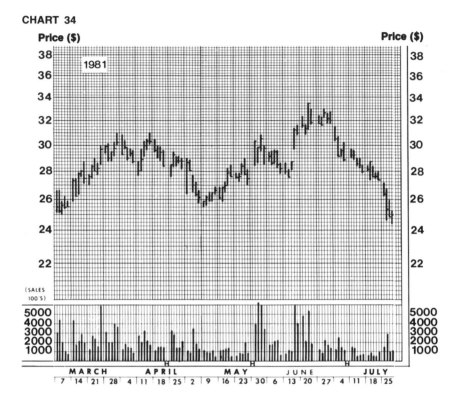

On May 28, Polaroid introduced the new camera and film, which they called the 600 SUN System. The system looked much like the SX-70 system but had a number of added features and technological improvements. The camera had a built-in flash and a far more sophisticated automatic exposure control system, which, combined with a faster film, enabled the user to take pictures in a wider range of lighting conditions, both indoors and out, with a higher proportion of successful shots. At the expected price for the new camera and film, Polaroid seemed to be offering the consumer a measurably better value for the price.

The stock, meanwhile, had moved back up to the $30 level as the May 28 introduction date approached. Immediately following the introduction, it settled back for two weeks before rebounding again to a high of $33 in June.

Reviews and opinions about the new SUN cameras and film were mixed. Analysts who were long-time followers of Polaroid generally agreed it was an impressive technological achievement, and was likely to be a modest spur to sales; but few seemed to think it was as revolutionary a change from the old SX-70 System as the SX-70 was from the older peel-apart products. Even so, it did seem to further Polaroid's technological lead over Kodak, which might enable Polaroid to further increase its market share lead over Kodak.

From late June through July 25, the stock declined back to the $25 level. As the end of the second quarter approached (June 30) the dollar continued to strengthen against foreign currencies and investors began to worry again about how much quarterly earnings would be hurt by the currency problem. The earnings problem that resulted from the translation of foreign subsidiaries' income statements and balance sheets to U.S. dollars might be viewed as temporary, because the dollar could not keep going up forever, and as soon as it stopped going up this problem would stop. But the strong dollar also presented another problem that might not go away. Since Polaroid's overseas operations buy many products and component parts from the United States, a permanently higher dollar (weaker foreign currencies) would make Polaroid products permanently more expensive to buy for the consumers in foreign countries and, as more consumers decided they could not afford the higher prices, unit sales overseas might decline to a lower level, implying lower earnings. Thus, while the *translation-of-financial-statement problems* would eventually disappear (when the dollar stabilized against foreign currencies), if the dollar stabilized at a higher rate than in prior years, it might permanently dampen sales due to the *higher price problem* in foreign countries. Thus stock market investors might be willing to ignore the translation-of-financial-statements problem, since it is inherently temporary; but the higher price problem, if it appeared likely to persist, could cause investors to permanently lower their earnings growth expectations for Polaroid's foreign operations. This was one factor depressing the stock.

While we have looked at the short-term ups and downs from early 1981 to late July 1981, if we step back from the short-term behavior of the stock we see that actually it has made little progress all year and, in fact, fluctuated in a relatively narrow range, given Polaroid's prior volatile history. In retrospect, there were two good short-term trading opportunities: one in anticipation of the annual meeting and the other in anticipation of the late May new-product introduction; but in both cases, you had to remember to sell "on the news" (i.e., there was a good short-term rally in anticipation of the introduction, but then the stock reversed itself on both occasions and went down shortly after the "news" was out). This is an excellent example of how the stock market anticipates.

Therefore, we might ask, did the stock decline in June and July because of lower earnings estimates and foreign exchange rate concerns, or was the stock simply following a classical stock market trading pattern ("selling on the news")? While that question is unanswerable, it is interesting to note that the timing of the up and down moves in Polaroid thus far in 1981 coincided surprisingly closely with the timing of the up and down moves in the Dow Jones Industrial Average.

Summer 1981—Another buying opportunity?

On July 21, Polaroid reported its second quarter earnings. EPS of $.41 versus $.46 in the year-ago quarter were generally better than Wall Street was looking for, given the currency translation problem.

POLAROID
2Q Results

	2Q 1980	2Q 1981	Comment
U.S. sales	$167.5	$196.2	Up 17.1%
Foreign sales.....	149.7	143.0	Off 4.5%
Total sales	$317.2	339.2	Up 6.9%
Pretax margin	7.8%	7.7%	
Pretax profit......	$ 24.8	26.0	Up 4.8%
Tax rate	39.1%	48.5%	Again distorted by currency problems
Net income	$ 15.1	$ 13.4	Off 11.3%
EPS.............	$ .46	$ .41	

Domestic sales were up a strong 17 percent, but recall that they were off 7.7 percent in the 1Q. Since both of these comparisons were distorted by dealers' pre-price-hike buying in the 1Q 1980, we might get a better indication of sales trends by comparing the first half of 1981 to the first half of 1980, rather than comparing the quarters. It is a good idea to compare semiannual results as well as quarterly results, because the semiannual results will eliminate any quarter-to-quarter distortions that may occur. The first-half 1981 versus first-half 1980 comparison reveals that domestic sales were up a modest 5.9 percent. When the effect of price increases is considered, it may be that unit sales in the U.S. were about flat.

The second quarter foreign sales comparison was again hurt by the currency translation problem. Although reported foreign sales declined 4.5 percent, Polaroid indicated that the actual sales in foreign countries were up. Even allowing for some currency translation problems, however, sales gains in the first half for Polaroid were not impressive.

Considering that currency translation was a problem, it is surprising that Polaroid was able to show an almost flat pretax margin. While we do not know why this happened, it may indicate that Polaroid is improving its manufacturing efficiency, perhaps due to the continuing reduction of workers on the payroll. This would be an encouraging sign for future earnings. Despite this, no analysts were publishing higher earnings estimates, probably because the dollar continued to strengthen—implying further foreign earnings disappointments in the third and possibly fourth quarters, and also because indications were that the U.S. economy and consumer-spending outlook were continuing to weaken, which implied poor sales of Polaroid products.

On July 21, Polaroid also issued a press release saying there would be a secondary offering of 1,500,000 shares of Polaroid stock from a foundation and an institution set up by Dr. Edwin H. Land. Recall that a secondary offering refers to already outstanding shares, so the company receives no money from the sale of these shares, and thus earnings are not diluted. However, 1½ million shares is still a large block to place on the market at once, and some people were concerned that it might put pressure on the stock near-term.

Would you buy or sell the stock today? Earnings were slightly better than expected, but foreign currency translation continued to look like a problem in upcoming quarters. In addition, there was a secondary offering planned. But the stock had come back to $25, where it started the year. At that price it was selling at a 17 percent discount from Polaroid's $30 book value and near the middle or low end of the recent years' P-E range (based on published Wall Street estimates).

Price	Earnings estimate range		P-E
$25	1981: Low	$2.00	11.4x
	High	2.70	9.3
	1982: Low	$3.00	8.3x
	High	3.80	6.6

Thus one might conclude that either the stock was "cheap," based on 1982 earnings estimates, or alternatively, perhaps Wall Street estimates for 1982 were much too high. **Is the stock a buy or a sell?**

CHART 35

CHART 36

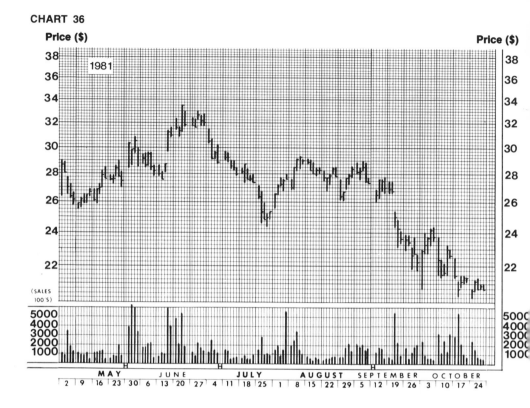

Bearish news—Near-term and long-term

Polaroid rallied into early August, as did the market in general. The market then fell sharply through the end of September, but Polaroid initially held up well, only declining slightly from mid-August until mid-September, before it, too, fell sharply. Possibly contributing to Polaroid's weakness were articles in magazines and newspapers about the coming of electronic photography. In late August, Sony announced it was developing a camera that would make its "negatives" on magnetic tape, which could then be played back through a television. The product would not be introduced for at least 18 months and then would cost in excess of $650. Thus, it seemed doubtful that it would really compete with Polaroid products despite Sony's statement that it would make conventional chemical photography obsolete.

Even though this product was probably years away and substantially more expensive, it is possible that it could impact Polaroid's stock now. Recall from Chapter 15 that the price-earnings ratio is the measure that reflects investors' confidence in a company's anticipated future earnings growth rate. While it seems doubtful now that electronic photography would ever totally displace conventional photography, it is possible that at least some users of conventional Polaroid products might eventually switch to electronic photography.[9] Thus the implication of the Sony product, although years away, was not that Polaroid would be put out of business, but that when electronic photography arrived it might cause a slowing of Polaroid's sales growth, or even a decline. Thus, the announcement of electronic photography should reduce either investors' future growth rate forecasts for Polaroid or at least their confidence that their best estimates would come to pass. The author knows of no one who has tried to forecast how much Polaroid's future growth would be impacted by electronic photography; but since some impact was probable, it was likely to be reflected in the price-earnings ratio investors would be willing to pay for Polaroid until that impact was known.

On the other hand, it is possible that Polaroid is also developing an electronic photographic process. Much of the excitement and high P-E ratios Polaroid enjoyed in earlier years was a result of the company's ability to accomplish technological feats that others had been unable to do. But Polaroid has given no such indications, and to assume it would be sheer speculation and hardly a basis for investing in Polaroid now.

While the market was declining sharply in late August and early September, Polaroid declined only slightly. On September 16, however, the stock was down sharply following the decision of a respected Wall Street analyst to lower his 1981 earnings estimate to $2.00 per share from the $2.45 per share he had been carrying. The analyst, Tom Henwood of First Boston Corporation, also said that he would "stand back" from the stock and that "the stock has held up extremely well and isn't ready for a disappointment." He went on to say, "Since our new estimate reflects currency accounting problems, rather than any problem with operations . . . we think it will be an extremely attractive buy again once the market has reacted." These views were quoted in *The Wall Street Journal's* widely read "Heard On the Street" column. The stock continued to decline sharply through September 28 with the rest of the market.

Here then, is another example of how short-term stock price behavior is extremely difficult to predict. Did the long-term outlook for Polaroid's earnings and dividend growth suddenly deteriorate because of Henwood's comments? Obviously not. But his comments did focus investor attention on Polaroid's short-term problems, and Polaroid had been holding up better than the market. With the market as a whole declining, any "bad news" at all would likely cause some stockholders to try to get out before other investors, and a bearish report from a respected Wall Street analyst was sufficient bad news in this case.

The stock bottomed along with the market on September 28 and

---

[9] Interestingly, it might be that the Sony system would use Polaroid film to make hard-copy positives. This would be a plus for Polaroid, but there was no reason to assume this at the time.

recovered with it for a week, until Polaroid announced on October 5 that the 3Q would be sharply lower than the 2Q 1981 earnings of $.41 per share. While currency concerns as well as general economic weakness had caused many analysts to lower their 1981 estimates in September, Polaroid's announcement caused yet another round of earnings forecast reductions, this time to a range of about $1.50–$1.90. In addition, 1982 estimates, which had been hovering in the $3.40–$4.00 range, now began to come down also—into the $2.35–$3.40 range.

Also adding to the stock's woes was the October 12 announcement by Fuji that it was introducing an instant photography system. The system would initially be introduced only in Japan, and Fuji did not say if and when it might be introduced in the United States. Although the Fuji system would initially be only a minor threat to Polaroid, it might eventually be introduced worldwide, including the United States. Thus, like electronic photography, the Fuji threat, while not currently a serious one, was a potential long-run negative for Polaroid and could put some downward pressure on the P-E investors would be willing to pay for Polaroid.

Another short-term negative was that although the price of silver had been declining now for 12 months, the higher silver prices paid early in 1980 were just now coming out of inventory and going into the Cost of goods sold as a result of Polaroid's FIFO inventory accounting system. This, of course, was only a temporary negative since once this higher-priced silver had been worked out of the system, the lower-priced silver purchased later in 1980 and in 1981 would be going to the earnings statements and therefore lowering expenses. In fact, a recently announced silver sale by the U.S. government suggested that silver prices could be coming down further in the immediate future.

Earnings were reported on October 19 and were off sharply, as preannounced.

POLAROID
3Q Results

	3Q 1980	3Q 1981	Comment
Domestic sales . . .	$218.8	$222.4	Up 1.6 percent
Foreign sales	145.9	136.6	Off 6.4 percent
Total sales	$364.7	359.0	Off 1.6 percent
Pretax margin.	9.3%	4.9%	
Pretax profit	$ 34.0	17.7	
Tax rate.	39.3%	63.8%	
Net profit.	$ 20.6	$ 6.4	Off 69 percent
EPS	$ .63	$ .19	

In the press release, Polaroid explained some of the reasons for the sharp earnings decline. First, camera shipments to dealers were down because dealers were reducing their inventory levels. The new SUN cameras and 600-speed color film, however, were drawing a "very favorable dealer and consumer response." Second, Polaroid took inventory write-downs and had production phase-out expenses associated with some of the SX-70 camera line that was being replaced by the SUN cameras. Management did not say how big the inventory write-down or production phase-out expenses were, and so there was no way for investors to know the exact size. The write-down, however, was obviously nowhere near as big as the $68 million write-down Polaroid took on its Polavision inventory in 1979.

Also, earnings were hurt by an increase in the effective tax rate to 63.8 percent. This was due "primarily to the translation impact of foreign currencies." Polaroid did not specify how big the foreign currency loss was, but we can infer that it was large, given the distortion it caused in the tax rate.

Finally, the release said earnings were adversely affected because sales "were below the company's plan." In other words, the company incurred a lot of expenses that would have been avoided if it had known sales would be as weak as they were.

Since each of these depressants on earnings could be viewed as essentially nonrecurring, if investors knew how big they were, they could be added back to reported earnings to get a better idea of Polaroid's real current earnings power. One respected analyst, Gary Bridge, with the brokerage firm of G.S. Grumman/Cowen, estimated that the negative impact on earnings resulting from translation was equivalent to about $.33 per share and that the write-downs were as much as $5 million, which was equivalent to about 9¢ per share. Other analysts made estimates that were similar to these. If they were right, then Polaroid's 3Q earnings would have been about flat with the year-ago earnings of $.63/share.

Nevertheless, with the dollar continuing strong and therefore currency problems likely to continue, and prospects for consumer spending in the U.S. and Europe remaining weak or worsening according to many economists, analysts who had not reduced their earnings estimates early in October following the announcement of sharply declining 3Q earnings were now reducing them for both 1981 and 1982.

While all of the above bad news had depressed the stock in October, there was more to come. On November 6, Polaroid issued a press release saying that because "worldwide economic conditions were having an adverse effect" on business, the company would have to reduce its employment by approximately 1,000 people. Since this layoff would necessitate severance pay, the company said it would take "an appropriate reserve" before year-end. The "reserve" simply means that the company would estimate the severance pay and add it to expenses on the income statement (probably in Cost of goods sold) in1981, even though it might not actually be paid until 1982.

This announcement caused some Wall Street analysts to lower their earnings estimates yet another time. In mid-November, the stock was selling at about $20, after having touched a low of $19.

Polaroid at $20—A long-term buy or sell?

It is now late November 1981. While thinking abou⁺ the investment outlook for Polaroid, an old friend calls and asks us to join him on a two-year trip around the world in which we would hit some really back-woods places. Since the offer is too good to refuse, we decide to go. Unfortunately, that will mean we will be out of touch with the market on a daily basis, and certainly be unable to get any useful information on which to make an investment decision on Polaroid. Thus, we must de-cide now whether to put the rest of our investable funds into Polaroid stock or to sell the shares we currently own and leave the money in a money market fund. Once our plane takes off, our decision will be irreversible for perhaps two years, so we must use our best investment judgment right now to decide if Polaroid should be bought today for a long-term holding period, or if it should be sold.

Let us review the long-term investment potential for the company and try to evaluate whether the stock at the current price of $20 is a buy or not. To begin, let's review the long term-historical summary table.

	EPS	Price range		P-E range		Aftertax return on equity	Pretax profit margin
		High	Low	High	Low		
1964	$ .58	$ 23 –	$ 16	40x –	28x	22.7%	25.8%
1965	.93	65 –	22	70 –	24	29.7	28.4
1966	1.51	87 –	54	58 –	36	38.1	30.0
1967	1.81	127 –	77	70 –	43	33.7	30.6
1968	1.86	134 –	88	72 –	47	26.6	32.1
1969	1.90	145 –	102	76 –	54	23.3	28.1
1970	1.86	130 –	51	70 –	27	14.4	25.6
1971	1.86	117 –	76	63 –	41	12.4	21.6
1972	1.30	150 –	87	115 –	66	7.8	13.0
1973	1.58	143 –	65	91 –	41	9.0	12.9
1974	.86	88 –	14	103 –	16	4.6	5.9
1975	1.91	44 –	15	23 –	8	9.8	14.9
1976	2.43	45 –	31	19 –	13	11.6	16.0
1977	2.81	39 –	25	14 –	9	12.2	14.9
1978	3.60	60 –	23	17 –	6	14.3	13.9
1979	2.10	56 –	22	27 –	10	7.5	8.4 Estimate
	1.10	56 –	22	51 –	20	3.9	2.6
1980	2.60	34 –	19	13 –	7	9.0	9.9

One thing that emerges from this table is that in the 1970s the stock has been cyclical. That is, it declined when going into recessions, as in 1969–70, 1973–74, and in 1979–80. Similarly, it has gone up at some point in economic growth periods (i.e., 1971–72 and 1975–78).

Since the economy now seems to be in a recession and the stock has declined to the $20 level, perhaps 1981 will be another bottom. In fact, the current experience is very reminiscent of 1974 and, to a lesser extent, 1979. At both of these times, sales were disappointing, the company was reducing its employment through layoffs, and Wall Street was lowering both its current-year and subsequent-year earnings estimates. In both subsequent years, however, 1975 and 1980, quarterly earnings came through better than expected and analysts were raising their estimates all year. Perhaps a similar recovery is being set up again. Perhaps the stock market is focusing too much on the short-term problems of the company and overlooking both the potential of sales to recover when the economy does and the potential of earnings to recover even more sharply, as a result of the lower-cost structure resulting from the layoffs. Perhaps we should not put too much emphasis on short-term problems, or we may become "nearsighted" as some Wall Street analysts have been, and miss a big recovery. With the stock having declined to new lows for the year, and earnings estimates coming down again for both 1981 and 1982, the stock appears to be totally out of favor, and so— perhaps now is the time to be a contrarian and buy it when everyone hates it and it is cheap.

However, because history does not always repeat itself, we should look as closely as possible to be sure we have not overlooked some important fundamental change in the investment outlook. Let us list some key investment variables and see if they are bullish or bearish.

1. Current earnings per share are not as bad as they look. Earnings in 1981 have been substantially depressed by currency translation problems, which are to some extent, possibly a large extent, non-recurring. EPS has also been depressed to a lesser degree by non-recurring writeoffs. Excluding these two factors, Polaroid might be earning something like $2.40–$2.50 per share, according to some Wall Street analysts. This is not bad for a poor economic year, and confirms the idea that EPS could move much higher when the economy picks up. Therefore, unless a prolonged recession is expected, the current depressed earnings is not a bad sign, and may in fact be good because it is depressing the stock and creating a great buying opportunity. This is especially true because the accounting profession has recently been talking about doing away with the foreign currency accounting regulations that caused Polaroid and other companies to report these large currency losses.

2. By historical standards the stock is cheap, based on book value. At $20 the stock is selling at 68 percent of book value of $29.35, slightly below the price-to-book ratio of 74 percent when the stock bottomed at $14 in 1974.

3. Now let us look at the price-earnings ratios. Published earnings estimates have now fallen to a range of about $1.30–$1.90 for 1981 and about $2.20–$3.40 for 1982. Since we want to be most cautious, because we will be unable to change our decision for two years and also because we have seen that Wall Street estimates are often too high in poor economic years, let us look at the P-Es based on the low end of these ranges.

Price	Earnings forecast	P-E ratio
$20	1981: $1.30	15.4x
	1982: 2.20	9.1

Comparing these figures to the historical summary table, Polaroid looks fully priced, based on 1981 earnings. However, it is now the end of November, so investors more likely than not are making their decisions based on 1982 forecasts. On this basis the stock, at 9.1x earnings does appear to be near the low end of its range in recent years.

Although the $2.20 EPS estimate for 1982 is near the low end of all the published estimates, perhaps we should assume an even lower earnings level just to be extra-conservative. Looking at the historical summary table, let us choose a worst-case estimate of $1.90 per share, equal to the 1975 earnings, which was also the end of a recession period.

Price	Earnings forecast	P-E ratio
$20	1982: $1.90	10.5x

At 10.5x earnings, Polaroid is selling at about the middle of its recent P-E range. So there is some downside risk if 1982 turns out to be a bad year. For a worst-case assumption, perhaps the stock would decline to a P-E of 7x EPS of $1.90, which would make it a $13 stock—a 35 percent decline from the current level.

However, there is also good upside potential. Since the stock has sold at at least 13x earnings in every year, let us use that P-E with our EPS estimates. Doing that, the stock appears to have reasonable upside potential in 1982.

Earnings estimate		Assumed P-E ratio		Derived price
1982 Extra-conservative	$1.90	×	13x	=	$25
1982 Conservative	$2.20	×	13x	=	$29
1982 High	$3.35	×	13x	=	$43½

Furthermore, the stock could easily go to a P-E higher than 13x, and may be likely to if earnings begin to recover sharply as in 1976.

Thus the risk/reward ratio could be interpreted favorably or not, depending upon one's viewpoint.

4. What factors could cause investors to change their P-E evaluation of Polaroid, compared to recent experience? Since P-Es are based on investors' future expected growth rates and their confidence that their best estimates will be correct, what has occurred that might alter investors' growth rate projections or their confidence?

First, there is the advent of electronic photography. While this threat is at least a couple of years away, perhaps a decade, it might still have a slight although unquantifiable impact on the P-E investors would be willing to pay for Polaroid. Second, there is the competitive entry by Fuji. While this threat also seems minimal in the foreseeable future, perhaps Fuji will at some time go worldwide and attempt to increase its market share by cutting prices, much like what happened when Kodak promoted its instant camera in the 1976–77 period, and this could hurt the earnings of all of the competitors. Thus the Fuji entry, although only expected to have a very minor impact on near-term earnings, must also be viewed as having some impact on investor confidence in Polaroid's future growth.

5. Two other near-term factors depressing earnings can both be viewed as temporary. These are the FIFO inventory accounting procedure, discussed earlier in the chapter, and the fact that dealers are currently shrinking their inventories. The latter is likely to reverse itself when the economy picks up again, and the former automatically ends when the high-cost materials are worked out of the inventory.

Weighing all these long-term positives and negatives, and considering the current near-term earnings pressures and any other factors that come to your mind, would you add to your holdings now or sell what you own, knowing that you cannot change your decision for an extended period of time?

CHART 37

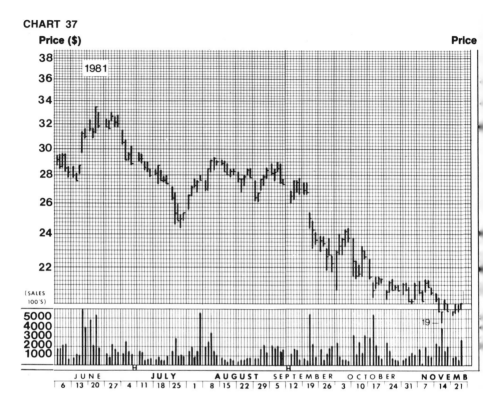

TO THE READER

We hope you have found the Polaroid story a useful way to sharpen your investment judgment. While much has been written analyzing statistics about stock performance and about the mechanics of investing, there is no substitute for the real-world experience of watching a stock's behavior in response to company announcements and the economic environment. This chapter attempted to create some of that experience. As the opportunities to make buy/sell decisions in this chapter arose, I hope you found that your judgment improved, and that your way of thinking about the stock changed. The sophistication you developed should help you in your approach to other stocks. Finally, this study of the ups and downs of Polaroid should suggest that there are usually many opportunities to buy or sell a stock, and one need not rush to buy upon first hearing about a stock with which you have no experience.

To answer your last question, I currently own 20 shares of Polaroid stock. Not because I made a well-thought-out investment decision, but because it is an exciting company and an active stock that always teaches me something new about investing, and therefore I want to be on the shareholders' mailing list to watch history unfold.

APPENDIX ONE

Short Selling

When an investor buys stock of a company, we say he is "long" that stock. That simply means he owns it. If the stock goes up and the investor sells it, he has a profit. If it goes down from where he bought it, he has a loss. Thus, one only "goes long" (i.e., buys a stock) if he expects it to go up. However, if an investor expects a stock to go down, he can make money by selling short, or *shorting* as it is called. Shorting essentially means borrowing a stock you do not own in order to sell it.

To see how shorting works, let's look at an example. Suppose Polaroid is selling at $100 per share. You do not own the stock and you feel certain it is going down. So you call your stockbroker and tell her to "short 10 shares of Polaroid." This means you want to sell 10 shares of Polaroid even though you do not own it. In order to sell stock you don't own, it is first necessary to borrow it. Then you can sell the shares that you borrowed. Normally, your brokerage firm will lend you the shares you want to sell. Let's assume you sold the 10 shares for $100 each or a total of $1,000. The brokerage firm will not give you the $1,000 yet because you have borrowed 10 shares which you still owe them, and the brokerage firm wants to hold the $1,000 as collateral for the loan. Now, assume you were right and the stock declined to $70, which is as low as you think it is going. At this point, you call your stockbroker and tell her to "cover your short." This means you want her to buy 10 shares of Polaroid for you in the market and use those 10 shares to pay back the 10 shares you

314

borrowed. Since Polaroid is now selling at $70 per share, you can buy 10 shares for $700. Since the broker is holding $1,000 of your money (received when you initially sold short the 10 shares), he uses $700 of it to buy the 10 shares and then sends you the remaining $300, which is your profit. The brokerage firm, of course, also keeps the 10 shares you just bought as replacement for those it loaned you earlier.

When selling short, what you are doing is betting that the stock is going down. You are borrowing stock in order to sell it, and hoping to buy it back later at a lower price to repay the loan.

The risk in shorting is that you may be wrong and the stock may go up. Suppose you shorted 10 shares of Polaroid at $100 per share. However, instead of declining, as you expected, the stock went up. You still have an obligation to replace the 10 shares you borrowed. But now that the stock has risen to $110, it will cost you $1,100 to buy back the 10 shares. Thus, if you "cover your short" now (i.e., buy back the 10 shares to repay the loan), then you will have lost $100. You sold the stock for $1,000 and bought it back for $1,100—so you have to pay your broker $100. The risk in shorting a stock is that if it keeps going higher, it will cost you more to buy it back. In short selling there is no limit to how much you can lose. Conversely, when you buy a stock "long" the most you can lose is what you paid for it if it goes to $0.

Why would an investor sell a stock short? Obviously because he felt the stock was overpriced and was likely to come down. Specifically, he might anticipate or know some bad news about the company that is not generally known yet; and, when it becomes known, he expects it will cause the stock to decline. For example, the investor may think that earnings are going to be lower than generally expected, or that a competitor is about to introduce a superior product. Or, as frequently occurs in market declines, some people simply short a stock because they think the stock is going down with the market and they want to make money on the decline. In doing so, of course, they add to the decline because they are selling.

APPENDIX TWO

Buying and Selling on Margin

Buying on margin simply means borrowing money from a brokerage firm to buy stock. The federal regulations about how much you can borrow and under what circumstances you might have to pay it back are quite detailed and will not be discussed here. You can get that information from your stockbroker. Margin buying and selling will be discussed here only so the reader can see the potential influence it can have on stock prices.

Do not confuse buying on margin with short selling. Short selling is *borrowing stock* you do not own in order to sell it. Margin refers to *borrowing money* so you can buy stock. Let's look at an example. Suppose Ms. Davis felt sure that Polaroid was going to rise sharply from its current level of $20 per share on November 15. Ms. Davis has $2,000 and so she could buy 100 shares. If she is right and the stock goes to $30, she would have a profit of $10 per share or $1,000 total profit. However, Ms. Davis is so confident Polaroid is going up that she decides to buy on margin, so she asks her broker to buy her 200 shares for a total of $4,000. She will pay the brokerage firm $2,000 for the first 100 shares and she will borrow $2,000 from the brokerage firm to pay for the second 100 shares. The stockbroker buys Ms. Davis 200 shares of Polaroid. Ms. Davis is now long 200 shares, that is, she owns them. Assume that she was right, and the stock goes to $30 three months later. Now she would have a profit of $10 per share × 200 shares or $2,000, except that she must pay interest on the $2,000 loan. But even if the interest on the loan was at a 15 percent annual rate, it would only come to $75 for three months, so her net profit would be $2,000 less $75 of interest, or $1,925. Even after the interest, this is more than the $1,000 she would have made if she had only bought the 100 shares she had enough money to pay for, and had not bought additional shares on margin.

Suppose she is wrong about the stock and it goes down. Instead of making more money because of her margin purchase, she loses more money. Suppose the stock declines to $15. Had Ms. Davis only bought the 100 shares she could afford to pay for, her loss would now be 100 shares × $5 per share decline for a $500 loss. Because she bought on margin, however, her loss is 200 shares × $5 per share decline for a $1,000 loss. Now she begins to worry, because the 200 shares of Polaroid are only worth 200 × $15 per share for a total market value of $3,000, and she owes the brokerage firm $2,000 (plus interest). Thus, she only has $1,000 of her original investment left (the $3,000 market value less the $2,000 loan) and she can see the stock going down daily. To make matters worse, if the stock falls below about $14, she may be required to pay off part of her loan, which, if she has no available cash, will require her to sell off some of her stock at a loss. This is called a "margin call." The price at which you get a margin call can be calculated precisely from the margin rules, which are available from your broker. It will vary depending on how much you borrowed relative to how much cash you put up. In this case it works out to about $14 per share.

Had Ms. Davis only bought the 100 shares she could afford to buy, she could hold her stock all the way down and never be forced to sell. But because she bought on margin she can be forced to sell if she cannot "meet the margin call" (i.e., pay off the required part of the loan).

When the market looks like it is going to decline, some investors who bought on margin will sell early to avoid the possibility of a margin call. Others might get a margin call and be forced to sell because they have no additional cash to put in. In either case, this selling forces the stock lower, which brings even more investors to the point where they are forced to sell, which in turn forces the stock lower. This forced "margin selling" can conceivably continue until all stockholders who have bought on margin have either sold or put up enough new cash to preclude having to sell. Suffice it to say, in a severe market decline, margin selling often adds to the sharpness of the decline.

Index